Disability Law and Policy in the Modern Era

An In-Depth Look at the Evolution of Employee Leave of Absence and Disability Claims in the Workplace

Scott Daniels

TEMPLE UNIVERSITY SCHOOL OF LAW

CAROLINA ACADEMIC PRESS

Durham, North Carolina

Library of Congress Cataloging-in-Publication Data

Names: Daniels, Scott author
Title: Disability law and policy in the modern era : an in-depth look at the evolution of employee leave of absence and disability claims in the workplace / Scott Daniels.
Description: Durham, North Carolina : Carolina Academic Press, 2026. | Includes bibliographical references and index.
Identifiers: LCCN 2026021198 | ISBN 9781531035525 paperback | ISBN 9781531035532 ebook
Subjects: LCSH: People with disabilities — Legal status, laws, etc. — United States | United States. Family and Medical Leave Act of 1993 | Family leave — Law and legislation — United States
Classification: LCC KF480 .D36 2026
LC record available at https://lccn.loc.gov/2026021198

Carolina Academic Press
700 Kent Street
Durham, North Carolina 27701
Telephone (919) 489-7486
www.cap-press.com

Printed in the United States of America

Disability Law and Policy in the Modern Era

Contents

Preface

Over the last thirty years, workplace leave of absence has undergone significant change. As a result of evolving workforce demographics, employee leave has transformed into more of an employee benefit and in some instances, a tool for talent retention and attraction. Traditional leave of absence options have included private and public disability benefits, as well as state and federal mandates requiring covered employers to provide specific allotments of leave. While this may sound straightforward, as more leave options have emerged, employers have struggled to keep up with the rigorous—and often highly elaborate—compliance requirements riddled with ambiguity and legal exceptions. With the variety of leave options available to employees through private plans and legal mandates, most employee leave events involve more than one claim type and may involve wage replacement and/or job protection. One single leave event often creates numerous employee entitlements and spurns a bevy of employer compliance requirements.

This book will focus on a broad set of disability laws, a rapidly changing regulatory environment and employee benefit offerings that continue to reshape the leave of absence space. With the advent of the Americans with Disabilities Act (ADA) in 1990, as well as the passage of the federal Family and Medical Leave Act (FMLA) in 1994, employee rights and employer obligations stemming from these pivotal laws have been transformed in the workplace. The ADA was a historic law designed to protect disabled individuals in the workplace and in public spaces. It was ultimately expanded in 2008, providing even greater employee rights. Throughout the course of this text, I'll focus heavily on the ADA's requirements for employers to consider reasonable workplace accommodations that enable employees to perform the essential functions of their job. These could be modifications, adjustments or changes in the workplace and can also involve "leave" as the accommodation.

Just four years after the passing of the ADA, another landmark law went into effect with the passing of the FMLA, which ushered in federally mandated unpaid, job protected, leave for covered employees that met specific eligibility requirements. Over time, the ADA and the FMLA have helped to shape the highly complex leave of absence space designed to (among many things):

- Protect employees from disability discrimination;
- Provide employees with more workplace flexibility when caring for oneself or a family member; and

- Ensure employers maintain workplace policies allowing employees to seek accommodations and/or leave without retaliation or reprimand.

Although rather inconspicuous, these laws gave employers a glaring opportunity to support employees that are potentially facing a dire situation involving their own medical condition or that of a loved one. Through policy design, human interaction and the development of new employee benefits intended to support employees during these vulnerable times, a variety of benefit trends and best practices emerged. However, like many new laws, following the passage of the ADA and FMLA, it took several years for employers to develop effective compliance measures and stable employee policies.

Although the ADA and FMLA played a large role in reshaping employee leave of absence options, this text will also cover private disability plans (short and long-term disability), state disability benefits, Social Security Disability benefits, Supplemental Security Income, state paid family and medical leave laws and newer and employer-sponsored benefit programs like parental leave that have gained popularity with employees over the last decade. These programs all carry their own eligibility criteria, funding mechanisms and most notably, their own rules for administration. These details are critical to understanding how an employee accesses these benefit options and what obligations both the employee and employer have throughout the process.

Lastly, like most areas of law, the already highly complex leave of absence environment was dramatically impacted by the COVID-19 pandemic. Employers were faced with navigating unchartered territory with how to administer and interpret their own private policies as well as state, local and federal leave mandates. Substantiating a medical condition through medical records immediately became a big challenge for employees where shelter-in-place orders were in effect and healthcare providers were only seeing patients through telehealth. As a result, healthcare providers were reluctant to provide disability evaluations or leave certifications through the modality of telehealth. This significantly impacted claims administration and in turn, decision making on leave and disability claims became quite difficult. With employers largely wanting employees to stay home if they tested positive for COVID-19 or exhibited symptoms, questions arose as to whether disability and leave claims should be "automatically approved" without traditional medical documentation to substantiate the claim.

The COVID-19 pandemic had a tremendously large impact on disability, leave and workplace accommodations by effectively highlighting the criticality of employees needing time off—or flexibility—to care for their own medical condition or that of a loved one. This put employer leave and disability policies in the spotlight with new, unique, highly complex, and often entangled, claims issues to consider.

Objectives

Develop a thorough understanding of the variety of disability and leave of absence options for employees through employer-sponsored programs, as well as federal and state laws.

Understand the interplay and overlap between federal and state leave laws and private, employer-sponsored disability and leave programs.

Compare how various disability and leave options carry different legal standards and assess how these differences impact employees and employers.

Identify areas where legal theory and the evolution of today's workforce has shifted a court's reasoning in the wake of litigation tied to disability, leave and accommodation issues.

Discover the business implications of a large, burgeoning disability and absence management industry that has experienced tremendous growth fueled by corporate sector needs, a growing external consultant industry and the rapid expansion of insurance products.

Disability Law and Policy in the Modern Era

Chapter I

Introduction and Overview

Over the last thirty years, employee leave of absence has transformed into a highly complex landscape with a variety of options for employees along with the necessity for employers to remain compliant under their own private policies and applicable federal and state laws. Dramatic shifts in workplace environments and workforce demographics have had a significant impact on how traditional leave and disability laws have changed over the years.

Advances in technology have also impacted the disability and leave claims process. For employees, there are more options to apply for and request leave of absence. Employers have progressed to leverage technology to make it easier for their employees to access, request and monitor their claims. But it has also fundamentally changed compliance requirements. The notion of working from home as a workplace accommodation in the mid-90s was likely a non-starter for employees who needed to be in the office to perform their job. Today, technology has enabled a significant number of jobs to be performed both inside and outside of the office—creating greater complexity within a workplace accommodation analysis. This is just one example of workforce changes and how technological advances have impacted the disability and leave of absence space.

This text will cover a broad range of the following: disability laws, regulations, employer-sponsored benefit offerings, as well as the business implications and corporate absence management models that have emerged to address rising compliance requirements. As disability and leave options have grown, employers have recognized the need to simplify the leave of absence process and in doing so, have partnered with insurance companies, third-party administrators and external consultants to develop policies, processes and procedures in the hopes of enhancing the employee experience while simultaneously mitigating risk.

Within these laws, regulations and benefit offerings, additional topics will include: legal burdens of proof, disability standards, threshold variance and eligibility requirements. Caselaw will examine examples of disability and employment discrimination, regulatory guidance and how there is rarely uniformity or consistency across the circuit courts. Additionally, I'll provide insights into the modernization of different laws and how employers have changed their approach to mitigating risk in today's complex environment.

The specific disability and leave programs to be covered will include:

- Short and long-term disability
- Family and Medical Leave Act (FMLA)
- State paid family and medical leave
- Parental benefits
- Workplace accommodations under the Americans with Disabilities Act (ADA)
- Social Security Disability Insurance (SSDI)
- Supplemental Security Income (SSI)

Throughout each section, references will also be made to workers' compensation benefits, state funded disability programs and some notable employer-sponsored benefit programs (i.e., caregiving leave) launched and deployed to serve the needs of changing employee needs.

Here is a summary chart of each disability and leave type:

Leave Type	Body of Law	Standard of Law	What It Provides
Short-Term Disability	Private policy; Various state laws	Depends on policy; In general, the inability to perform your own job	Wage replacement
Long-Term Disability	Private policy; Employee Retirement Income Security Act (ERISA)	Depends on policy; Often combines the inability to perform your own job + the inability to perform any other job ("own occupation, any occupation")	Wage replacement
Family & Medical Leave Act (FMLA)	29 U.S.C. 2601 29 CFR Part 825	To care for oneself, a spouse, parent or child with "serious health condition"	Unpaid, job protection
State Paid Family & Medical Leave	Varies by state law	To care for oneself, a spouse, parent, child, extended family members *Each state law has varied in coverage, benefits, eligibility, funding, etc.*	Portion of wage replacement, sometimes job protection
Workplace Accommodations (specifically leave as the accommodation)	The Americans with Disabilities Act	Physical or mental impairment that "substantially limits one or more major life activities"	Unpaid, job protection

Social Security Disability Insurance (SSDI)	Social Security Act; Code of Federal Regulations section 404	Unable to perform "past relevant work" and/or "substantial gainful employment"	Wage replacement
Supplemental Security Income (SSI)	Code of Federal Regulations section 416	Same as SSDI, but with strict asset/ resource thresholds ("limited to no resources")	Income *It's not 'wages' here because for SSI, the claimant either doesn't have a work history, isn't eligible for SSDI or is a child*
Workers Compensation	Varies by state law	Work-related injury "arising out of" and "in the scope of" employment	Wage replacement
Parental Leave (offered by employers)	Varies by employer program	Employer policy cannot discriminate	Wage replacement and/or job protection

Within each specific area, I will address how the COVID-19 pandemic has impacted employee rights, employer obligations, claims management, employer policies and decision-making. We'll examine how the pandemic forced employers and their vendor partners to tweak—and in some instances rethink—their policies to ensure claims were adjudicated fairly and accurately. For instance, in the early stages of the pandemic, many states implemented shelter-in-place mandates, forcing individuals to remain in their homes. In some of these locations, hospitals were either overwhelmed with COVID-19 patients or specifically reserved for the seriously ill. This prevented people from treating with their medical providers and consequently, if these individuals had an open disability or leave claim, they were unable to obtain medical documentation to substantiate their claim. We'll also examine how telehealth was leveraged during the pandemic and how it is used today with respect to disability and leave claims.

Lastly, in addition to understanding each specific disability and leave option that may be available, recognition must be given to the multitude of legal considerations within each area. Here is a short list of common considerations:

- How does this specific disability or leave type interact with other leaves and/or federal or state law?
- What rights are afforded to the employee under this law or program?
- What are the employer responsibilities and/or legal obligations?
- Who bears the burden of proof?
- What are the applicable regulations governing this specific disability or leave program?

- Is there a governmental agency responsible for enforcement? (Equal Opportunity Employment Commission, EEOC; Department of Labor, DOL)
- Have specific legal issues been tested by the courts?
- Has the law changed over the years or has it been applied differently? Have interpretations of the law by various courts changed?
- Have workforce variations changed the way these programs are viewed?

Chapter II

Short- and Long-Term Disability Programs

The concept of disability insurance spans all the way back to the 19th-century England to insure railway riders against the rising number of injuries and fatalities on the railway system.[1] Depending on the class of fare purchased, riders were able to also purchase a premium and the insurance was limited initially to accidents on the railway. Over the years, the Railway Passengers Assurance Company expanded, took on additional lines of business, and by 1971, was only insuring fire and accident. The company ultimately dissolved in 2005 but remains the early pioneer of disability insurance.

In the United States, the Social Security Act was signed into law in 1935. The intent of this piece of legislation was to establish a retirement program to fund old-age pensions through payroll taxes on employees and employers. It also created an unemployment insurance program to help vulnerable families. Significantly, the concept of disability insurance within the Social Security Act was not passed into law until twenty years later. In 1956, President Dwight D. Eisenhower signed into law the Social Security Disability Insurance program.[2] This was a landmark addition to the Social Security Act and sought to provide a means of disability insurance for workers suffering from a disability. The program would be funded through payroll taxes and it is still in existence today.

In the United States, private disability policies, also known as, individual disability income (IDI) insurance became quite popular in the 1980s. In a paper titled, "Individual Disability Income Insurance in the United States," by Robert W. Beal, FSA, he describes how favorable market conditions (rising interest rates) made IDI insurance

---

1. A Brief History of Insurance, The Insurance Centre, August 2, 2018, accessed March 25, 2026, https://www.tic-insurance.co.uk/a-brief-history-of-insurance/#:~:text=Gamblers%20placed%20bets%20on%20whether,hence%20the%20term%20%E2%80%9Cunderwriter%E2%80%9D.&text=Destroying%20more%20than%2013%2C000%20houses,fatalities%20on%20the%20railway%20system.&text=80%20years%20after%20Edward%20Lloyd,most%20famous%20names%20in%20insurance.

2. John R. Kearney, "Social Security and the 'D' in OASDI: The History of a Federal Program Insuring Earners Against Disability, *Social Security Bulletin* 66, no. 3, August, 2006, https://www.ssa.gov/policy/docs/ssb/v66n3/v66n3p1.html.

a desirable protection for white collar professionals and executives.[3] According to Beal, traditional life insurance carriers began to recognize the market opportunity with IDI and soon thereafter entered the space. These insurance carriers began targeting employers to offer group disability insurance to an entire population of employees rather than target a single employee.

Since 1980, the insurance industry has developed a variety of disability insurance products, ancillary services and an array of administrative options for employers. Although I will not be focusing on the historical components of private disability insurance, Robert Beal's paper provides an excellent historical analysis of the birth and evolution of the private disability industry.

What Is Short-Term Disability?

Short-term disability (STD) benefits traditionally offer temporary income protection for individuals if they become unable to work due to an injury or illness. The focus of this section is on private STD plans offered by employers. There are however a handful of state-sponsored disability programs for employees working in that specific state (i.e., New York, California).

It is important to note that most, if not all, employer-sponsored STD policies require an employee to provide medical documentation to substantiate their claim. This can include: treatment records, lab reports, hospital records, surgical reports and written medical opinions that explain why the person is incapable of performing their job. These records, in the aggregate, are helpful in determining whether an employee can be found disabled.

Further, while a medical diagnosis, or even a lab report, can be helpful to confirm a specific medical condition, documentation explaining why a person is unable to perform their job and opinions on why their condition is hindering their job performance is often the key to a disability determination. Lastly, STD claim approvals are not automatic and are completely independent of the employee's tenure or performance track record.

Employers offering STD benefits can choose to provide the benefit to employees at no cost to them or they can offer it as a voluntary benefit, giving the employee the choice to purchase the insurance. At the discretion of the employer, an STD benefit can provide full wage replacement (100% of pay) or a percentage of the employee's wages. There are various ways to design the actual wage replacement benefit, including a gradual step-down in the benefit over time (see example below). Another popular benefit design option is an initial waiting period (usually 7 days) where there is a minimum requirement of continuous disability before the benefit is paid.

3. Robert Beal, FSA, "Individual Disability Income Insurance in the United States," accessed March 25, 2026, https://www.soa.org/globalassets/assets/Files/resources/research-report/2018/claim-incidence-trend-study-note.pdf.

Most STD benefits last for 26 weeks, but this can vary at the discretion of the employer. Twenty-six weeks, or approximately 180 days, can be tied to the start of a long-term disability benefit, which often requires at least six months, or 180 days, of continuous disability. Again, employers can choose to design their programs without being discriminatory but this six-month window, or 180 days, is common for long term disability (LTD) plans.

Here is an example of an STD benefit with a gradually decreasing wage replacement rate:

Sample Company STD Benefit
(up to 26 weeks)

Weeks 1–6:	100% pay
Weeks 7–12:	70% pay
Weeks: 13–26:	60% pay

STD benefits are highly customizable on almost every aspect of the plan design. The funding, eligibility, criteria, administrative process, benefit rate and duration are at the discretion of the employer. Note that all these components could factor into an employer's return-to-work strategy as well. Looking at the example STD benefit wage replacement above, there is industry sentiment that this gradual reduction in wage replacement can serve as a motivator to get employees back to work. Alternatively, when the benefit rate is 100% wage replacement for twenty-six weeks, one could argue there is no incentive for the employee to return to work faster.

What Does Short-Term Disability Provide?

Generally speaking, STD benefits provide wage replacement when an employee is temporarily unable to work due to an injury or illness. In addition to wage replacement, employers have the discretion to add things to their policy like job protection, but this will vary depending on the employer's policy. Another leave option that often runs parallel to STD benefits is leave under the Family and Medical Leave Act (FMLA). This will be covered extensively in the next section, but it is a federal leave mandate that provides unpaid, job protected leave, to care for one's own "serious health condition" if eligibility criteria is met. So while an employer may only choose to provide wage replacement with their STD benefit, an employee may still receive job protection through the FMLA.

The interplay between an STD benefit and a family medical leave entitlement can be rather confusing for an employee who is experiencing a single leave event. With a general rule being that employees may be entitled to both benefits at the same time. It is imperative that an employer, or their leave administrator, explain the difference between the two, the benefits of each and the potential documentation requirements for each one.

To illustrate the interplay between an STD benefit and family medical leave entitlement for an employee unable to work due to their own medical condition, here is a sample timeline with hypothetical benefits and entitlements:

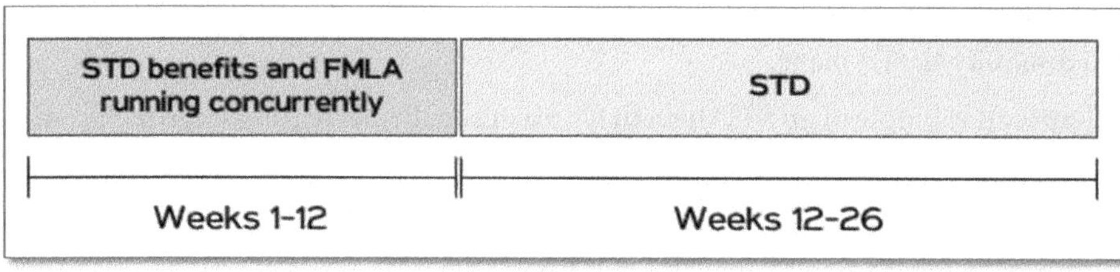

This illustration depicts an STD benefit that can last for up to 26 weeks (again, this will vary by employer, but 26 weeks seems to be the industry norm), with a family medical leave claim running concurrently for the first 12 weeks. For this initial 12-week period, the employee will receive wage replacement from the STD benefit and will have federal mandated job protection through the FMLA. It is important to note the definition of disability under an STD policy may vary and is typically different than FMLA's "serious health condition" standard. However, the latter is typically a much easier threshold to meet so if an employee meets the criteria for disability under an STD plan, they are almost always likely to be approved for family medical leave (assuming they meet the eligibility criteria). Job protection under FMLA generally prohibits an employer from discharging or discriminating against an employee because they have taken leave.[4] It also typically entitles an employee to return to their same or an equivalent job with the same pay, benefits and other terms and conditions of employment.[5]

We will revisit the above illustration as we move onto different leave types as singular leave of absence events often involve multiple leave types.

STD Insurance Models (Self-Insured versus Fully-Insured)

Employers will carry a variety of insurance to protect almost every aspect of their business. Disability benefits have become very common within employer benefit portfolios to protect employees when they are faced with an injury or illness that is preventing them from working. For STD plans specifically, employers are generally choosing between two types of plans:

1. **Self-insured plans:** also referred to as "self-funded," employers carry the risk here and pay for STD claims as they are approved. Under this structure, the

4. Fact Sheet #28: The Family and Medical Leave Act, United States Department of Labor, Wage and Hour Division (Revised March 2025), accessed 2006.

5. *Id.*

employer can still leverage a claims administrator to manage the claims process, but the employer is responsible for paying the cost of the disability benefits.

Potential advantages of a self-insured plan include cost savings (if claim volume is lower), more control over plan design and the ability to influence claim decisions.

2. **Fully-insured plans:** under this model, employers negotiate with a disability insurance carrier to pay a fixed premium in exchange for employee coverage. The insurance company is responsible for administering each claim and paying the disability benefit if approved under the policy.

   The primary advantage of leveraging a fully-insured disability plan is mitigating financial risk by locking in a fixed premium cost in providing protection for employees.

There are multiple pros and cons for self-insured and fully-insured STD plans, but it will primarily hinge on the employer's risk tolerance. Simply put, does the employer want to assume the risk of paying STD claims (self-insured), which could result in paying more or less than expected, or would they prefer to lock in a set cost through an insurance premium so they know what the spend will be each year—regardless of STD claim volatility.

To fund these benefits, employers can choose to cover this benefit entirely and offer it at no cost to the employee or they can subsidize it. In a subsidized model, employees will typically have to "opt in" to coverage and agree to pay a certain amount for coverage. While a subsidized funding structure might help an employer with overall costs to provide coverage, it could result in low, or sporadic enrollment, resulting in lack of disability coverage for employees who choose not to enroll. Industry practice to ensure disability coverage for all employees is typically through an employer-sponsored STD program with no cost to the employee.

Here is a side-by-side comparison for these two STD models:

	Self-Funded	Fully-Insured
Assumption of Risk	Employer	Insurance carrier
STD Benefit Payments	Employer paid	Insurance carrier paid
Claims Administration	Employer or claims administrator	Insurance carrier
Plan Design	Employers have more flexibility, creativity	Plan design options are driven by insurance carrier, in collaboration with employer
Decisional Influence	Employer discretion	Insurance carrier makes claim decisions with no influence by employer
Funding	Employer paid (can be shared with employee)	Employer pays premiums to insurance carrier
Compliance	Employer is responsible	Insurance carrier is responsible

Employee Retirement Income Security Act (ERISA)

ERISA is a large federal law that sets minimum standards for most voluntarily established retirement and health plans in the private sector to provide unified protections for employees in these plans.[6] ERISA covers a broad range of health and welfare programs—most notably health insurance plans—but our focus will be with short and long-term disability plans, specifically how ERISA governs these plans.

The purpose of ERISA is to protect both employees and employers through a specific set of unified rules around the claims process within these plans. Employees, otherwise known as "participants," in the plan, must follow rules related to claim deadlines, evidence and an appeals process. Employers must also follow these rules and ensure the employee is aware of the process and how to file a claim or appeal.

One of the major components of ERISA is the fiduciary responsibility imposed on employers and insurance carriers to put the best interests of the employee above company interests. In the disability space, this is often the subject of contention when a claimant is denied benefits, and they disagree with the decision. An appeal can involve a claim that the employer, or more likely, the insurance carrier, breached their fiduciary duty.

ERISA governed disability plans are required to have plan documents or summary plan descriptions explaining things like eligibility, disability criteria, the benefit rate, any offsets plan rules and appeal rights. These plan descriptions can vary in terms of transparency and the level of detail provided. Under ERISA, employers must adhere to strict rules designed to protect participants (claimants) and employers must notify all eligible employees of any plan changes that are made (i.e., benefit rate, deadlines, appeals).

In contrast to ERISA governed STD plans, employers have the option of offering something called a non-ERISA STD plan which is exempt from ERISA rules. These disability plans are deemed as a "payroll practice" where the benefits—or wage replacement—are funded out of general company assets rather than an insurance policy or trust. In order to meet the payroll practice exception so that a plan can be deemed Non-ERISA, the payment of short-term disability benefits must not be insured nor can it be funded by a trust (it must come from the employer's general assets), and the payment of benefits cannot exceed more than the employee's normal compensation.[7]

Employers have the sole discretion of choosing whether to have an ERISA or Non-ERISA STD plan. There are advantages to both, but the primary reason an employer might decide to implement a Non-ERISA STD plan is so they can dictate plan design and maintain discretion to determine benefits eligibility. It is important to note that choosing a Non-ERISA plan does not allow employers to create an unrea-

6. United States Department of Labor, "Employee Retirement Income Security Act (ERISA)," https://www.dol.gov/general/topic/retirement/erisa.

7. Code of Federal Regulations, "29 CFR Section 2510.3-1, Employee welfare benefit plan," https://www.ecfr.gov/current/title-29/section-2510.3-1.

sonable, or arbitrary, claims process that would be overtly challenging for claimants. Even with these Non-ERISA plans, employers are still required to act in good faith in making their claims decisions.

The issue of whether employers retain the discretion to determine benefits eligibility has been tested in the courts over the years.

The case of *Leone v. Tyco Electronics*, No. 5:08-CV-290-F (E.D.N.C. June 26, 2009), illustrates the distinction between a disability policy subject to ERISA and an employer-sponsored non-ERISA plan (case below).

Joseph S. Leone v. Tyco Electronics Corporation

407 Fed. Appx. 749 (4th Cir. 2011)

KEENAN, Circuit Judge:

Joseph Leone brought this action against his former employer, Tyco Electronics Corporation (Tyco). Leone alleged that Tyco breached a contractual provision of its short-term disability policy by refusing to pay him short-term disability benefits from June 6, 2007 through December 5, 2007. Leone also alleged that Tyco's refusal to pay these short-term disability benefits violated the North Carolina Wage and Hour Act (the Act), N.C. Gen. Stat. § 95-25.1, et seq.

The district court granted summary judgment in favor of Tyco on both claims. On the breach of contract claim, the district court held that Tyco processed Leone's application in compliance with the short-term disability policy, and that Leone failed to produce evidence that Tyco's actions in denying the claim were unreasonable, unfair, or in bad faith. The district court also held that Leone failed to establish a claim for wages under the Act. We affirm.

I.

Between 1996 and 2006, Leone worked as a "mold maker" for Tyco. In November 2006, he filed a claim for short-term disability benefits. At that time, Leone was being treated for a bipolar disorder by Dr. Jason Crandell and for a sleep disorder by Dr. Baldwin Smith. On November 14, 2006, Tyco's short-term disability administrator, Hoover Rehabilitation Services, Inc. (Hoover), informed Leone that his short-term disability claim had been approved effective November 7, 2006.

Leone returned to work without restrictions on May 1, 2007. One month later, however, he filed a new claim for short-term disability benefits. Upon receipt of Leone's application, Hoover's representative contacted Tyco's corporate medical director, Dr. Mark A. Bates, and asked him to review Leone's claim. After reviewing Leone's medical documentation and speaking with Dr. Smith, Dr. Bates recommended that Leone's claim be denied. According to Dr. Bates, the medical documentation did not substantiate any change in Leone's medical condition that would explain how Leone could have been disabled from working for almost six months, then able to work without restrictions for thirty-one days, and immediately thereafter be unable to work again. Hoover later informed Leone that Tyco had denied his claim for short-term disability benefits, and advised Leone of his appeal rights under Tyco's short-term disability policy.

Leone filed an appeal with Hoover challenging the denial of his claim. In support of his appeal, Leone enclosed records from Dr. Smith and a letter from Leone's wife. These documents were sent to Dr. Bates for review.

After receiving these documents, Dr. Bates contacted Dr. Smith to discuss Leone's condition. Based on Dr. Bates' review of the medical documents and his conversation with Dr. Smith, Dr. Bates informed Hoover of his opinion that although Leone had "some sort of sleep disturbance," there was no change in Leone's condition between the period that he was working without restriction and the time that he requested resumption of short-term disability benefits. Dr. Bates therefore recommended to Hoover that Leone's appeal be denied. On July 18, 2007, Hoover sent Leone a letter notifying him that his appeal had been denied.

After receiving Hoover's denial letter, Leone asked for the opportunity to submit additional documentation to support his claim. Hoover agreed and conducted a review of Leone's additional documentation, including Leone's physicians' letters. These letters were forwarded to Dr. Bates for further review of Leone's claim. When Dr. Bates again recommended that the claim be denied, Hoover informed Leone of the final denial of his claim for a resumption of short-term disability benefits.

On July 26, 2007, Tyco sent Leone a letter stating that his employment was terminated, effective June 6, 2007. Tyco stated that its decision was based on the fact that Leone had been absent from work since June 6, 2007, that his short-term disability claim and appeal had been denied, and that he had exhausted his leave under the Family Medical Leave Act.

In June 2008, Leone filed an action against Tyco in Wake County Superior Court in North Carolina. In the complaint, Leone alleged that Tyco breached a contractual provision in the short-term disability policy by refusing to pay him short-term disability benefits. He also alleged that Tyco's refusal of his claim violated the Act.

Tyco removed the case to the federal district court and later moved for summary judgment on all of Leone's claims. The district court granted Tyco's motion for summary judgment on Leone's breach of contract claim, holding that "Leone proffered no evidence that Tyco's processing of his second [short-term disability] claim was anything other than compliant with Tyco's Policy." The district court also granted summary judgment to Tyco on Leone's claim under the Act, concluding that Tyco did not owe Leone wages after the effective date of his termination. Leone filed a timely an appeal in this court challenging the district court's judgment.

II.

We review an award of summary judgment de novo. *Homeland Training Ctr., LLC v. Summit Point Auto. Research Ctr.*, 594 F.3d 285, 290 (4th Cir.2010). Under this standard, summary judgment is appropriate when "there is no genuine dispute as to any material fact and the movant is entitled to judgment as a matter of law." Fed. R. Civ. P. 56(a).

III.

We first address Leone's argument that Tyco breached its contract by refusing to pay Leone short-term disability benefits. The parties agree that we apply North Carolina law to this breach of contract claim.

Under North Carolina law, Tyco's short-term disability policy is a unilateral contract in which Tyco offered its employees an opportunity to apply for and to receive short-term disability benefits. *See White v. Hugh Chatham Mem'l Hosp., Inc.*, 97 N.C. App. 130, 387 S.E.2d 80, 81 (1990); *Hamilton v. Memorex Telex Corp.*, 118 N.C. App. 1, 454 S.E.2d 278, 282–83 (1995). A Tyco employee accepts that offer by entering or maintaining employment. *See White*, 387 S.E.2d at 81.

North Carolina law provides that a contract is construed as a whole, and that individual clauses are construed in their context. *Sec. Nat'l Bank v. Educators Mut. Life Ins. Co.*, 265 N.C. 86, 143 S.E.2d 270, 275 (1965). If a contract provides a party "discretionary power affecting the rights of others," then that party must exercise its discretionary power "in a reasonable manner based upon good faith and fair play." *Mezzanotte v. Freeland*, 20 N.C. App. 11, 200 S.E.2d 410, 414 (.1973). A contract confers "discretionary power" when the contract language provides one party with the right to exercise its sole judgment. *See Midulla v. Howard A. Cain Co.*, 133 N.C. App. 306, 515 S.E.2d 244, 246 (1999).

We consider the plain language of the short-term disability contract. *See Holshouser v. Shaner Hotel Group Props. Ltd. P'ship*, 134 N.C. App. 391, 518 S.E.2d 17, 18 (1999). The stated purpose of Tyco's short-term disability policy is to "establish the procedure to determine an employee's eligibility to receive Short-Term and Long-Term Disability Benefits for non-occupational illness/injury." The policy defines a "Short Term Disability" as "a condition that renders an employee incapable of performing the required duties of his/her occupation ... due to non-occupational injury or illness." The policy states that a short-term disability benefit "may" be available to an employee who has a short-term disability.

The policy includes a section entitled "Short-Term Disability Procedure." In that section, the policy explains that an employee must notify his supervisor when he is unable to work due to an illness or injury. The policy further details the responsibilities of the supervisor in contacting the short-term disability "vendor." According to the policy, the vendor is responsible for contacting the employee and the employee's medical provider to verify the employee's medical information.

The procedure section of the policy also explains the various requirements imposed after the approval or denial of an employee's disability claim. For example, if a claim is approved, the employee must provide medical updates to the vendor on a regular basis. However, if the disability claim is denied, the employee must return to work immediately or appeal the denial of the claim within fourteen days.

A "disclaimer" is provided at the end of the policy. The disclaimer states that "[t]he Vice President of Human Resources, or designee, whose decision shall be final, shall make any interpretation(s) of, or exception(s) to [the] policy."

The plain language of Tyco's policy demonstrates that the policy does not guarantee that an employee will receive short-term disability benefits if the employee meets the policy's requirements for establishment of a short-term disability. Instead, the policy merely provides that short-term disability benefits "may" be available to an employee who has a short-term disability. This language also must be construed in light of other policy provisions, including the disclaimer and the statement that a claim may be "approved" or "denied." *See Sec. Nat'l Bank,* 143 S.E.2d at 275.

These provisions, when viewed together, provide employees alleging a disability with the right to file a claim for benefits, and with an established claims procedure that allows Tyco the right to exercise its judgment when reviewing claims made under the policy. This policy language provides Tyco with "discretionary power" to approve or deny claims. *See Mezzanotte,* 200 S.E.2d at 414. An employee's right to short-term disability benefits therefore is contingent upon Tyco's exercise of its discretionary power.

We are not persuaded by Leone's argument that Tyco lacks discretionary power to approve or deny benefit claims because such power is not stated expressly in the policy. In advancing this argument, Leone exclusively relies on court decisions involving claims brought under the Employee Retirement Income Security Act (ERISA). *See Gallagher v. Reliance Standard Life Ins. Co.,* 305 F.3d 264, 268–69 (4th Cir.2002); *Herzberger v. Standard Ins. Co.,* 205 F.3d 327, 331–32 (7th Cir.2000). These ERISA cases, which reflect the fiduciary relationship of an employer to its employees in certain contexts not applicable here, are not relevant to our breach of contract analysis. *See Griggs v. E.I. DuPont de Nemours & Co.,* 237 F.3d 371, 379–80 (4th Cir.2001) (discussing the responsibilities of a fiduciary under ERISA). As explained above, we reach our conclusion concerning Tyco's contractual authority upon consideration of the plain language of the entire policy.

We also observe that, under North Carolina contract law, Tyco was required to exercise its discretionary power "in a reasonable manner based upon good faith and fair play." *Mezzanotte,* 200 S.E.2d at 414. The evidence in the record shows that Tyco acted reasonably in reviewing Leone's second claim for short-term disability benefits. Tyco referred Leone's claim to Dr. Bates for multiple reviews, considered Leone's appeal and additional documentation, and relied on Dr. Bates' various recommendations to deny Leone's claim. Additionally, Leone has not presented any evidence that Tyco failed to exercise its discretionary power in a reasonable manner. Therefore, we hold that the district court did not err in granting summary judgment to Tyco on Leone's breach of contract claim.

IV.

Leone next challenges the district court's decision awarding summary judgment to Tyco on Leone's claim for wages under the Act. The relevant provision of the Act states that employers must pay "all wages and tips accruing to the employee on the regular payday." N.C. Gen. Stat. § 95-25.6. The Act further provides that "[e]mployees whose employment is discontinued for any reason shall be paid all wages due." N.C. Gen. Stat. § 95-25.7.

The Act defines "wages" as "compensation for labor or services rendered by an employee." N.C. Gen. Stat. § 95-25.2(16). The Act states that a "wage" includes "sick pay, vacation pay, severance pay, commissions, bonuses, and other amounts promised when the employer has a policy or a practice of making such payments." N.C. Gen. Stat. § 95-25.2(16).

The Act does not require that an employer have a policy providing wage-related benefits. *Narron v. Hardee's Food Sys., Inc.,* 75 N.C. App. 579, 331 S.E.2d 205, 207 (1985). However, if the employer decides to offer wage-related benefits, then the Act requires, among other things, that an employer notify its employees of the benefits policy, inform its employee of the conditions that must be met to earn the benefits, and provide the benefits due when the employee performs the work required to earn the benefits. *Id.*

Even if we assume, without deciding, that short-term disability benefits are considered wage-related benefits payable as "wages" under the Act, we conclude that Leone does not have a valid claim under the Act. Tyco's policy did not guarantee short-term disability benefits to disabled employees. Under the language of the policy, a claim for benefits accrues after Tyco approves an employee's benefits claim. Leone's final claim for short-term disability benefits was not approved by Tyco and, thus, Leone never accrued short-term disability benefits for that later time period. *See Moses Cone Mem'l Health Servs. Corp. v. Triplett,* 167 N.C. App. 267, 605 S.E.2d 492, 496 (2004). Therefore, we conclude that the district court did not err in awarding summary judgment to Tyco on Leone's claim for wages under the Act.

For these reasons, we affirm the district court's award of summary judgment to Tyco.

AFFIRMED.

Issues for Consideration

1. How did the Fourth Circuit treat Tyco's STD plan? What was their explanation?
2. Did Tyco breach its contract with Leone by refusing to pay STD benefits?
3. Was Tyco entitled to make decisions around eligibility here?
4. What was wrong with Leone's reliance on court decisions involving claims brought under ERISA?
5. Did Tyco act reasonably and in good faith?

Long-Term Disability Plans

Employer-sponsored long-term disability (LTD) plans, or "group" disability plans, are typically offered to provide financial protection to employees who are unable to work for extended periods of time. Not to be confused with "individual disability plans" that can be purchased on the open market by individual consumers, we will focus on LTD insurance offered through the employer. With traditional STD programs providing benefits through 26 weeks (or 180 days), employers will generally align the LTD plan design to begin following an employee's continuous disability for more than 180 days. This ensures that a disabled employee will not collect both STD and LTD benefits at the same time. Like STD plans, employer-sponsored LTD plans can be customized, but if the plan is fully-insured—which most are—employers, and the carriers, are subject to the rules of ERISA.

We previously reviewed the interplay between STD benefits and the Family and Medical Leave Act running concurrently with each other, providing wage replacement and job protection for employees. Now that LTD benefits have been introduced, here is an updated illustration of the benefit and leave entitlement interplay. Note this is an example based on an STD plan that would provide benefits for up to 26 weeks and an LTD plan that would begin after 26 weeks of continuous disability.

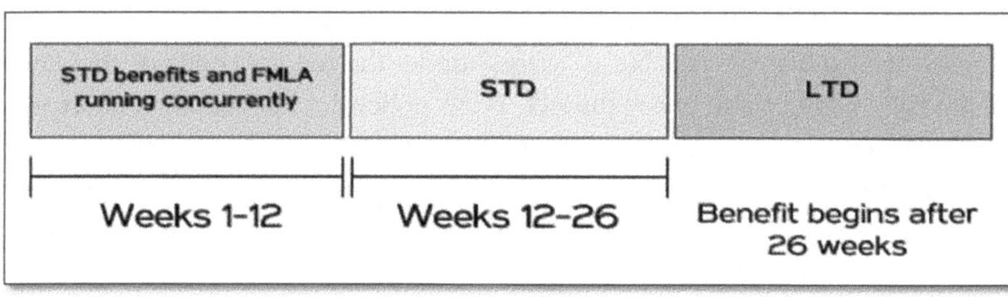

It's important to recognize the interplay between an STD plan that may be self-funded through a pay-practice and an LTD plan that is fully insured and administered by an insurance carrier. At a high level, STD and LTD benefits are critical pieces to an employer-sponsored benefits package. They provide significant financial protection when their employees are faced with the daunting prospect of being unable to work due to a physical or mental impairment(s). But each benefit may have a different definition of disability, as well as different eligibility and claim processing rules. What might be considered a disability under an employer's STD plan may not rise to the level of disability under the employer's LTD plan—which is likely to be insured and administered by an insurance carrier. Remember that with self-funded STD plans, employers have the ability to influence a claims decision whereas they do not with fully insured LTD plans. Even if an employee is approved for STD benefits through the entire duration of the benefit (26 weeks), they may need to provide additional medical information or evidence to the LTD insurance carrier. The main point here is that when there are separate disability plans in place, a finding of disability is not automatic. This can be confusing for employees seeking benefits through what can sometimes be an arduous claims process, so it is critical for employers to have resources that can help guide employees around the process and benefit interaction.

Another significant component of LTD insurance is how the employer chooses to offer it to employees. The employer has the discretion whether to subsidize the benefit, pay for it entirely or offer it up for employees to purchase. There are numerous factors that go into these decisions, but here are a few more common options (not an exhaustive list):

- **Fully subsidized:** The LTD benefit would be fully paid for by the employer at no cost to the employee. Employer pays the benefit premium and the insurance carrier administers the claim and pays the benefit if rendered disabled.
- **Partially subsidized:** Employers may opt to subsidize a "base-LTD benefit" which represents a percentage of salary, usually with a maximum limit. Then in addition to this base LTD benefit, the employer may offer its employees the option to "buy-up" a supplemental LTD benefit, which would give the employee a higher benefit rate. The employee would pay for the cost of this supplemental buy-up but it would give them additional disability protection. This buy-up is completely optional and employees typically receive this option to bolster their LTD benefit through a traditional, annual open enrollment for benefits.

Example

Fully Subsidized LTD Plan	Partially Subsidized LTD Plan
• 60% of salary • Maximum of $5,000/month • Employer paid—no cost to employee	• 40% of salary (LTD base) • Maximum of $5,000/month • Employer paid—no cost to employee for this 40% base ***Optional Supplemental Buy-Up*** • 20% Buy-up • Maximum of $10,000/month with both Base and Buy-up • Employee-paid—cost is paid through monthly premiums to insurance carrier *In this example, the employee is electing to increase their LTD benefit to 60% by paying for the 20% Supplemental Buy-up.*

The supplemental buy-up option where employees can elect to increase their disability coverage can be advantageous for employers that want to personalize their benefit options recognizing there is not a one-size-fits-all approach to disability benefits. It also enables employers to offer both short and long-term disability coverage through mutually beneficial cost-effective measures. Under the above example, employees not interested in the buy-up option will still have group LTD insurance paid for by their employer. And for those employees interested in more disability coverage, they can purchase through the buy-up option.

Employer-sponsored disability coverage is often the most overlooked, but also the most critical benefit in a total rewards portfolio when an employee is sick or injured. Unlike a parental benefit where an employee may have aspirations to start, or expand, their family, they simply do not expect to become disabled during their career (nor do they want to).

Employees tend to focus on paid time off and other wellness benefits in addition to their compensation package. Unfortunately, according to the Social Security Administration, "about 1 in 4 of today's 20-year-olds will become disabled and entitled to Social Security disabled workers [benefits] before reaching age 67."[8] This statistic that 1 in 4 people will eventually become disabled is a staggeringly high number that substantiates the importance of disability insurance. It can prove to be the most critical benefit because it replaces income (usually a percentage of it) when an employee is in their most vulnerable state and unable to work either temporarily or permanently.

Impact of COVID-19

The global pandemic ushered in a title wave of new issues in the leave, disability and employee benefit space. For disability claims, the immediate question that employers and claims administrators faced was whether an STD claim could be approved based on a positive COVID test, COVID symptoms or even potential exposure. With little to no information about COVID in the early stages of the pandemic (approximately 2020), employers were forced to acknowledge new, sporadic policies like encouraging employees to stay home if they aren't feeling well, as opposed to determining how this would impact a potential claim for STD benefits. For many customer facing jobs, if an employee was asked to stay home because they either tested positive for COVID-19, were experiencing symptoms, or might have been exposed, STD benefits became an option for some kind of wage replacement in lieu of the employer continuing to pay the employee.

Positive Tests and Medical Documentation

If an STD policy had a 7-day waiting period (very common), there was also a question of whether one's experience of COVID-19 would rise to the level of disability in these private plans. Remember that for disability claims, while a medical diagnosis is helpful to better understand the employee's overall condition, it is the medical opinions and explanations of why the employee is unable to perform their job that is critical to determining whether the employee is able to work.

8. Social Security Administration, "Fact Sheet, 2024 Beneficiary data," published by SSA in 2025, https://www.ssa.gov/news/press/factsheets/basicfact-alt.pdf.

Obtaining these opinions during the pandemic was extremely challenging. Many healthcare providers stopped seeing patients out of an abundance of caution and emergency rooms were jammed up across the country (and globe for that matter). With access to care proving to be a major challenge, employees were unable to receive appropriate—or optimal—care for their conditions and in many cases, they were unable to get an opinion from their providers as to whether they could work. These opinions, proof of treatment and documentation are used by claims administrators to make decisions on a disability case. The medical documentation is used to determine whether the individual does in fact have a medical condition and associated symptoms, limitations and restrictions that prevent them from working. Employer-sponsored disability plans, claims administrators and insurance carriers had very difficult decisions as to whether they would approve claims based on either a COVID-19 diagnosis or employee's word if they were unable to gather medical documentation. Lastly, throughout the pandemic, availability of COVID-19 tests were sporadic in nature depending on where one lived, even validating a positive COVID-19 diagnosis became a challenge. This was significant because if an employer, through their claim administration process, chose to automatically approve a disability claim based on a validated COVID-19 diagnosis, even this became a challenge if employees were unable to acquire tests.

"High-Risk" Individuals and Underlying Medical Conditions

Another issue impacting the determination of a disability claim was whether or not a person could be found disabled based solely on the fact that they were considered to be "high-risk" for severe medical complications if they contracted COVID-19 because they had an underlying medical condition or autoimmune disorder. These situations presented the question of whether a disability claim could be approved based on their risk factor of contracting the virus, rather than a person actually having a debilitating medical condition. Below is an example of how this played out:

> ***Example: Employee with asthma***
>
> John, a store clerk at The Grocery Store, had asthma that was medically managed. John took medication and used an inhaler. But during the COVID-19 pandemic, John was instructed by his pulmonologist to be overly careful about avoiding situations where he could be exposed to the virus. John's physician opined that because of this medical condition, he would be very high-risk for asthmatic complications that could be fatal.
>
> With John's role as a grocery store clerk, his job required him to be in-person at the grocery store. This would inherently put him at risk for contracting the virus even with mitigating measures like wearing a mask. So while John's asthma was medically managed under normal circumstances—and would not qualify him for disability benefits—with the emergence of the COVID-19 virus and the high-risk factors that accompanied his diagnosis, John claimed the

inability to work and perform his job based on the opinions of his provider and his high-risk factors.

Would John be entitled to disability benefits based on his risk factor rather than experiencing symptoms, limitations and restrictions that would prevent him from working?

In this example above, a major question was whether a disability claim could be approved based someone being "high-risk." This idea of approving someone for disability benefits out of an abundance of caution is essentially in conflict with the notion that under a hypothetical policy, a claimant has the burden of proof to show that they have a medical condition with associated symptoms, limitations and restrictions that has rendered them unable to perform their job. In the example above, John did have a medical condition, but without exposure or infection of the COVID-19 virus, it was managed with medication so that he could essentially perform work activities. But with his job being located in a public space and open to the public, his potential exposure and infection was extremely dangerous for him. The question of whether to approve these claims became a dilemma.

Approval Timelines

Another associated question of whether to approve a disability claim based on a "high-risk" factor that generally speaking, was not typically addressed in a traditional short-term or long-term disability plan, is if the decision is made to approve these claims, what was the length of time for approval? During the pandemic, there was so much uncertainty that a person could conceivably be high-risk forever. So the question became, if the decision was to approve these claims (based on a positive diagnosis or symptoms), for how long should the claim be approved before?

Prior to the widespread rollout of vaccinations, there was really no timetable for an individual to no longer be deemed "high-risk" because of their underlying medical condition or autoimmune disorder. Even with the rollout of vaccinations, individuals that were deemed to be "high-risk" remained in that category, further complicating an employer's decision to either approve them for disability benefits or leave, or utilize something like administrative pay and keep their claim open until they felt comfortable returning.

Long COVID

As the pandemic wore on, each individual's experience of becoming infected with the COVID-19 virus was very different. Despite a positive test, symptoms ranged from mild to extremely severe. This meant the range of severity was incredibly vast and reports of little to no symptoms or an experience like the common cold were frequent. But you also had reports of individuals who had near fatal experiences where they were immobile for several days or needed to be under appropriate medical care for multiple days at a time. This range of severity also contributed to the difficulty of how to treat COVID-19 disability claims.

Another relatively new condition that emerged in parallel with the COVID-19 pandemic was something called "long COVID," which essentially is the term for one's experience of a variety of symptoms after a COVID-19 infection. According to the Center for Disease Control (CDC)[9], long COVID is described as:

- A serious illness that can result in chronic conditions requiring comprehensive care and may cause disability.
- Long COVID can include a wide range of ongoing symptoms and conditions that can last weeks, months, or even years after COVID-19 illness.
- Living with Long COVID can be difficult and isolating, especially when there are no immediate answers or solutions.

The CDC goes on to explain that anyone can experience long COVID and the symptoms, as well the frequency and severity of them, are sporadic in nature. We'll come back to the topic of Long COVID with workplace accommodations and it's recognition as a disability by the EEOC, but within the context of disability claims, long COVID was not only a new term, but the medical community was still researching how it impacted individuals. This made making a disability determination quite challenging.

Ultimately, employers, administrators and insurance carriers were faced with new and complex challenges with the COVID-19 pandemic. Industry practices of validating a medical condition and appropriate care were questioned—especially when many were unable to get into treatment during the pandemic (i.e., shelter-in-place mandates across the country). If the pandemic taught us anything from a claims management perspective, it was that disability policies are helpful in outlining eligibility, policy rules and disability criteria, but, depending on the circumstances at play, flexibility should always be considered to ensure fairness and to maintain access to a critical benefit at a time of great vulnerability.

9. Center for Disease Control, "Long COVID basics," accessed February 3, 2025, https://www.cdc.gov/covid/long-term-effects/index.html.

Chapter III

Family and Medical Leave Act (FMLA)

The Family and Medical Leave Act (FMLA) was signed into law by President Bill Clinton in January 1993. This was a landmark federal law that gave eligible employees access to federally protected leave from their workplace stemming from their own medical condition, to care for a family member, bonding with a child or to care for a military service member. This legislation was first introduced in 1984 through the help of an organization known as the Women's Legal Defense Fund who advocated for almost a decade for this to become law. In fact, FMLA was introduced in Congress every year from 1984 to 1993 but ultimately failed to become law until 1994. The Women's Legal Defense Fund is now known as the National Partnership for Women and Families and they continue to advocate for a variety of leave and paid leave laws at the federal level.[1]

When President Clinton signed the FMLA into law on February 5, 1993, he commented that the FMLA addressed a "substantial and growing need" of a changing workforce.[2] At the time, it truly was a groundbreaking piece of legislation that not only provided job-protected leave to most employees, but it contributed to the idea that in many cases, employees did not have to choose between their career or taking care of themselves or their family.

Upon passage, the law was relatively simple, but as we'll delve into further, it has become challenging for both employees and employers alike. Generally speaking—and per the Department of Labor—FMLA provides certain employees with up to 12 weeks of unpaid, job protected leave year. It also requires that their group health benefits be maintained during the leave.[3] Employees' eligibility includes 1 year of service (12 months) with their employer and they must have worked at least 1,250 hours in the last year. They must also work at a location where there are 50 or more employees within

1. National Partnership for Women & Families, "History of the FMLA," https://nationalpartnership.org/economic-justice/family-medical-leave-act/history-of-the-fmla/.

2. Ryan Golden, "FMLA: The 30-year legacy of a celebrated—and complicated—employment law" *HR Dive*, (February 3, 2023), https://www.hrdive.com/news/fmla-30th-anniversary-history-paid-leave/641972/.

3. United States Department of Labor, "Family and Medical Leave (FMLA)," https://www.dol.gov/general/topic/benefits-leave/fmla.

a 75-mile radius.[4] In this section, we'll dissect the FMLA's qualifying reasons for leave, key legal definitions and how the law is enforced.

The FMLA was an exceptional piece of legislation that bolstered employee rights with respect to leave in the workplace, but it also had a tremendous impact on the employer. To maintain compliance with a new law that enabled employees to take federally protected leave of absence, employers had to establish mechanisms for tracking and administering this law. Individual employee eligibility was (and still is) based on having at least one year of service, but also a minimum of 1,250 hours worked in the past year. If employers were not tracking that at the time, this law essentially forced them to do so for compliance reasons. While time-tracking at the employer level was not necessarily a novel idea—especially for hourly workers—vendors that provided this service became much more sophisticated with their services to ensure tracking for all workers, not just hourly ones. Notably, the law includes provisions around recordkeeping requirements, so it was incumbent for covered employers to start tracking hours worked. And lastly, as we'll see with caselaw that followed the passage of the FMLA, the concept of "interference" emerged as a large threat to employers that intended to be compliant with the law, but may have failed to ensure that leaders and supervisors were well versed in the mechanics of the law and protections it provided.

What Is the Family and Medical Leave Act (FMLA)?

United States Code Title 29, Subtitle B, Chapter C, Part 825 contains the provisions of the FMLA in its entirety. In this text, we will cover the pertinent sections of the law and how claim administration, the employee experience and employer compliance have evolved over the years.

Starting with what the law provides and taken directly from Title 29, Code of Federal Regulations, Part 825,[5] The Family Medical and Leave Act of 1993, Subpart A, Coverage Under the Family and Medical Leave Act, states (in pertinent):

(a) FMLA allows eligible employees of a covered employer to take job-protected, unpaid leave ... for up to 12 workweeks in any 12 months because of:

- Birth of child and to care for the newborn;
- Placement of a child with the employee for adoption or foster care;
- Employee needs to care for family member (child, spouse or parent) with a "serious health condition";
- Employee's own "serious health condition" makes the employee unable to perform the functions of their job; or

---

4. *Id.*

5. Code of Federal Regulations, "Part 825, The Family and Medical Leave Act of 1993," accessed 2025 https://www.ecfr.gov/current/title-29/subtitle-B/chapter-V/subchapter-C/part-825#_top.

- Any qualifying exigency arising out of the fact that the employee's spouse, son, daughter, or parent is a military member on active duty or call to covered active-duty status (also referred to as military exigency).

In certain cases, FMLA leave may be taken on an intermittent basis rather than all at once, or the employee may work a part-time schedule.

(b) An employee on FMLA leave is also entitled to have health benefits maintained while on leave as if the employee had continued to work instead of taking the leave. If an employee was paying all or part of the premium payments prior to leave, the employee would continue pay their share during the leave period.

(c) An employee generally has a right to return to the same position or an equivalent position with equivalent pay, benefits, and working conditions at the conclusion of the leave. The taking of FMLA leave cannot result in the loss of any benefit that accrued prior to the start of the leave.

(d) The employer generally has a right to advance notice from the employee. In addition, the employer may require an employee to submit certification to substantiate that the leave is due to the serious health condition of the employee or the employee's covered family member, due to the serious injury or illness of a covered servicemember, or because of a qualifying exigency.

Following details of the leave and associated employee protections, the Act describes the purpose and overall intent of the law. These excerpts are taken directly from Section 825.101, Purpose of the Act:[6]

(a) FMLA is intended to allow employees to balance their work and family life by taking reasonable unpaid leave for medical reasons, for the birth or adoption of a child, for the care of a child, spouse, or parent who has a serious health condition, for the care of a covered servicemember with a serious injury or illness, or because of a qualifying exigency arising out of the fact that the employee's spouse, son, daughter, or parent is a military member on covered active duty or call to covered active duty status. **The Act is intended to balance the demands of the workplace with the needs of families, and to promote national interests in preserving family integrity.** It was intended that the Act accomplish these purposes in a manner that accommodates the legitimate interests of employers, and in a manner consistent with the Equal Protection Clause of the Fourteenth Amendment in minimizing the potential for employment discrimination on the basis of sex, while promoting equal employment opportunity for men and women.

(b) The FMLA was predicated on two fundamental concerns—the needs of the American workforce, and the development of high-performance organizations. Increasingly, America's children and elderly are dependent upon family

6. *Id.*

members who must spend long hours at work. **When a family emergency arises, requiring workers to attend to seriously-ill children or parents, or to newly-born or adopted infants, or even to their own serious illness, workers need reassurance that they will not be asked to choose between continuing their employment, and meeting their personal and family obligations or tending to vital needs at home.**

(c) The FMLA is both intended and expected to benefit employers as well as their employees. A direct correlation exists between stability in the family and productivity in the workplace. FMLA will encourage the development of high-performance organizations. When workers can count on durable links to their workplace they are able to make their own full commitments to their jobs. The record of hearings on family and medical leave indicate the powerful productive advantages of stable workplace relationships, and the comparatively small costs of guaranteeing that those relationships will not be dissolved while workers attend to pressing family health obligations of their own serious illness.

The first section (825.100) of the FMLA provides a healthy description of the leave entitlement, what it covers, what family members are covered and some additional protections tied to the leave (job protection, continuation of health benefits, right to return to same or similar position). Essentially, this introductory section provides the foundational components of what the law provides.

Section 825.100(a) details covered reasons for taking leave but also indicates who the family member is under the Act. A family member under the FMLA is defined as a spouse, child or parent and later, we'll see how state paid family and medical leave programs expanded this definition to provide more coverage for employees. It is important to note that the FMLA defines a parent as "an employee's biological, adoptive, step or foster parent, or someone who stood ***in loco parentis*** to the employee when the employee was a child. Standing in loco parentis means a person is in the role of a parent.[7]" This is significant because it expands the use of this leave through a concept of standing in a familial relationship rather than a biological or even legal (guardian) one. Acknowledging that in many cases, employees standing in the place of a parent and providing caregiving support, won't have documentation to prove their status so it becomes a difficult decision by the employer to request documentation to prove their status. The FMLA does allow employers to request "reasonable" documentation, but employees can satisfy this requirement with a statement asserting the family relationship exists.[8]

In the following section (825.101), the Act goes into great detail on ***why*** this leave is so critical for employees—honing in on the spirit and intent of the law. Highlighting the traditional demands of the workplace that often conflict with an employee's need

7. United States Department of Labor, "Fact Sheet #28C: Using FMLA Leave to Care for Someone Who Was in the Role of a Parent to You When You Were a Child" (March 2025), https://www.dol.gov/agencies/whd/fact-sheets/28C-fmla-eldercare.

8. *Id.*

to tend to family emergencies, the Act emphasizes its intent to provide protections that eradicate the need for an employee to choose between their family and their career. It is worth noting that while FMLA provides federally mandated leave for covered employers, the leave itself is unpaid. While the FMLA was a landmark law and first of its kind to require employers to grant leave for specific situations, some employees were still faced with economic hardships when taking this leave. Since the inception of the FMLA in 1993, the "unpaid" component of this law would go on to spark a movement across state legislatures over the next twenty years. The concept of state paid family leave would eventually become yet another leave type that resembled family medical leave under the FMLA, but differed in many ways too. The FMLA was ultimately the beginning of a larger conversation about the need for more employee protections in the workplace when faced with the daunting proposition of one's own serious health condition or that of a family member's.

What Is a Serious Health Condition?

One of the primary components of the FMLA's criteria for taking leave is what the Act calls a "serious health condition." This is the FMLA's threshold for taking leave specifically for one's own medical condition or to care for a spouse, child or parent. Taken on its face, a serious health condition is rather vague and could be interpreted differently depending on who you ask. Fortunately, the FMLA addresses this in Section 825.113, Serious Health Condition.[9]

Before examining the specific provisions that detail what a serious health condition is under the FMLA, it is important to note how an employee substantiates, or justifies, the need for leave. This is done through medical documentation and most commonly through what's generally known as an FMLA certification form or another medical record that supports—and in many cases—explains the need for continuous or intermittent leave. Per the Department of Labor (DOL), "employers must accept a complete and sufficient certification, regardless of the format."[10] To assist both employees and employers with this, the DOL has provided several templates and guides to assist in this process with the goal of eliciting key information to substantiate the need for leave.

The following sections and provisions within are taken directly from the regulations in Part 825. This is not an exhaustive list of the regulations, but for purposes of understanding the key components of FMLA, employee rights and employer impact, I'm providing the relevant sections to understand how this leave of absence is utilized and managed within the workplace.

Section 825.113 (copied in full from Code of Federal Regulations)

(a) For purposes of FMLA, serious health condition entitling an employee to FMLA leave means an illness, injury, impairment or physical or mental con-

9. *Id.*

10. United States Department of Labor, "FMLA: Forms," accessed 2025, https://www.dol.gov/agencies/whd/fmla/forms.

dition that involves inpatient care as defined in Section 825.114 or continuing treatment by a health care provider as defined in Section 825.115.

(b) The term incapacity means inability to work, attend school or perform other regular daily activities due to the serious health condition, treatment therefore, or recovery therefrom.

(c) The term treatment includes (but is not limited to) examinations to determine if a serious health condition exists and evaluations of the condition. Treatment does not include routine physical examinations, eye examinations, or dental examinations. A regimen of continuing treatment includes, for example, a course of prescription medication (e.g., an antibiotic) or therapy requiring special equipment to resolve or alleviate the health condition (e.g., oxygen). A regimen of continuing treatment that includes the taking of over-the-counter medications such as aspirin, antihistamines, or salves; or bed-rest, drinking fluids, exercise, and other similar activities that can be initiated without a visit to a health care provider, is not, by itself, sufficient to constitute a regimen of continuing treatment for purposes of FMLA leave.

(d) Conditions for which cosmetic treatments are administered (such as most treatments for acne or plastic surgery) are not serious health conditions unless inpatient hospital care is required or unless complications develop. Ordinarily, unless complications arise, the common cold, the flu, ear aches, upset stomach, minor ulcers, headaches other than migraine, routine dental or orthodontia problems, periodontal disease, etc., are examples of conditions that do not meet the definition of a serious health condition and do not qualify for FMLA leave. Restorative dental or plastic surgery after an injury or removal of cancerous growths are serious health conditions provided all the other conditions of this regulation are met. Mental illness or allergies may be serious health conditions, but only if all the conditions of this section are met.

Section 825.113 defines what a serious health condition is, but it also calls out two important terms that help to determine whether something is a serious health condition. Under subsection (a), a serious health condition is one that inpatient care (825.114) or continuing treatment by a health care provider (825.115). These terms are very important to be able to distinguish a serious health condition and can often make an FMLA claim determination much easier to resolve if either one is present.

Section 825.114 defines inpatient care as an "overnight stay in a hospital, hospice or residential medical care facility, including any period of incapacity as defined in 825.113(b), or any subsequent treatment in connection with such inpatient care."[11] Per this section, if an employee is admitted to the hospital overnight, it would in all likelihood qualify them for FMLA leave.

11. *Id.*

Section 825.115 (copied in full from Code of Federal Regulations)

The Act goes into great detail on how lawmakers defined "continuing treatment. They expand on the type of treatment, the length of time for that treatment and even call out specific conditions. I've included the provisions of Section 825.115 in its entirety to fully grasp how this section encapsulates such a wide variety of medical treatment and in doing so, creating a very low threshold for approval under the FMLA.

A serious health condition involving continuing treatment by a health care provider includes any one or more of the following:

(a) ***Incapacity and treatment.*** A period of incapacity of more than three consecutive, full calendar days, and any subsequent treatment or period of incapacity relating to the same condition, that also involves:

   (1) Treatment two or more times, within 30 days of the first day of incapacity, unless extenuating circumstances exist, by a health care provider, by a nurse under direct supervision of a health care provider, or by a provider of health care services (e.g., physical therapist) under orders of, or on referral by, a health care provider; or

   (2) Treatment by a health care provider on at least one occasion, which results in a regimen of continuing treatment under the supervision of the health care provider.

   (3) The requirement in paragraphs (a)(1) and (2) of this section for treatment by a health care provider means an in-person visit to a health care provider. The first (or only) in-person treatment visit must take place within seven days of the first day of incapacity.

   (4) Whether additional treatment visits or a regimen of continuing treatment is necessary within the 30-day period shall be determined by the health care provider.

   (5) The term *extenuating circumstances* in paragraph (a)(1) of this section means circumstances beyond the employee's control that prevent the follow-up visit from occurring as planned by the health care provider. Whether a given set of circumstances are extenuating depends on the facts. For example, extenuating circumstances exist if a health care provider determines that a second in-person visit is needed within the 30-day period, but the health care provider does not have any available appointments during that time period.

(b) ***Pregnancy or prenatal care.*** Any period of incapacity due to pregnancy, or for prenatal care (referencing Section 825.120).

(c) ***Chronic conditions.*** Any period of incapacity or treatment for such incapacity due to a chronic serious health condition. A chronic serious health condition is on which:

(1) Requires periodic visits (defined as at least twice a year) for treatment by a health care provider, or by a nurse under direct supervision of a health care provider;

(2) Continues over an extended period of time (including recurring episodes of a single underlying condition); and

(3) May cause episodic rather than a continuing period of incapacity (e.g., asthma, diabetes, epilepsy, etc.)

(d) ***Permanent or long-term conditions.*** A period of incapacity which is permanent or long-term due to a condition for which treatment may not be effective. The employee or family member must be under continuing supervision of, but need not be receiving active treatment by, a health care provider. Examples include Alzheimer's, a severe stroke, or the terminal stages of disease.

(e) ***Conditions requiring multiple treatments.*** Any period of absence to receive multiple treatments (including any period of recovery therefrom) by a health care provider or by a provider of health care services under of, or on referral by, a health care provider for:

(1) Restorative surgery after an accident or other injury; or

(2) A condition that would likely result in a period of incapacity of more than three consecutive, full calendars in the absence of medical intervention or treatment, such as cancer (chemotherapy, radiation, etc.), severe arthritis (physical therapy), or kidney disease (dialysis).

(f) Absences attributable to incapacity under paragraph (b) or (c) of this section qualify for FMLA leave even though the employee or the covered family member does not receive treatment from a health care provider during the absence, and even if the absence does not last more than three consecutive, full calendar days. For example, an employee with asthma may be unable to report for work due to the onset of an asthma attack or because the employee's health care provider has advised the employee to stay home when the pollen count exceeds a certain level. An employee who is pregnant may be unable to report to work because of severe morning sickness.[12]

Upon a review of the regulations contained in section 825, one can infer that beyond the standard eligibility criteria of service year and hours worked in the prior year, the threshold for utilizing leave under the terms "serious health condition" and "continuing health care" are relatively low. The intent was not to make it difficult for employees to pursue leave, but make it much more accessible than ever before.

The FMLA regulations also go into great detail on defining things like "continuing health care" so that they remain all-encompassing. The effect over the last 30 years has been just that. The law continues to be a large safety net for employees needing leave for a variety of reasons based on their own care, bonding, the care of a family member

12. *Id.*

or military servicemember. The law is not without criticism, however. FMLA's biggest limitation is the unpaid component and as we'll see later in this text, individual state legislatures have addressed this piece with their own state laws. And lastly, FMLA's definition of "family member" only includes spouse, child or parent. This has been a significant limitation where household inhabitants may not necessarily fall into one of these categories. This too has been addressed by various states with individual state paid family and medical leave laws.

Family and Medical Leave Entitlement Under the FMLA

Historically speaking, one of the more unique aspects of the FMLA and it's leave entitlement is the way employees can utilize the leave from work. In thinking about short and long-term disability leave, typical usage had minimum requirements for being able to take such leave. For example, most short-term disability plans require that an individual be unable to work for at least 7 days. Otherwise known as a "waiting period," an employee could not have eligibility until they've been out, or expect to be out, for at least 7 days before they could even be considered for the paid benefit. For long-term disability benefits, that waiting period has traditionally been set at 182 days, or 6 months, to align with the end of most short-term disability plans. The main point here is that under most employer short and long-term disability plans, disability leave must be taken on a continuous basis.

In contrast to traditional disability plans, the FMLA allows for leave to be taken on both a continuous and intermittent basis. Under the regulations (see below), intermittent leave refers to taking FMLA leave in separate blocks of time. This could include, but is not limited to, a few hours down to 15-minute increments. This component of the FMLA highlights yet another aspect of ushering in workplace flexibility so that the employee can attend to the needs of themselves or their family without having to fully unplug from work. But as we'll look at shortly, this aspect of the FMLA has effectively forced employers to implement sophisticated systems to ensure leave tracking, compliance and to prevent abuse.

FMLA eligible employees are entitled to 12 workweeks of job-protected, unpaid leave per year. Workweeks will apply differently to employees and are based the employee's actual work schedule. This is an important distinction in the context of intermittent usage of FMLA because depending on the employee's regular work schedule, they could leverage more intermittent leave under the FMLA if their regular schedule has more hours than say, a regular 40 hour per week employee.

Here are a few examples of how an employee's regular workweek could impact their FMLA bucket of leave time when factoring in intermittent usage:

Example 1: Sally, a secretary, works Monday–Friday, 9am–5pm (40 hours/week)

- FMLA entitlement by weeks: 12 weeks

- FMLA entitlement by hours: 480 hours

Example 2: Jim, a delivery driver, works Monday–Saturday, 8am–8pm (72 hours/week)

- FMLA entitlement by weeks: 12 weeks
- FMLA entitlement by hours: 864 hours

Example 3: Mary, a salesperson, works Mondays and Tuesdays, 10 hours per day

- FMLA entitlement by weeks: 12 weeks
- FMLA entitlement by hours: 240 hours

Based on these examples, you can see how an employee's regularly scheduled hours impact the amount of leave they can utilize under the FMLA. And when taken intermittently, they haven't actually left their job or the performance of their duties like they would for a continuous leave. Intermittent leave can essentially be defined as approved, sporadic instances of leave depending on an employee's, or their family member's, experience of symptoms or treatment schedule.

Moving ahead in the regulations to "Subpart B—Employee Entitlements Under the Family and Medical Leave Act," the Act goes into detail on how much leave an employee can use throughout the year, employer options for determining a 12-month period for which the leave can be taken and additional details on the allowance for intermittent leave. Below are a few provisions pertaining employer calculations and intermittent leave, but note that Subpart B contains a variety of other provisions tied to FMLA coverage, eligibility, interaction with other laws (Fair Labor Standards Act), and much more.

Section 825.200(b)

Under this section, the Act reiterates the 12 workweeks of leave available for employees to take under the FMLA. In highlighting that the leave needs to be taken within a 12-month period, Section 825.200(b) details the options that employers have for determining—and ultimately, administering—the 12-month period where the leave can be taken. This subsection is taken directly from the regulations:

> An employer is permitted to choose any one of the following methods for determining the 12-month period in which the 12 weeks of leave entitlement described in paragraph (a) of this section occurs:
>
> (1) The calendar year;
>
> (2) Any fixed 12-month leave, such as a fiscal year, a year required by State law, or a year starting on an employee's anniversary date;
>
> (3) The 12 month period measured forward from the date any employee's first FMLA leave ... or
>
> (4) A "rolling" 12-month period measured backward from date an employee uses any FMLA leave.

In subsection (c), the Act describes the various ways these options could be applied. Each one of these options listed in subsection (b) have different implications on when an employee has more leave if they've used up their 12 weeks in a specific period. These methods for calculating leave eligibility can be rather complex—especially if an employer has both hourly and salaried employees. This is yet another example of how these regulations required employers to develop not only an infrastructure for tracking these leaves, but also a very detailed policy for employees to understand what is available to them and when.

The following sections are not copied in entirety. I've included the pertinent sections and provisions to lay the foundation for use of intermittent leave under the FMLA.

Section 825.202(a)

Section 825.202(a) provides a thorough definition of "intermittent leave or reduced schedule." This is the primary section that distinguishes the use of leave under the FMLA in specific blocks of time.

(a) Definition. FMLA leave may be taken intermittently or on a reduced leave schedule under certain circumstances. *Intermittent leave* is FMLA leave taken in separate blocks of time due to a single qualifying reason. A *reduced leave* schedule is a leave schedule that reduces an employee's usual number working hours per workweek, or hours per workday. A reduced leave schedule is a change in the employee's schedule for a period of time, normally from full-time to part-time.

With employees able to leverage leave under the FMLA on an intermittent basis, it is incumbent on them to provide medical documentation that substantiates their need for leave. This typically comes in the form of medical records that indicate the medical condition (note that some states prevent employers from asking about a diagnosis), the frequency and duration of symptoms and possibly other information that helps to support the leave request. Whether the leave is continuous or intermittent, an employer always has the right to request medical information to substantiate the leave and today, most employers have standard forms that employees can provide to their providers to complete.

One of the more notable provisions related to the use of intermittent leave under the FMLA is the requirement for employees to make efforts to notify and schedule treatments that won't disrupt the operations of the employer. This is, of course, much easier said than done and conventional wisdom suggests that the experience of symptoms, as well as corresponding treatment, is not only hard to predict, but for many conditions, incredibly sporadic in nature. This provision does however give employer's some recourse, albeit small, to ask employees to make their best efforts on scheduling treatments with respect to an intermittent leave request. Section 825.203 states, in pertinent:

Section 825.203 (in pertinent)

> ... [I]f an employee needs leave intermittently or on a reduced leave schedule for planned medical treatment, then the employee must make a reasonable

effort to schedule the treatment so as not to disrupt unduly the employer's operations.

Practically speaking, Section 825.203 makes sense since intermittent leave could create workforce gaps that are difficult to plan for. When leave is taken on a continuous basis, employers have somewhat of an opportunity to plan for the intended leave. Alternatively, intermittent leave is not always so easy to predict. If it's treatment for a specific medical condition, that might have some consistency versus a leave allotment (4–5 days per month) due to the sporadic frequency and duration of symptoms an employee might be experiencing from an autoimmune disorder. Below are a few examples that help to illustrate intermittent leave usage.

Example—Set Treatment Schedule: Mary, a secretary for a building company, is receiving chemotherapy for cancer treatment and needs dialysis every week on Fridays for 3 months. Her provider completes an FMLA certification that indicates the need for her cancer treatment to include dialysis 1 x week over 3 months. Can Mary's employer dictate what day Mary's dialysis takes place?

Legal Analysis: In Mary's case, her provider indicates the need for dialysis on a consistent, weekly, basis. Depending on the nature of Mary's work, her employer could ask if the appointment could be modified to avoid the disruption of operations, but her employer cannot require it. That said, the consistent nature of Mary's request does make it a bit easier for her employer to plan for. They know she'll be out Friday, so they can determine how to manage Mary's work on that day or decide to bring in temporary help. This will always depend on the nature of the employer's operations, but it is important to remember Mary's employer cannot force her to change her treatment schedule based on business needs.

Example 2—Unpredictable Experience of Symptoms: Tim, a golf pro at a major golf store in town, suffers from fibromyalgia where his symptoms include fatigue, body aches, instability, brain fog and pain. The frequency of these symptoms are sporadic and unpredictable. Tim's physician completes an FMLA certification indicating that due to his unpredictable experience of symptoms, he will likely be unable to work 4–5 days per month. Tim's physician is estimating the amount of days in a month that Tim will be suffering from a serious health condition (fibromyalgia) that will render him unable perform the duties of his job. What, if anything, can Tim's employer do to manage this need for leave throughout the month?

Legal Analysis: To differentiate from the last example, Tim does not have an exact day of the week or time of the month where he'll expect to be using leave under the FMLA. Assuming Tim's FMLA certification is approved, he will have an allotted 4–5 days to take his intermittent medical leave should he need it throughout the month. Since the frequency and duration of his symptoms are sporadic, there is no way for him to "plan" his need for intermittent leave. This impacts both Tim and his employer, but the FMLA cared for this conundrum with intermittent leave provisions. One's experience of medical symptoms are highly individualized so it would be impossible to plan the need for leave when it is convenient for the employer. Under this scenario, Tim's employer can ask Tim to notify them at the earliest possible time when he would be utilizing his medical leave under the FMLA. Most employers have policies that may include reaching out the work location, supervisor or a third-party administrator that may be tracking the leave.

The FMLA's provisions under Part 825 are vast. The regulations are quite specific and other provisions detail employee protections, employer rights, impact to other benefits, the interplay with paid leave (if applicable through a private plan or state/local law) and much more. I've only included specific provisions of the FMLA within this text to highlight the foundational components of the federally mandated leave and to illustrate how it's played out in the workforce. Now that you have a baseline of what the leave is, we'll explore the specific employee protections from the Act and what happens if an employer "interferes" with these protections.

Employee Protections Under the FMLA

As a quick refresh, eligible employees who possess at least 12 months of service, have at least 1,250 hours of service with their employer in the last year and work at a location where the employer has at least 50 employees within 75 miles, have access to job-protected leave and the continuation of group health benefits. Additionally, "employees must be restored to the same or virtually identical position when they return to work after the FMLA leave.[13] This essentially protects an employee's job and benefits if they utilize this leave. It's an important distinction because it prohibited employers from making adverse employment decisions based on the utilization of this leave. That being said, it does not protect a job that is eliminated or part of a larger, company-wide reduction-in-force as long as the employer can delineate that the job elimination was completely separate from the leave. We will see examples of this in the caselaw.

Taken directly from the DOL's Fact Sheet #28, revised in March 2025, the agency details the primary employee protections under the FMLA:

> **Job protection.** Employees who use FMLA leave have the right to go back to work at their same job or to an equivalent job that has the same pay, benefits, and other terms and conditions of employment at the end of their FMLA leave. Violations of an employee's FMLA rights may include changing the number of shifts assigned to the employee, moving the employee to a location outside of his or her normal commuting area, or denying the employee a bonus for which the employee qualified before taking FMLA leave.[14]

---

13. United States Department of Labor, "Fact Sheet #28: The Family and Medical Leave Act" (Revised March 2025), https://www.dol.gov/agencies/whd/fact-sheets/28-fmla.

14. *Id.*

Note that under this DOL guidance, "job protection" extends beyond just reserving the employee's job. It includes adverse, or detrimental, impacts to the employee by way of changing some of the core functions of the job or promotional opportunities. As we'll see with the relevant caselaw, these things can be difficult to prove but will depend heavily on the specific facts and circumstances in each situation.

> **Group health plan benefits.** Employers are required to continue group health insurance coverage for an employee on FMLA leave under the same terms and conditions as if the employee had not taken leave. For example, if family member coverage is provided to an employee, family member coverage must be maintained during the employee's FMLA leave.[15] In most cases, an employee is responsible for paying their share of any healthcare premiums while on unpaid leave. This is at the discretion of the employer but is typically done through direct billing to the employee (as opposed to automatic payroll deductions when the employee is working and receiving a paycheck.

Job protection and maintaining health benefits are fairly straightforward, the DOL goes further and specifically emphasizes that employers are also prohibited from "interfering with, restraining, or denying the exercise of, or the attempt to exercise, any FMLA right."[16] This final piece is a protection against retaliation for taking FMLA leave and the concept of "interference" can take shape in many different ways.

A further examination of the job protection piece for employees is the right to be returned to the same or equivalent position with the same pay, benefits and other terms of employment. This is covered specifically within sections 825.214, 825.215 and 825.216.

One important provision to highlight specifically because it serves as the primary exception to the job reinstatement piece is section 825.217, key employee, general rule. Here, the FMLA lists the primary reason where an employer is allowed to deny job restoration to the employee because it would cause "substantial and grievous economic injury." This is covered in sections 825.217 and 825.218.

> **§ 825.218 Substantial and grievous economic injury**
>
> (a) In order to deny restoration to a key employee, an employer must determine that the restoration of the employee to employment will cause substantial and grievous economic injury to the operations of the employer, not whether the absence of the employee will cause such substantial and grievous injury.
>
> (b) An employer may take into account its ability to replace on a temporary basis (or temporarily do without) the employee on FMLA leave. If permanent replacement is unavoidable, the cost of then reinstating the employee can be considered in evaluating whether substantial and grievous economic injury will occur from restoration; in other words, the effect on the operations of the company of reinstating the employee in an equivalent position.

15. *Id.*
16. *Id.*

(c) A precise test cannot be set for the level or hardship or injury to the employer which must be sustained. If the reinstatement of a key employee threatens the economic viability of the firm, that would constitute substantial and grievous economic injury. A lesser injury which causes substantial, long-term economic injury would also be sufficient. Minor inconveniences and costs that the employer would experience in the normal course of doing business would certainly not constitute substantial and grievous economic injury.

(d) FMLA's substantial and grievous economic injury standard is different from and more stringent than the undue hardship test under the ADA [Americans with Disabilities Act].[17]

In summary, under this key employee rule, employers can ultimately deny job restoration to this "key" employee if they are FMLA eligible, salaried and among the highest-paid 10% of all employees within 75 miles, but the employer also needs to establish:

- Substantial and grievous economic injury to its operations would result from the restoration;
- They must have provided notice to the employee that they are a key employee and that the restoration will be denied; and
- They must provide the employee a reasonable opportunity to return to work.

It is important to recognize this rule is referring to the "reinstatement" of an employee rather than the allowance of using leave under the FMLA. The need for—and utilization of—leave under the FMLA, even for key employees is not impacted here. FMLA §825.219 establishes the rights of a key employee and details employer notice requirements and the impact of whether the key employee returns to work.

The final provision of the FMLA, Subpart B, is §825.220, which lays out the protections for employees who request or otherwise assert FMLA rights. This is the primary section where the FMLA lists, in detail, what is specifically prohibited by employers if and when an employee requests, or otherwise asserts, the need for leave under the FMLA. Outside of an employer flat out denying the use of leave under the Act, the provisions specifically address "interference" and the various ways that can take place. With respect to employee recourse if their leave has been denied, restrained or interfered with, this is a pivotal section for understanding the most basic employee protections under the Act. Lastly, interference claims over the years have evolved as changes to the workplace have transformed how an employee could be interfered with during their leave. An example of this can be illustrated with the advent of technology and the ability of employee's to work—or perform common functions of a job—from anywhere (calls, video meetings, etc.).

---

17. Code of Federal Regulations, "Title 29, Subtitle B, Chapter V, Subchapter C, Part 825.218, The Family and Medical Leave Act of 1993," accessed 2025, https://www.ecfr.gov/current/title-29/subtitle-B/chapter-V/subchapter-C/part-825#_top.

Below is § 825.220, copied in full from the regulations, which is critical for purposes of determining whether an FMLA violation occurred based on the fact patters we'll see with the caselaw in this section.

§ 825.220 Protection for employees who request leave or otherwise assert FMLA rights

(a) The FMLA prohibits interference with an employee's rights under the law, and with legal proceedings or inquiries relating to an employee's rights. More specifically, the law contains the following employee protections:

(1) An employer is prohibited from interfering with, restraining, or denying the exercise of (or attempts to exercise) any rights provided by the Act.

(2) An employer is prohibited from discharging or in any other way discriminating against any person (whether or not an employee) for opposing or complaining about any unlawful practice under the Act.

(3) All persons (whether or not employers) are prohibited from discharging or in any other way discriminating against any person (whether or not an employee) because that person has—

i. Filed any charge, or has instituted (or cause to be instituted) any inquiry or proceeding relating to a right under this Act;

ii. Given, or is about to give, any information in connection with an inquiry or proceeding relating to a right under this Act;

iii. Testified, or is about to testify, in any inquiry or proceeding relating to a right under this act.

(b) Any violations of the Act of or these regulations constitute interfering with, restraining, or denying the exercise of rights provided by the Act. An employer may be liable for compensation and benefits lost by reason of the violation, for other actual monetary losses sustained as a direct result of the violation, and for appropriate equitable or other relief, including employment, reinstatement, promotion, or any other relief tailored to the harm suffered. *See § 825.400(c).* Interfering with the exercise of an employee's rights would include, for example, not only refusing to authorize FMLA leave, but discouraging an employee from using such leave. It would also include manipulation by a covered employer to avoid responsibilities under the FMLA, for example:

(1) Transferring employees from one worksite to another for the purpose of reducing worksites, or to keep worksites, below the 50-employee threshold for employee eligibility under the Act;

(2) Changing the essential functions of the job in order to preclude the taking of leave;

(3) Reducing hours available to work in order to avoid employee eligibility.

(c) The Act's prohibition against interference prohibits an employer from discriminating or retaliating against an employee or prospective employee for having exercised or attempted to exercise FMLA rights. For example, if an employee on leave without pay would otherwise be entitled to full benefits (other than health benefits), the same benefits would be required to be provided to an employee on unpaid FMLA leave. By the same token, employers cannot use the taking of FMLA leave as a negative factor in employment actions, such as hiring, promotions or disciplinary actions; nor can FMLA leave be counted under no fault attendance policies. *See § 825.215.*

(d) Employees cannot waive, nor may employers induce employees to waive, their prospective rights under the FMLA. For example, employees (or their collective bargaining representatives) cannot trade off the right to take FMLA leave against some other benefit offered by the employer.

In breaking down § 825.220 a bit, we see the Act goes into great detail on what could constitute an interference claim or retaliation. In addition to an outright denial of leave under the FMLA or in some way hindering an employee's ability to request, and ultimately use, this leave, interference and retaliation can take shape in several ways.

For reference, § 825.220(b) describes how transferring an employee to another worksite or changing the job functions of the position could be deemed as interference. FMLA § 825.220(c) expressly prohibits adverse employment by employers if an employee requests and/or utilizes leave under the FMLA.

Now that the FMLA is over 35 years old, interference claims have evolved with workforce changes and the advent of technology. These advances have changed the way jobs are performed so while the Act lists a few examples of how interference could play out, it is important to recognize that it's not an exhaustive list. The Department of Labor did publish "Fact Sheet #77B: Protection for Individuals under the FMLA," which summarizes § 825.220 and provides the following examples of prohibited conduct:

- Refusing to authorize FMLA leave for an eligible employee,
- Discouraging an employee from using FMLA leave,
- Manipulating an employee's work hours to avoid responsibilities under the FMLA,
- Using an employee's request for or use of FMLA leave as a negative factor in employment actions, such as hiring, promotions, or disciplinary actions, or,
- Counting FMLA leave under "no fault" attendance policies.[18]

The following case law reflects different ways how an employee's FMLA leave could be potentially interfered with. Depending on the functions of the job and the specific tasks associated with that job, if an employee is asked, or told, to perform specific work tasks while on leave, the issue of interference will emerge. As for whether an employee's claim will rise to the level of interference as described in the Act, the circumstances and specific facts regarding the actions of the employer and what the employee was

18. United States Department of Labor, "Fact Sheet #77B: Protection for Individuals under the FMLA" (December 2011), https://www.dol.gov/agencies/whd/fact-sheets/77b-fmla-protections.

asked to perform will dictate whether they were interfered with or restrained from using the leave.

Neal Goad v. Milwaukee County

2018 WL 1440338 (E.D. Wisc. March 21, 2018)

DAVID E. JONES, Magistrate Judge.

Neal Goad was employed by Milwaukee County (the County) as a facilities maintenance worker from February 2012 until December 2015. During the course of Mr. Goad's employment, the County ranked the members of his maintenance crew based on seniority. This ranking was used, among other things, to establish the workers' schedules.

Mr. Goad began his employment ahead of only one crew member on the seniority list, but he then moved to third-to-last after the County hired a new maintenance worker. From June 2013 until September 2013, Mr. Goad was out on medical leave after breaking his arm. Mr. Goad's supervisor erroneously believed that this leave period did not count as accrued time toward the County's seniority system. Consequently, by the time Mr. Goad returned from leave, he had been passed by the only two co-workers beneath him in seniority.

As the last-ranked crew member, Mr. Goad had the worst schedule. He was frequently required to return to work just eight hours after finishing a shift. As a result, Mr. Goad became sleep deprived, depressed, anxious, and irritable. When Mr. Goad complained about his schedule, he learned that the supervisor erred in holding the missed time against him. By that time, however, Mr. Goad did in fact have the least amount of seniority on his crew. Mr. Goad was eventually terminated following an altercation with a co-worker.

Following his termination, Mr. Goad filed suit in federal court, alleging that the County interfered with his rights under the Family and Medical Leave Act (FMLA) of 1993 and the ADA Amendments Act (ADAAA) of 2008 and retaliated against him for exercising his FMLA rights. The County has moved for summary judgment on all of Mr. Goad's claims. For the reasons that follow, the Court finds that the County is entitled to summary judgment on Mr. Goad's FMLA retaliation and ADAAA claims but not his FMLA interference claim. The County's motion will therefore be granted in part and denied in part, as explained below.

I. Factual Background[19]

On February 12, 2012, Milwaukee County hired Neal Goad as a facilities maintenance worker. Defendant's Proposed Findings of Fact in Support of Its Motion for

---

19. [1] This factual background is taken from the parties' statements of fact and the responses thereto. The Court notes that the County filed a reply in support of its own facts. See Defendant's Replies to Plaintiff's Responses to Defendant's Proposed Findings of Fact, ECF No. 36. This document was not necessary to the disposition of the motion and is not ordinarily permitted by this district's local rules. See E.D. Wis. Civil L. R. 7(i) & 56(b)(3). As such, it will not be referred to herein. See, e.g.,

Summary Judgment (Def.'s Facts) ¶¶ 1–2, ECF No. 30. In that capacity, Mr. Goad was responsible for lawn care, salting, snow removal, light bulb replacement, general maintenance, and grounds maintenance. Def.'s Facts ¶ 3.#Mr. Goad's initial assignment was at the Vel R. Phillips Juvenile Justice Center, labeled by the County as Facilities West. Def.'s Facts ¶ 4.

The County used a seniority system for its facilities maintenance workers. See Def.'s Facts ¶¶ 10–16. Workers were ranked based on the hours they had accrued, excluding overtime. This ranking was used, in part, to determine the workers' schedules. Workers with the same number of seniority hours were ranked based on the last four digits of their social security numbers: the worker with the highest number received the highest seniority ranking and so on and so forth.

Mr. Goad was initially (and incorrectly) ranked second-to-last on his maintenance crew, ahead of only Devin Richard. See Def.'s Facts ¶ 22. Although both were hired and began work on the same day, Mr. Richard's social security number is higher than Mr. Goad's, entitling Mr. Richard to higher seniority under the applicable work rules. Def.'s Facts ¶ 23. But for the County's mistake, Mr. Goad would have been the lowest ranked facilities maintenance worker at the outset of his employment. Def.'s Facts ¶ 24.

In May 2013, Mr. Goad broke his arm. Plaintiff's Proposed Findings of Fact (Pl.'s Facts) ¶ 4, ECF No. 33. He informed his supervisor, Jason McCarthy, of the injury and indicated that he needed time off to allow his arm to heal. Pl.'s Facts ¶ 4. Mr. Goad took a leave of absence under the FMLA. See Amended Complaint ¶ 10, ECF No. 13. On August 9, 2013, Mr. Goad's doctor told him that he could return to work on September 3, 2013. Am. Compl. ¶ 11. When Mr. Goad called Mr. McCarthy to inform him of his impending return to work, Mr. McCarthy told Mr. Goad that he had "lost time" as a result of his unpaid leave. See Am. Compl. ¶ 12–14; Pl.'s Facts ¶ 5; Def.'s Facts ¶¶ 26, 28–33. Mr. Goad therefore would have the least amount of seniority of the workers on his maintenance crew upon his return.

When Mr. Goad returned to work as planned in September 2013, he was listed last on the schedule, immediately behind Mr. Richard and Derrick Watson, a maintenance worker who started in late February 2012—two weeks after Mr. Goad and Mr. Richard. See Def.'s Facts ¶¶ 25, 40. Facilities workers were scheduled for multiple different shifts (i.e., first, second, or third) during the same two-week pay period, which sometimes required them to return to work just eight hours after finishing a shift. See Am. Compl. ¶ 15–17; Pl.'s Facts ¶ 7; Def.'s Facts ¶ 57–58. Mr. Goad was informed during the interview process that the facilities maintenance position involved working such "swing shifts." Def.'s Facts ¶ 58.

Upon his return, Mr. Goad was required to work more swing shifts than he had prior to taking FMLA leave. Pl.'s Facts ¶ 7. Before going out on leave, Mr. Goad had worked twelve swing shifts; he worked fourteen such shifts upon his return. Similarly, upon

---

J.M. v. City of Milwaukee, 249 F. Supp. 3d 920, 933 n.8 (E.D. Wis. 2017) (noting that such replies are "neither contemplated nor permitted by this District's Local Rules").

his return, Mr. Goad was required to work more swing shifts than his closest peers in seniority. Prior to Mr. Goad's leave, Mr. Richard had worked fifteen swing shifts while Mr. Watson had worked twelve. After Mr. Goad returned, Mr. Richard worked four and Mr. Watson worked five.[20] See Pl.'s Facts ¶¶ 40–50; Def.'s Facts ¶¶ 42–48, 61–71 (citing Exhibit 11 to Declaration of Kristofor L. Hanson, ECF No. 28-11).

In Spring 2014, Mr. Goad learned that he should not have lost seniority for taking unpaid leave. See Pl.'s Facts ¶¶ 8–11. He subsequently called Mr. McCarthy to question why he was last on the schedule. See Am. Compl. ¶ 20; Pl.'s Facts ¶¶ 22–24, 26, 30–31; Def.'s Facts ¶¶ 94–99. Mr. McCarthy explained that Mr. Goad and Mr. Richard had the least amount of time accrued, but Mr. Goad was listed last as a result of the County's tiebreaking system. By that time, Mr. McCarthy had learned that unpaid leave time did not affect seniority. See Plaintiff's Response to Def.'s Facts ¶ 99, ECF No. 34 (citing Exhibit 9 to Declaration of Brenda Lewison, ECF No. 35-9). On June 10, 2014, Mr. Goad received a written reprimand for the conduct he exhibited during his phone conversation with Mr. McCarthy. Am. Compl. ¶ 21; Pl.'s Facts ¶ 25; Def.'s Facts ¶ 93.

Mr. Goad claims that he developed "swing shift syndrome" (also known as shift work disorder) as a result of having to work more swing shifts. See Am. Compl. ¶ 18. This condition "is characterized by depression, anxiety, irritability, and sometimes, increased absenteeism and accidents due to sleep deprivation." *Id.* Mr. Goad testified, however, that he did not inform anyone at the County about his medical conditions. Def.'s Facts ¶¶ 86–88 (citing Exhibit 3 to Supplemental Declaration of Kristofor L. Hanson, ECF No. 39-3 at 13). But he did take advantage of the County's Employee Assistance Program—a program used to provide employees with opportunities to address workplace issues, see Def.'s Facts ¶ 119—and voluntarily sought mental health treatment for depression and anxiety, see Am. Compl. ¶ 22; Pl.'s Facts ¶ 21.

Mr. Goad continuously had conflicts with co-workers while stationed at Facilities West. Def.'s Facts ¶¶ 91–95. The conflicts became so disruptive that Gary Waszak, the facilities maintenance manager, decided to consult the human resources manager assigned to the facilities division, Sean Moore. Def.'s Facts ¶¶ 34, 79, 117. Given the concerns from Mr. Goad's supervisors, in October 2014, Mr. Moore determined that Mr. Goad should participate in the Employee Assistance Program. See Def.'s Facts ¶¶ 115–18. He issued the mandatory referral during a meeting he arranged with Mr. Goad and Mr. Waszak. Pl.'s Facts ¶ 33. During that meeting, Mr. Goad indicated that he was already seeing someone from the Employee Assistance Program and questioned why he had to see someone else. Pl.'s Facts ¶ 34.

The mandatory referral letter, which was addressed to Mr. Goad, stated as follows: "A review of your past/current performance has indicated a problem with/history of not following directions of [your] supervisor, raising your voice and being defensive

20. [2] Mr. Watson was transferred from Facilities West on February 8, 2014. See Def.'s Facts ¶¶ 43, 55, 67; Defendant's Responses to Pl.'s Facts ¶ 48, ECF No. 37.

and accusatory with your supervisor, having a poor attitude and not being helpful with clients when responding to work orders." See Exhibit 12 to Hanson Decl., ECF No. 28-13 at 5–6. The letter also described Mr. Goad's specific behavioral problems, indicated that Mr. Goad would be referred to a licensed clinician or treatment facility "to help address the workplace issues," and emphasized that Mr. Goad's compliance with any recommended "treatment" was mandatory. Id.; see also Pl.'s Facts ¶ 56.

Upon returning to work following the mandatory referral, Mr. Goad was involuntarily transferred to the Milwaukee County Courthouse. Def.'s Facts ¶¶ 5, 91, 125. Mr. Goad was pleased with his new schedule at the Courthouse, but he continued to have problems with co-workers. See Def.'s Facts ¶¶ 126–27. For example, on March 17, 2015, Mr. Goad slapped a radio out of the hands of Anthony Dailey. Def.'s Facts ¶¶ 128–30; see also Am. Compl. ¶¶ 30–32. The following day, Mr. Goad and Mr. Dailey were involved in a verbal confrontation while working at the Courthouse loading dock. Def.'s Facts ¶ 135; see also Am. Compl. ¶¶ 33–35.

The incidents between Mr. Goad and Mr. Dailey were investigated by Mary Beth Buechel, the County's human resources business partner. See Def.'s Facts ¶¶ 134–39 (citing Exhibit 13 to Hanson Decl., ECF No. 28-14). Mr. Dailey received a written reprimand for his actions. Ms. Buechel determined, however, that Mr. Goad escalated the March 17 incident and instigated the one on March 18. Based on those findings, as well as Mr. Goad's prior discipline, on April 21, 2015, Ms. Buechel recommended that Mr. Goad be discharged. Ex. 13; see also Pl.'s Facts ¶ 61; Def.'s Facts ¶ 137. Ms. Buechel listed Mr. Goad's mandatory referral to the Employee Assistance Program as "prior discipline." See Ex. 13 at 3; see also Pl.'s Facts ¶ 59.

Ms. Buechel prepared the written charges, which were signed by Jeremy Theis, the County's director of facilities management, on May 21, 2015. See Exhibit A to Declaration of Mary Beth Buechel, ECF No. 25-1; see also Def.'s Facts ¶ 147. The charges stemmed from the March 18, 2015 verbal confrontation with Mr. Dailey; the March 17, 2015 physical confrontation with Mr. Dailey; the June 2014 written reprimand; and the October 2014 mandatory referral. Ex. A. Mr. Goad was suspended without pay pending the final decision of the County's Personnel Review Board. Ex. 12 at 1.

Following several hearings, on December 8, 2015, the Review Board upheld the charges for discharge. See Exhibit B to Buechel Decl., ECF No. 25-2; Pl.'s Facts ¶ 63; Def.'s Facts ¶¶ 147–49. The Review Board determined that Mr. Goad had violated the following civil service rules of the County: threatening, intimidating, coercing, or harassing employees or supervision at any time; interference with normal work flow or departmental procedures; indecent, criminal, or inappropriate conduct on county premises during working hours; and offensive conduct or language toward the public or toward county officers or employees. Ex. B at 2. The Review Board's decision also referenced the mandatory referral and questioned why the investigation of the charges against Mr. Goad took so long. See Ex. B at 5–7.

II. Procedural Background

Mr. Goad filed the present action on August 7, 2015, see Complaint, ECF No. 1, and he timely filed an amended complaint on April 1, 2016, see Scheduling Order, ECF No. 12. The matter was reassigned to this Court in August 2016 after the parties consented to magistrate judge jurisdiction. See Consent to Proceed Before a Magistrate Judge, ECF Nos. 15, 16 (citing 28 U.S.C. § 636(c) and Fed. R. Civ. P. 73(b)).

In his Amended Complaint, Mr. Goad alleges that the County "interfered with [his] rights as guaranteed under the Family and Medical Leave Act (FMLA), the Americans with Disabilities Act, as amended (ADAAA), the Rehabilitation Act, and the Age Discrimination in Employment Act and retaliated against him for his use of those rights." Am. Compl. ¶ 42. He seeks lost wages, damages, and equitable relief. Am. Compl. ¶¶ 43–44.

On May 12, 2017, the County filed a motion for summary judgment on all of Mr. Goad's claims. Defendant's Motion for Summary Judgment, ECF No. 24; see also Defendant's Brief in Support of Its Motion for Summary Judgment, ECF No. 29. In responding to the County's motion, Mr. Goad expressly abandoned his age discrimination claim but continued to press his FMLA claims and his disability discrimination claim. See Plaintiff's Brief in Response to Defendant's Motion for Summary Judgment 1, ECF No. 31. The County filed its reply brief on July 11, 2017. Defendant's Reply Brief in Support of Its Motion for Summary Judgment, ECF No. 38. Accordingly, the matter is now ready for disposition.

III. Summary Judgment Standard

"The court shall grant summary judgment if the movant shows that there is no genuine dispute as to any material fact and the movant is entitled to judgment as a matter of law." Fed. R. Civ. P. 56(a). "Material facts" are those that, under the applicable substantive law, "might affect the outcome of the suit." See *Anderson v. Liberty Lobby, Inc.*, 477 U.S. 242, 248 (1986). A dispute over a material fact is "genuine" "if the evidence is such that a reasonable jury could return a verdict for the nonmoving party." *Id.*

A moving party "is entitled to a judgment as a matter of law" when "the nonmoving party has failed to make a sufficient showing on an essential element of [his] case with respect to which [he] has the burden of proof." *Celotex Corp. v. Catrett*, 477 U.S. 317, 323 (1986) (first internal quotation marks omitted). Still,

> a party seeking summary judgment always bears the initial responsibility of informing the district court of the basis for its motion, and identifying those portions of the pleadings, depositions, answers to interrogatories, and admissions on file, together with the affidavits, if any, which it believes demonstrate the absence of a genuine issue of material fact.

Id. (internal quotation marks omitted).

To determine whether a genuine issue of material fact exists, the court must review the record, construing all facts in the light most favorable to the nonmoving party and drawing all reasonable inferences in that party's favor. See *Heft v. Moore*, 351

F.3d 278, 282 (7th Cir. 2003) (citing *Liberty Lobby*, 477 U.S. at 255). "However, [the court's] favor toward the nonmoving party does not extend to drawing inferences that are supported by only speculation or conjecture." *Fitzgerald v. Santoro*, 707 F.3d 725, 730 (7th Cir. 2013) (quoting *Harper v. C.R. Eng., Inc.*, 687 F.3d 297, 306 (7th Cir. 2012)). That is, "to survive summary judgment, the nonmoving party must establish some genuine issue for trial 'such that a reasonable jury could return a verdict' in [his] favor." *Fitzgerald*, 707 F.3d at 730 (quoting *Makowski v. SmithAmundsen LLC*, 662 F.3d 818, 822 (7th Cir. 2011)).

IV. Discussion

Mr. Goad claims that the County interfered with his FMLA rights and retaliated against him for taking FMLA leave by demoting his seniority within the facilities maintenance crew. He also claims that the County violated the ADAAA when it terminated his employment. The County seeks summary judgment on all of these claims.

A. Whether Milwaukee County is entitled to summary judgment on Mr. Goad's FMLA interference claim

Mr. Goad maintains that the County interfered with his FMLA rights because after he returned from leave he lost seniority and was required to work disproportionally more swing shifts than Mr. Richard and Mr. Watson, his two closest peers in seniority on the facilities maintenance crew. Pl.'s Br. 15–16.

"To prevail on an FMLA interference claim, an employee need only show that his employer deprived him of an FMLA entitlement; no finding of ill intent is required." *Burnett v. LFW Inc.*, 472 F.3d 471, 477 (7th Cir. 2006) (citing *Hoge v. Honda Am. Mfg., Inc.*, 384 F.3d 238, 244 (7th Cir. 2004)). Specifically, the employee must establish that: "(1) he was eligible for the FMLA's protections, (2) his employer was covered by the FMLA, (3) he was entitled to leave under the FMLA, (4) he provided sufficient notice of his intent to take leave, and (5) his employer denied him FMLA benefits to which he was entitled." *Id.* The County does not contest the first four requirements. See Def.'s Br. 17. The only issue is whether the County improperly denied benefits to which Mr. Goad was entitled.

The FMLA "provides eligible employees of a covered employer the right to take unpaid leave for a period of up to twelve work weeks in any twelve[-]month period for a serious health condition." *King v. Preferred Tech. Grp.*, 166 F.3d 887, 891 (7th Cir. 1999) (citing 29 U.S.C. § 2612(a)(1)). The Act "also requires that an employee be reinstated to his former position or an equivalent one upon returning from leave." *Breneisen v. Motorola, Inc.*, 512 F.3d 972, 977 (7th Cir. 2008) (citing 29 U.S.C. § 2614(a)(1)). It is "unlawful for an employer to interfere with these entitlements." *Breneisen*, 512 F.3d at 977 (citing 29 U.S.C. § 2615(a)(1)).

"The test for equivalence is strict." *Breneisen*, 512 F.3d at 977. Jobs are equivalent within the meaning of the FMLA only "if they entail 'equivalent employment benefits, pay, and other terms and conditions of employment.'" *Breneisen*, 512 F.3d at 977 (quoting 29 U.S.C. § 2614(a)(1)(B)). The undisputed facts demonstrate that Mr. Goad had the same benefits and pay upon his return from FMLA leave. The parties dispute whether the terms and conditions of Mr. Goad's employment were equivalent given his placement on the bottom of the seniority list.

"An equivalent position must have substantially similar duties, conditions, responsibilities, privileges and status as the employee's original position." 29 C.F.R. § 825.215(e). As such, an employee returning from leave "is ordinarily entitled to return to the same shift or the same or an equivalent work schedule." 29 U.S.C. § 825.215(e)(2). The equivalence requirement, however, "does not extend to de minimis, intangible, or unmeasurable aspects of the job." 29 C.F.R. § 825.215(f).

Upon returning from FMLA leave in September 2013, Mr. Goad was placed at the bottom of the seniority list, immediately behind Mr. Richard and Mr. Watson. As a result, Mr. Goad was required to work more swing shifts than he had prior to taking leave. In the sixteen-month period prior to taking leave, Mr. Goad worked twelve swing shifts. Mr. Goad acknowledged that his schedule improved after he was transferred to the Milwaukee County Courthouse in October 2014. Accordingly, the issues with his schedule persisted for fourteen months. During that period, Mr. Goad worked fourteen swing shifts.

By comparison, before Mr. Goad went out on leave, Mr. Richard worked fifteen swing shifts while Mr. Watson worked twelve. After Mr. Goad returned from leave, Mr. Richard worked only four swing shifts; Mr. Watson worked five before he was transferred from Facilities West in February 2014. The following charts depict these comparisons:

Table 1—Number of swing shifts worked

	Mr. Goad	Mr. Richard	Mr. Watson
Feb. 2012–May 2013	12	15	12
Sept. 2013–Oct. 2014	14	4	5*

* Through February 8, 2014

Table 2—Average number of swing shifts worked per month

	Mr. Goad	Mr. Richard	Mr. Watson
Feb. 2012–May 2013	0.7500	0.9375	0.7500
Sept. 2013–Oct. 2014	1.0000	0.2857	0.9524**

** 0.9524 = 5 swing shifts/5.25 months

The above figures show that, prior to Mr. Goad's leave, the swing shifts were split relatively evenly between the three maintenance workers. Upon his return, however, Mr. Goad was required to work more swing shifts than Mr. Richard or Mr. Watson. A reasonable jury could therefore conclude that Mr. Goad's position upon returning from FMLA leave was not equivalent to his pre-leave position. Accordingly, this case is distinguishable from *Karaffa v. Montgomery Twp.*, CIVIL ACTION No. 12-1184, 2013 U.S. Dist. LEXIS 39185 (E.D. Pa. Mar. 21, 2013), a case relied upon by the County.

The County argues that, to the extent Mr. Goad worked more swing shifts after returning from leave, "the difference is *de minimis.*" See Def.'s Br. 19–21; Def.'s Reply 4–7. According to the County, Mr. Goad was incorrectly listed ahead of Mr. Richard on the schedule prior to taking leave due to an error in how the County applied its seniority tiebreaking system. Thus, after Mr. Watson was transferred from Facilities West in February 2014, the schedule was correct: Mr. Goad was properly listed last, directly below Mr. Richard. During the only period when Mr. Goad was improperly listed lower on the schedule than he should have been (September 2013 through February 8, 2014), he worked "just three" more swing shifts than Mr. Watson. Def.'s Reply 5. "These differences become even more de minimis," according to the County, "when the number of multiple shifts these workers were scheduled to work during each two-week pay period is taken into account." Def.'s Reply 6.

The County's arguments are unavailing for several reasons. First, whether Mr. Goad's placement on the schedule resulted from a mistake or an intentional act is irrelevant to his FMLA interference claim. See *Burnett,* 472 F.3d at 477 (noting that ill intent is not a required to prove an FMLA interference claim). Second, the County did not realize its misapplication of the tiebreaking system until Spring 2014 when Mr. Goad started complaining about being placed last on the schedule—that is, after the mistake was self-corrected upon Mr. Watson's transfer. It is unknown when (or if) the County would have discovered this mistake had Mr. Goad not been improperly demoted. It is therefore reasonable to infer that Mr. Goad would have been listed ahead of both Mr. Richard and Mr. Watson if the County had (correctly) not held his taking FMLA leave against him, just as he was prior to taking leave. The County's suggestion that Mr. Goad "was not entitled to return to" the schedule he had prior to taking leave is therefore based on an unreasonable assumption.

Third, the County's argument rests on a misunderstanding of how the Court views the evidence. At this stage in the proceedings, the Court must construe all facts in the light most favorable to Mr. Goad, the non-moving party, and draw all reasonable inferences in his favor. In defining the relevant periods of comparison, the County essentially asks the Court to consider the evidence in its favor. That would be improper. The evidence, when viewed in favor of Mr. Goad, shows that he worked more swing shifts upon his return from leave and worked disproportionately more swing shifts than either Mr. Richard or Mr. Watson.

Finally, even if the Court were to adopt the County's periods of comparison, a reasonable jury still could conclude that Mr. Goad was not reinstated to an equivalent position upon his return for leave. The average number of swing shifts Mr. Goad worked per month increased from 0.7500 to 1.0000 upon his return. From September 2013 through February 8, 2014, Mr. Goad worked three more swing shifts than Mr. Watson. Thus, Mr. Goad averaged 1.5238 swing shifts per month over that period while Mr. Watson averaged 0.9524. During this same time period, Mr. Richard worked only one swing shift, an average of 0.1905 per month. The County has not provided any explanation for why the Court should ignore the stark difference in schedules between Mr. Goad and Mr. Richard before and after Mr. Goad's leave.

The Court cannot say that these differences are *de minimis* as a matter of law. At best, the County's interpretation of the evidence creates a factual dispute on the equivalence issue. The County therefore is not entitled to summary judgment on Mr. Goad's FMLA interference claim.

B. Whether Milwaukee County is entitled to summary judgment on Mr. Goad's FMLA retaliation claim

Mr. Goad similarly maintains that the County placed him at the bottom of seniority list in retaliation for his taking FMLA leave. Pl.'s Br. 16–17. The County argues that Mr. Goad's placement at the bottom of the seniority list does not constitute a materially adverse employment action under the FMLA. Def.'s Br. 9–12; Def.'s Reply 8–10. The County further argues that Mr. Goad's loss of seniority was an unintentional error, not payback for his taking leave. Def.'s Br. 13–16; Def.'s Reply 7–8.

It is unlawful for employers to discriminate against an employee who has exercised his FMLA rights. See 29 U.S.C. § 2615(a)(2). "A retaliation claim requires proof of discriminatory or retaliatory intent, which can be established directly or indirectly." *Nicholson v. Pulte Homes Corp.*, 690 F.3d 819, 828 (7th Cir. 2012) (citing *Kauffman v. Fed. Express Corp.*, 426 F.3d 880, 884 (7th Cir. 2005)). "To establish a *prima facie* case using the direct method, [the employee must] 'present evidence of (1) a statutorily protected activity; (2) a materially adverse action taken by the employer; and (3) a causal connection between the two.'" *Langenbach v. Wal-Mart Stores, Inc.*, 761 F.3d 792, 799 (7th Cir. 2014) (quoting *Scruggs v. Carrier Corp.*, 688 F.3d 821, 826 (7th Cir. 2012)). Under the indirect method, the employee must present evidence that (1) he was meeting the employer's legitimate expectations; (2) he suffered an adverse employment action; and (3) he was treated less favorably than similarly situated employees who did not request FMLA leave. See *Langenbach*, 761 F.3d at 800 (citing *Caskey v. Colgate-Palmolive Co.*, 535 F.3d 585, 592 (7th Cir. 2008)).

The United States Court of Appeals for the Seventh Circuit has consistently held that "the adverse action giving rise to an FMLA retaliation claim" must be "materially adverse." *Cole v. Illinois*, 562 F.3d 812, 816 (7th Cir. 2009). "Materially adverse actions are not limited to employment-related activities but include any actions that would dissuade a reasonable employee from exercising his rights under the FMLA." *Breneisen*, 512 F.3d at 979 (citing *Burlington N. & Sante Fe Ry. v. White*, 548 U.S. 53, 57 (2006)); see also *Thomas v. Potter*, 202 F. App'x 118, 119 (7th Cir. 2006) (applying Title VII's analogous materiality requirement). According to the Seventh Circuit, a reassignment that does not affect the employee's pay or promotion opportunities ordinarily does not constitute a material adverse employment action. See *Washington v. Ill. Dep't of Revenue*, 420 F.3d 658, 662 (7th Cir. 2005).

A reassignment, however, may be material if the employee presents evidence that his employer "sought to exploit a 'known vulnerability' by altering [his] work schedule upon return from FMLA leave." *Langenbach*, 761 F.3d at 799–800 (citing *Porter v. City of Chicago*, 700 F.3d 944, 955 (7th Cir. 2012); *Washington*, 420 F.3d at 662); see also *Thomas*, 202 F. App'x at 119; *Koty v. Zaruba*, No. 15 C 2600, 2017 U.S. Dist. LEXIS

152207, at *33–34 (N.D. Ill. Sept. 19, 2017); *Wink v. Miller Compressing Co.*, Case No. 14-CV-367, 2015 U.S. Dist. LEXIS 70491, at *19–20 (E.D. Wis. June 1, 2015). For example, the Seventh Circuit determined that a reasonable jury could conclude that the Illinois Department of Revenue set out to exploit a known vulnerability of its former employee, Chrissie Washington, when it altered her work schedule after she returned from unpaid leave. *Washington*, 420 F.3d at 662–63. Despite knowing that Ms. Washington needed a flexible schedule so that she could care for her disabled son, the Department reassigned her to a position with a standard 9-to-5 schedule. This scheduling change resulted in Ms. Washington having to exhaust all of her vacation and sick leave before she found a new supervisor who allowed her to work from 7:00 a.m. to 3:00 p.m.

Here, Mr. Goad has failed to demonstrate that his placement on the bottom of the seniority list constituted a materially adverse employment action. The undisputed facts show that this reassignment did not result in "a decrease in wage or salary, a less distinguished title, a material loss of benefits, [or] significantly diminished material responsibilities." *Porter*, 700 F.3d at 954. Mr. Goad claims that the increase in swing shifts caused him to be sleep deprived and to be sick so often that he had to take unpaid leave. But he has not provided any evidence to suggest that he was more vulnerable than the average person to lack of sleep, let alone that the County was aware of such vulnerability and sought to exploit it. See *Koty*, 2017 U.S. Dist. LEXIS 152207, at *33–34 (denying ADA retaliation claim where employee was reassigned to the midnight shift upon his return from leave because, "[w]hile losing sleep is certainly an annoyance, the schedule change does not rise to the level of an adverse action"). This case is therefore distinguishable from *Washington*.

Accordingly, any effects Mr. Goad suffered from being placed on the bottom of the seniority list do not rise to the level of harm sufficiently serious to dissuade a reasonable employee to forego exercising his rights under the FMLA. See *Burlington N.*, 548 U.S. at 68 (adopting materiality standard articulated by the Seventh Circuit in Washington). The County is therefore entitled to summary judgment on Mr. Goad's FMLA retaliation claim.[21]

C. Whether Milwaukee County is entitled to summary judgment on Mr. Goad's ADAAA claim

Mr. Goad also claims that the County discharged him because he had, or was perceived to have, a disability. Pl.'s Br. 18–19.

"The ADA makes it unlawful for an employer to discriminate against a 'qualified individual on the basis of disability.'" *Severson v. Heartland Woodcraft, Inc.*, 872 F.3d 476, 480 (7th Cir. 2017) (quoting 42 U.S.C. § 12112(a)). "A plaintiff claiming disparate treatment in violation of the ADA can rely on two different methods of proof to survive a summary judgment motion." *Bunn v. Khoury Enters.*, 753 F.3d 676, 683 (7th Cir.

21. [3] Because Mr. Goad has failed to establish the second requirement of an FMLA retaliation *prima facie* case, the Court does not need to address whether the County acted with retaliatory intent when it reduced his seniority.

2014). Mr. Goad has not identified any similarly situated co-worker. Thus, it appears he is proceeding under the direct method of proof.

To establish disparate treatment via the direct method, the employee must show: (1) that he is disabled within the meaning of the Act; (2) that he is qualified to perform the essential functions of the job with or without accommodation; and (3) that he has suffered an adverse employment action because of his disability. *Bunn,* 753 F.3d at 683 (citing *Timmons v. Gen. Motors Corp.,* 469 F.3d 1122, 1127 (7th Cir. 2006)). An employee survives a motion for summary judgment only if he presents "the court with evidence that, if believed by a trier of fact, would establish all three elements of his claim." *James v. Hyatt Regency Chi.,* 707 F.3d 775, 782 (7th Cir. 2013).

Mr. Goad has failed to provide sufficient evidence from which a reasonable jury could conclude that the County discriminated against him because he had, or was regarded to have, a disability. For one, Mr. Goad has not produced any evidence to satisfy the first two elements of an ADAAA claim. He vaguely claims to have suffered from "swing shift syndrome" but has not provided any evidence to support this allegation. Moreover, none of the circumstantial evidence Mr. Goad has presented is sufficient to create a genuine issue of fact as to whether he was terminated on account of a disability.

Mr. Goad claims in his declaration that he told Mr. Moore, the human resources manager assigned to the facilities division, that he was sleep-deprived, anxious, and frequently ill from having to work so many swing shifts. See Declaration of Neal Goad ¶¶ 14–15, ECF No. 32. But this claim directly contradicts Mr. Goad's deposition testimony, in which he testified that he did not tell anyone at the County about any of his medical conditions. See Ex. 3 at 13.

Mr. Goad also indicates that Mr. Moore and Mr. Waszak knew he was getting help from the Employee Assistance Program prior to the mandatory referral. While true, this fact does not establish that the County knew Mr. Goad had a medical condition, let alone a disability within the meaning of the ADAAA. The County's Employee Assistance Program was used to address a wide range of workplace issues. Mr. Goad has not provided any evidence that he told Mr. Moore or Mr. Waszak that he was seeking mental health treatment through the program.

To further support his disparate treatment claim, Mr. Goad points out that the mandatory referral to the Employee Assistance Program required him to seek treatment and that this referral formed part of the basis for discharge. Although the referral letter did use the term "treatment," the referral was clearly designed to address Mr. Goad's behavioral issues and conflicts with others. See Ex. 12 at 5–6. Treatment in this sense simply meant that Mr. Goad had to attend counseling sessions and comply with the provider's recommendations. The letter did not reference any medical condition. Consequently, Ms. Buechel's listing of the mandatory referral under the category of "prior discipline," see Ex. 13, does not suggest that Mr. Goad was disciplined for having a disability. Rather, this reference accurately captured Mr. Goad's ongoing workplace issues with supervisors, coworkers, and clients.

Finally, Mr. Goad claims that the encounter with Mr. Dailey was a pretext for a discriminatory discharge. Mr. Goad asserts that, during the investigation into that incident, Mr. Waszak asked him what medications he was taking. See Goad Decl. ¶ 37. He further asserts that the length of the investigation—approximately seven weeks—creates suspicion that the County was using that time to devise a non-discriminatory reason for his discharge.

Mr. Goad's pretext argument is unavailing. The disciplinary proceedings demonstrate one inescapable conclusion: Mr. Goad was discharged due to his history of workplace violations. See Ex. B. The violent encounter with Mr. Dailey was merely the final straw.

Because Mr. Goad has not produced evidence from which a reasonable jury could conclude that he was discharged because of his disability, the County is entitled to summary judgment on his ADAAA claim.

V. Conclusion

For all the foregoing reasons, the Court finds that the County is entitled to summary judgment on Mr. Goad's FMLA retaliation and ADAAA claims. The County is not, however, entitled to summary judgment on Mr. Goad's FMLA interference claim. Its motion will therefore be granted in part and denied in part.

NOW, THEREFORE, IT IS HEREBY ORDERED that Defendant's Motion for Summary Judgment, ECF No. 24, is GRANTED in part and DENIED in part, as stated herein.

Issues for Consideration

- Was Goad's FMLA leave interfered with? Did Milwaukee County's actions rise to level of interference?
- How did the concept of swing shifts impact whether Goad had an interference claim?
- Did Milwaukee County prevent, deny or restrain Goad from his rights under the FMLA?
- Was Goad returned to an equivalent position in compliance with FMLA rules?

Noemi Valdivia v. Township High School District 214

2018 WL 1403221 (N.D. Ill. Mar. 20, 2018)

SIDNEY I. SCHENKIER, United States Magistrate Judge

Plaintiff, Noemi Valdivia, filed a two-count first amended complaint ("complaint") against defendant Township High School District 214 ("District 214" or defendant) seeking damages and injunctive relief on the grounds that defendant subjected her to a racially offensive and hostile work environment, in violation of Title VII of the Civil Rights Act of 1964, 42 U.S.C. § 2000e, *et seq.* ("Title VII"), and interfered with her right to take job-protected leave, in violation of the Family and Medical Leave Act of 1993, 29 U.S.C. §2601, *et seq.* ("FMLA") (doc. # 29: Compl., at ¶¶ 49–58). On May 15, 2017, after briefing by the parties, this Court denied defendant's motion to dismiss. *Valdivia v. Twp. High Sch. Dist. 214*, No. 16 C 10333, 2017 WL 2114965, at *5 (N.D. Ill. May 15, 2017). Subsequently, defendant answered the complaint, and the parties engaged in discovery. After completion of discovery, defendant moved for summary judgment (doc. # 58). For the reasons set forth below, the Court grants defendant's motion for summary judgment as to plaintiff's Title VII claim, but denies the motion as to plaintiff's FMLA claim.

I.

The legal standards governing motions for summary judgment are well-established. Summary judgment is appropriate where the moving party establishes that there is no genuine issue as to any material fact and he or she is entitled to judgment as a matter of law. Fed. R. Civ. P. 56(a); *Celotex Corp. v. Catrett*, 477 U.S. 317, 323 (1986). A genuine issue exists when "the evidence is such that a reasonable jury could return a verdict for the nonmoving party." *Anderson v. Liberty Lobby, Inc.*, 477 U.S. 242, 248 (1986). The substantive law identifies which facts are material. *Zaya v. Sood*, 836 F.3d 800, 804 (7th Cir. 2016).

In deciding a motion for summary judgment, we construe the facts and draw reasonable inferences in the light most favorable to the nonmoving party. *Sommerfield v. City of Chicago*, 863 F.3d 645, 649 (7th Cir. 2017). However, "we need not draw inferences that are supported by only speculation and conjecture." *Woods v. City of Berwyn*, 803 F.3d 865, 869 (7th Cir. 2015); *See also Aguilar v. Gaston-Camara*, 861 F.3d 626, 630–31 (7th Cir. 2017). "[T]he non-movant must 'go beyond the pleadings (*e.g.*, produce affidavits, depositions, answers to interrogatories, or admissions on file), to demonstrate that there is evidence upon which a jury could properly proceed to find a verdict in her favor.'" *Sterk v. Redbox Automated Retail, LLC*, 770 F.3d 618, 627 (7th Cir. 2014) (quoting *Modrowski v. Pigatto*, 712 F.3d 1166, 1169 (7th Cir. 2013)). In other words, the non-moving party "must do more than raise some metaphysical doubt as to the material facts; [it] must come forward with specific facts showing that there is a genuine issue for trial." *Citizens for Appropriate Rural Roads v. Foxx*, 815 F.3d 1068, 1074 (7th Cir. 2016). At this stage, "[t]he parties are required to put their evidentiary cards on the table.... Summary judgment is not a time to be coy...." *Sommerfield*, 863 F.3d at 649 (internal citations and quotations omitted).

II.

In support of its motion for summary judgment, defendant submitted a Local Rule 56.1 statement of material facts (doc. # 58: DSOF).[22] Plaintiff responded to defendant's statement of material facts (doc. # 60: Pl.'s Resp. to DSOF, pp. 1–19), and filed a Rule 56.1(b)(3)(C) statement of additional facts (doc. # 60: PSOF, pp. 19–24), to which

22. [2] Defendant filed its DSOF in the same document as its motion for summary judgment, beginning on page two of the document (doc. # 58).

defendant responded (doc. # 63: Def.'s Resp. to PSOF). The following facts are undisputed unless otherwise indicated.

Ms. Valdivia emigrated from Mexico as a child (Def.'s Resp. to PSOF, ¶ 2). In May 2010, she began working at Elk Grove High School ("Elk Grove") in District 214 (Pl.'s Resp. to DSOF, ¶ 1). Ms. Valdivia worked as an assistant to the associate principal of instruction (*Id.*), and served as a bilingual support staff member; in that capacity, she spoke Spanish with some of the school's Hispanic families (Def.'s Resp. to PSOF, ¶ 3). During the 2010–2011 school year, the associate principal of instruction position was split between Carmela Sacchitello and Janet Reed (DSOF, Ex. A: Valdivia Dep. at 28–30). Nancy Holman was the principal at Elk Grove, and the associate principal of operations was Kyle Burritt (*Id.*). Ms. Valdivia worked in the same office as Diane Free (Ms. Holman's assistant) and Denise Heinol (Mr. Burritt's assistant) (*Id.* at 31; Def.'s Resp. to PSOF, ¶ 1).

On June 1, 2011, plaintiff complained in writing (by text message) to Ms. Sacchitello about racially derogatory remarks Ms. Heinol allegedly made about Latino families (Def.'s Resp. to PSOF, ¶ 4). In the text to Ms. Sacchitello, Ms. Valdivia wrote that Ms. Heinol's remarks included, among other things, that she was sick and tired of Mexicans or illegal aliens coming to the United States because they: do not speak English, want and expect everything to be handed to them for free, get to have a bilingual secretary instead of having to learn English for themselves, keep having babies because everything is handed to them, and do not file tax returns and get paid under the table (DSOF, Ex. H: Kelly Dep., Ex. 2: June 2011 text). Ms. Valdivia requested that Ms. Sacchitello ask Mr. Burritt not to "bring the racist thing up to Nancy [Holman]. We all need to survive with the way things are currently. She [Ms. Heinol] just needs to be told to relax her attitude" (*Id.*). On June 2, 2011, Ms. Sacchitello emailed the text conversation to Mr. Burritt (Def.'s Resp. to PSOF, ¶ 7). That year, plaintiff also complained to Ms. Reed or Ms. Sacchitello that Ms. Heinol stated that District 214 was catering to its Latino families by hiring a bilingual secretary (Pl.'s Resp. to DSOF, ¶ 24).

Glen Simon replaced Ms. Reed and Ms. Sacchitello as associate principal of instruction for the 2012–2013 school year (Valdivia Dep. at 43). Ms. Valdivia does not recall if she complained to Mr. Simon that her co-workers made racist comments (*Id.* at 46). In the summer of 2013, Paul Kelly replaced Ms. Holman as principal at Elk Grove, and Judi Miller took over the position as assistant to the principal (*Id.* at 31, 45, 49; Kelly Dep. at 14–16). In 2014, Megan Knight replaced Mr. Simon as associate principal of instruction (Valdivia Dep. at 104).

Ms. Valdivia alleges that Ms. Heinol continued to make derogatory comments about Latino families, including in 2015, when she stated that she hoped Donald Trump won the election and ended illegal immigration (Pl.'s Resp. to DSOF, ¶ 23). Plaintiff also claims that Ms. Miller twice told her to stop speaking Spanish because they were in America (Def.'s Resp. to PSOF, ¶ 10). At some point, Ms. Valdivia complained to

Valerie Norris, the Assistant Principal of Student Services at Elk Grove,[23] about her office-mates' comments, work habits and work distribution; Ms. Valdivia also told Ms. Norris that she thought Ms. Heinol was a racist (Pl.'s Resp. to DSOF, ¶¶ 36, 39).

In 2015, plaintiff complained to Mr. Kelly that her co-worker made derogatory comments about Latinos, Mexicans and illegal immigration (Pl.'s Resp. to DSOF, ¶¶ 23, 26). On August 31, 2015, Mr. Burritt sent the 2011 chat conversation between Ms. Sacchitello and Ms. Valdivia to Mr. Kelly and Ms. Knight (Def.'s Resp. to PSOF, ¶ 8). Plaintiff cannot recall how many times her co-workers made derogatory comments about Latinos but she asserts that they did so frequently (Pl.'s Resp. to DSOF, ¶ 25). Mr. Kelly recalls Ms. Valdivia complaining to him about interoffice disputes with Ms. Miller and Ms. Heinol, but he does not recall that Ms. Valdivia ever complained that they made racist or harassing comments (*Id.*, ¶¶ 29–32).

While at Elk Grove, Ms. Valdivia received positive annual reviews and never received any discipline or reprimands (Pl.'s Resp. to DSOF, ¶ 3). In March 2016, she applied for a position as assistant to the principal—Angela Sisi—at District 214's Wheeling High School ("Wheeling"); this job offered more pay and prestige than Ms. Valdivia's Elk Grove position (Def.'s Resp. to PSOF, ¶¶ 14–15). Ms. Sisi is the daughter of Ms. Sacchitello; Ms. Sacchitello recommended Ms. Valdivia as the best assistant she had ever had (*Id.*, ¶ 16). Ms. Sisi first met plaintiff at Ms. Sacchitello's home in 2011, and they had bumped into each other about five times at Elk Grove (Pl.'s Resp. to DSOF, ¶ 8). In April 2016, Wheeling hired Ms. Valdivia for a 12-month position, which Ms. Valdivia began in mid-June 2016 (Def.'s Resp. to PSOF, ¶¶ 17–20). Plaintiff did not discuss problems she had at Elk Grove with anyone at Wheeling (Pl.'s Resp. to DSOF, ¶ 41).

In June 2016, Ms. Valdivia asserts that she began to feel overwhelmed and experienced racing thoughts, obsessive worrying, anxiety, insomnia and loss of appetite (Def.'s Resp. to PSOF, ¶ 21). Ms. Valdivia had never received mental health treatment, and she did not understand what was happening to her (Pl.'s Resp. to DSOF, ¶¶ 48–49).

On July 14, 2016, Ms. Valdivia applied for a job closer to her home, with School District 300; she was offered the position, and she accepted on or before July 27, 2016 (Pl.'s Resp. to DSOF, ¶¶ 16–17, 50). Ms. Valdivia was emotional when she discussed her decision to leave District 214 with Ms. Sisi; Ms. Valdivia told Ms. Sisi that she had not been sleeping and she was worried about her career and about leaving Ms. Sisi (*Id.*, ¶ 54). Ms. Valdivia asserts that she cried in front of Ms. Sisi and experienced crying fits at work, but defendant disputes this (Def.'s Resp. to PSOF, ¶¶ 21–22; Pl.'s Resp. to DSOF, ¶ 53). On August 4, 2016, Ms. Valdivia submitted her letter of resignation to Ms. Sisi; Ms. Valdivia asserts that she was crying when she did so, but defendant disputes this, acknowledging only that Ms. Valdivia was "emotional" (*Id.*; Pl.'s Resp. to DSOF, ¶¶ 55–57). Ms. Valdivia told Ms. Sisi she was going to take the District 300 job at least partly because it was closer to her home (*Id.*, ¶ 58).

---

23. [3] Ms. Norris worked in a separate office and was not Ms. Valdivia's direct supervisor (DSOF, Ex. I: Norris Dep. at 11).

On August 9, 2016, Ms. Valdivia showed up unannounced at Ms. Sisi's home at 7:00 a.m., asking to rescind her resignation from Wheeling (Def.'s Resp. to PSOF, ¶ 26). Ms. Valdivia asserts that she was crying, but defendant disputes this (*Id.*) Ms. Sisi did not allow Ms. Valdivia to rescind her resignation, and the District 214 school board accepted Ms. Valdivia's resignation on August 11, 2016 (*Id.*, ¶ 28; Pl.'s Resp. to DSOF, ¶ 12). Ms. Sisi never discussed FMLA leave with plaintiff (Pl.'s Resp. to DSOF, ¶ 59).

Ms. Valdivia started work for District 300 on August 12, 2016; she had completed her employee physical for District 300 on August 5, 2016, which indicated she had no work restrictions (Pl.'s Resp. to DSOF, ¶¶ 18–20). On August 20, 2016, plaintiff was hospitalized for four days and given medication for severe depression and anxiety, and treated for her inability to sleep (Def.'s Resp. to PSOF, ¶ 31). She began seeing a psychiatrist on August 31, 2016, who diagnosed her with severe major depressive disorder and moderate to severe generalized anxiety disorder (*Id.*, ¶¶ 32–33).

III.

Defendant contends that this Court should grant summary judgment in its favor because Ms. Valdivia has not raised a genuine issue as to any fact material to her hostile work environment and FMLA claims. We first address plaintiff's hostile work environment claim.

In the complaint, Ms. Valdivia alleged that defendant "knowingly and continually subjected [her] to a racially offensive and hostile work environment" on the basis of her Hispanic race, in violation of Title VII (Compl., ¶¶ 51–53). Title VII prohibits "employers from requiring people to work in a discriminatorily hostile or abusive environment." *Boss*, 816 F.3d at 920. "To survive summary judgment on a racially hostile work environment claim, an employee must provide sufficient evidence that demonstrates: (1) that the work environment was both subjectively and objectively offensive; (2) that the harassment was based on membership in a protected class; (3) that the conduct was severe or pervasive; and (4) that there is a basis for employer liability." *Nichols v. Michigan City Plant Planning Dep't*, 755 F.3d 594, 600 (7th Cir. 2014). "If there is no triable issue of fact on even one essential element of the nonmovant's case, summary judgment is appropriate." *Boss*, 816 F.3d at 916.

District 214 argues that Ms. Valdivia has failed to provide sufficient evidence that she was subjected to actionable conduct that was severe or pervasive (doc. # 59: Def.'s Mem. in Supp. of Summ. J. at 7). In its briefing, defendant erroneously states on several occasions that plaintiff must establish that the alleged conduct was "severe *and* pervasive" (*Id.* (emphasis added)). Defendant made this same error in briefing its motion to dismiss. As we explained in our earlier opinion, "[t]his is the wrong standard. This element of a hostile work environment claim 'is in the disjunctive—the conduct must be either severe or pervasive. This means that one extremely serious act of harassment could rise to an actionable level as could a series of less severe acts.'" *Valdivia*, 2017 WL 2114965, at *3 (quoting *Hall v. City of Chicago*, 713 F.3d 325, 330 (7th Cir. 2013)). "[P]ervasiveness and severity are, to a certain degree, inversely related; a sufficiently severe episode may occur as rarely as once, while a relentless pattern of lesser harassment that extends over a long period of time also violates the statute." *Cerros v. Steel Techs., Inc.*, 398 F.3d 944, 951 (7th Cir. 2005) (internal quotations omitted). "[W]hile there is no magic number of slurs that indicates a hostile work environment, an unambiguously racial epithet falls on the more severe end of the spectrum." *Nichols*, 755 F.3d at 601 (internal quotations omitted).

Under either the severe or pervasive standard, "[t]he key inquiry is whether the conduct... altered the conditions of the employment relationship. In determining whether the conduct is sufficiently severe or pervasive to be actionable, we look at the totality of the circumstances, including: (1) the frequency of the discriminatory conduct; (2) how offensive a reasonable person would deem it to be; (3) whether it is physically threatening or humiliating conduct as opposed to verbal abuse; (4) whether it unreasonably interferes with an employee's work performance; and (5) whether it was directed at the victim." *Nichols*, 755 F.3d at 601.

Construing the facts and drawing all reasonable inferences in her favor for summary judgment purposes, Ms. Valdivia has established (by way of her own deposition) that during the six years they worked in the same office, Ms. Heinol stated multiple times—in the presence of Ms. Valdivia or to her—that she was sick and tired of Mexicans or illegal aliens coming to the United States because they: do not speak English, want and expect everything to be handed to them for free, get to have a bilingual secretary instead of having to learn English for themselves, keep having babies because everything is handed to them, and do not file tax returns and get paid under the table. Ms. Heinol also voiced support for Mr. Trump and his desire to end illegal immigration. In addition, Ms. Miller at least twice told Ms. Valdivia to stop speaking Spanish because they were in America.[24]

However, that evidence is not adequate to allow a reasonable jury to find that the conduct of which Ms. Valdivia complains was sufficiently severe or pervasive to be actionable, Below, we address the factors, and the evidence, relevant to our determination.

A.

Regarding the frequency of the alleged discriminatory conduct, Ms. Valdivia contends that over several years, she heard Ms. Heinol—and, to a lesser extent, Ms. Miller—"consistently," "frequently" and "regularly" make derogatory comments about Latinos and illegal immigrants (doc. # 61: Pl.'s Resp. at 1–3, 7). However, this contention "provides no detail on the regularity [of the conduct] and so we cannot consider the few comments detailed in the briefs to be pervasive." *Ezell v. Potter*, 400 F.3d 1041, 1048 (7th Cir. 2005) (noting that "a regular basis could be daily, weekly, monthly or even yearly"). "[V]ague and conclusory allegations of being 'harassed' and 'intimidated' by her supervisors... without more detail" do not present a triable issue as to whether the

24. [4] Ms. Valdivia states that in July 2016, she also heard Angela Ginnan, Associate Principal of Operations at Wheeling, make a derogatory comment about a Hispanic family that "those people never paid their bills" (Pl.'s Resp. to DSOF, ¶¶ 42–45). Plaintiff did not report this comment to anyone (*Id.*, ¶ 46).

complained-of conduct was objectively offensive, severe, or pervasive. *Porter v. City of Chicago*, 700 F.3d 944, 956 (7th Cir. 2012).

Ms. Valdivia asserts that she has adequately supported her claim that the conduct occurred consistently, frequently and regularly with "evidence of multiple instances of specific racially derogatory comments" (Pl.'s Resp. at 8). However, Ms. Valdivia only specifically recalled a few instances of the alleged harassing conduct, and besides an example from 2011, Ms. Valdivia's examples are not at all specific. Ms. Valdivia recalled that: in 2011, she complained of Ms. Heinol's conduct in a text message to Ms. Sacchitello; in 2015, she verbally complained to Mr. Kelly about her co-worker's comments; also in 2015, her co-workers expressed hope that Donald Trump would win the election and end illegal immigration; at some undefined point after 2013, when Ms. Miller began working in the office, she twice told Ms. Valdivia to stop speaking Spanish; and at another unspecified time or times, Ms. Valdivia told Ms. Norris that she thought Ms. Heinol was a racist.

Ms. Valdivia's general recollections of alleged discriminatory conduct are not sufficient to raise a triable issue of fact that she was subjected to such frequent discriminatory conduct that it could be considered pervasive. The Seventh Circuit has described the pervasiveness standard as "a concentrated or incessant barrage" of conduct. *Whittaker v. N. Ill. Univ.*, 424 F.3d 640, 646 (7th Cir. 2005). "[R]elatively isolated instances of non-severe misconduct will not support a claim of a hostile environment." *Id. See also Mannie v. Potter*, 394 F.3d 977, 983 (7th Cir. 2005) (affirming summary judgment where "[m]ost of the conduct that forms the basis of [the plaintiff's] claim consists of derogatory statements made by supervisors or co-workers out of her hearing," and the rest was "isolated and not particularly severe"); *Compare Jackson v. Cty. of Racine*, 474 F.3d 493, 499–500 (7th Cir. 2007) (holding that while alleged conduct was not particularly severe, it could be considered "pervasive enough and corrosive enough" to meet the standard for liability where the plaintiff provided evidence that her supervisor engaged in harassing conduct on a daily basis).

The evidence Ms. Valdivia provides does not support a finding of pervasive conduct. She recalls only "[a] handful of comments" spread over six years, including a gap in the evidence of three to four years within that, which is the kind of conduct the Seventh Circuit has found is insufficient to sustain a hostile work environment claim. *Whittaker*, 424 F.3d at 646; *see also Malekpour v. Chao*, 682 Fed.Appx. 471, 475 (7th Cir. 2017) (affirming the district court's determination that the alleged discriminatory incidents did not evidence a hostile work environment because they were "infrequent (the district court noted that they were spaced out over six years) and were not so hostile as to alter the conditions of the victim's employment and create an abusive working environment"); *Patt v. Family Health Sys., Inc.*, 280 F.3d 749, 754 (7th Cir. 2002) (holding that eight offensive gender-based comments made to the plaintiff during her multi-year employment with the defendant "were too isolated and sporadic to constitute severe or pervasive harassment").

The other conduct that Ms. Valdivia asserts is too vague and unspecific to allow a jury to evaluate its severity or pervasiveness. *See Lucas v. Chicago Transit Auth.*, 367 F.3d 714, 726 (7th Cir. 2004) (holding that general examples that African-American employees were treated "more harshly" was not sufficient to avoid summary judgment where the plaintiff did not set forth "any of the times, dates or places which led to these conclusions"); and *Gabrielle M. v. Park Forest-Chicago Heights, IL. Sch. Dist. 163*, 315 F.3d 817, 822 (7th Cir. 2003) (affirming grant of summary judgment in Title IX case because the plaintiff had failed to specify the "when, where, or how often" the alleged conduct occurred). In sum, the lack of specific evidence showing the frequency of the alleged discriminatory conduct undermines Ms. Valdivia's claim that the alleged conduct was severe or pervasive.

B.

We next consider how offensive a reasonable person would deem the alleged conduct. *Nichols*, 755 F.3d at 601. As we explained above, even if the conduct is not frequent enough to be considered pervasive, it may support a hostile work environment claim if the conduct is sufficiently severe or extreme. *Cerros*, 398 F.3d at 951.

Here, Ms. Heinol's alleged derogatory comments and her political views on immigration issues and the 2016 presidential race, and Ms. Miller's demand that Ms. Valdivia speak English, are far from the kind of "unambiguously racial epithet[s]" that "fall[ ] on the more severe end of the spectrum." *Nichols*, 755 F.3d at 601. The Seventh Circuit has held that conduct far more extreme than Ms. Valdivia alleges was not severe enough to sustain a hostile work environment claim. *See, e.g., Id.* (holding that calling colleague "black n----r" was "disrespectful" and "deplorable," but "one utterance of the n-word has not generally been held to be severe enough to rise to the level of establishing liability"); *Mercer v. Cook Cty., Ill.*, 527 Fed.Appx. 515, 521 (7th Cir. 2013) (holding that supervisors' comments such as calling employees "bitches" was "certainly boorish and rude," but not sufficiently severe to create a hostile work environment); *Porter*, 700 F.3d at 956 (supervisor's conduct calling the plaintiff a church girl and speaking to her in a high-pitched voice was "inappropriate and rude," but "[o]ffhand comments, isolated incidents, and simple teasing do not rise to the level of conduct that alters the terms and conditions of employment"); *Overly v. KeyBank Nat'l Ass'n*, 662 F.3d 856, 862 (7th Cir. 2011) (supervisor's comments calling subordinate "cutie" were "inappropriate and condescending" but not sufficiently severe to create a hostile work environment); *Ezell*, 400 F.3d at 1048 (7th Cir. 2005) (comments "reflect[ing] some ignorant stereotypes of men, of older workers and of Caucasian workers [we]re rude and inappropriate," but were "not so severe as to change the conditions of [the plaintiff's] employment").

In addition, the evidence Ms. Valdivia presents suggests that she herself did not consider Ms. Heinol's or Ms. Miller's conduct to be severe. Ms. Valdivia took pains not to elevate her complaints about Ms. Heinol up the District 214 chain of command. In 2011, when Ms. Valdivia contacted Ms. Sacchitello by text to complain about Ms. Heinol, she explicitly asked that Ms. Sacchitello not raise the issue with the Elk Grove principal. Ms. Valdivia also does not recall mentioning Ms. Heinol's or Ms. Miller's alleged conduct to Mr. Simon, the associate principal who replaced Ms. Sacchitello. Although Ms. Valdivia recalls that years later she told Ms. Norris (who was outside Ms. Valdivia's direct chain of command) that Ms. Heinol was a racist, Ms. Valdivia presents no evidence that she asked Ms. Norris to follow up on this allegation. Ms. Valdivia's "inaction in following up on h[er] complaints or taking them up the chain when no apparent action was taken by [her supervisors], belies the notion that [Ms. Heinol's or Ms. Miller's] harassment was severe or pervasive." *Yancick v. Hanna Steel Corp.*, 653 F.3d 532, 545 (7th Cir. 2011).

C.

The Court also takes into consideration the fact that neither Ms. Heinol's nor Ms. Miller's conduct ever became physically threatening or humiliating to Ms. Valdivia. *Nichols*, 755 F.3d at 601. While Ms. Valdivia contends that she was offended by their alleged comments, she does not suggest that their conduct ever became physically threatening or humiliating. Indeed, as we address further below, most of their comments were not even directed at Ms. Valdivia. This consideration thus weighs against Ms. Valdivia's contention that the conduct was severe or pervasive. *See, e.g., Luckie v. Ameritech Corp.*, 389 F.3d 708, 714 (7th Cir. 2004) (affirming summary judgment where the conduct in question consisted of "isolated events that were not physically threatening or humiliating and in some cases were not even directed" at the plaintiff).

D.

We next address whether Ms. Valdivia has presented evidence from which a reasonable jury could conclude that the derogatory comments at issue unreasonably interfered with her work performance. *Nichols*, 755 F.3d at 601. It is undisputed that for the six years Ms. Valdivia worked at Elk Grove, she excelled at her job, received consistently positive reviews and was never disciplined or reprimanded (Pl.'s Resp. to DSOF, ¶ 3). When Ms. Valdivia eventually left Elk Grove to work at Wheeling, she did so because the position at Wheeling offered more pay and prestige than Ms. Valdivia's Elk Grove position (Def.'s Resp. to PSOF, ¶¶ 14–15).[25]

The fact that Ms. Valdivia excelled at her job—and stayed at her job for five years after the alleged discriminatory conduct began—belies her contention that the conduct at issue interfered with her work performance. *See Rosario v. Aunt Martha's Youth Serv. Ctr.*, No. 16-05648, 2017 WL 4882365, at *4–5 (N.D. Ill. Oct. 30, 2017) (granting summary judgment on hostile work environment claim where the plaintiff testified that she continued receiving good performance reviews, indicating that the

25. [5] In her response brief, Ms. Valdivia appears to suggest for the first time that the work environment at Elk Grove may have caused or contributed to her mental health issues in June or July 2016 (*see* Pl.'s Resp. at 3, "two months after Noemi left Elk Grove, Noemi started psychiatric treatment and she told her psychiatrist how stressed she had been working in this hostile environment for so long"). However, Ms. Valdivia does not develop this argument or cite any specific evidence in support of this contention. Therefore, we need not address the contention here. *See, e.g., Aparicio-Brilo v. Lynch*, 824 F.3d 674, 685 (7th Cir. 2016) (court need not consider conclusory allegations that lack factual and legal support).

harassment did not affect her job performance); *Venton v. Million Dollar Round Table*, No. 13-7725, 2015 WL 3777543, at *4 (N.D. Ill. June 16, 2015) (granting summary judgment on hostile work environment claim where the record showed that the plaintiff liked working for her employer and praised her supervisor); *Fudali v. Napolitano*, No. 10-6744, 2014 WL 1097840, at *18 (N.D. Ill. Mar. 20, 2014) (granting summary judgment on hostile work environment claim where there was no evidence that any comments or conduct unreasonably interfered with the plaintiff's ability to perform his job; the plaintiff stated that he demonstrated impeccable job performance, passed all of his tests on the first attempt, and had a perfect attendance record); *Mannie v. Potter*, 394 F.3d 977, 983 (7th Cir. 2005) (affirming summary judgment for the defendant on a hostile work environment claim in part because the plaintiff offered no proof that she "was unable to perform her job because of the conduct of her supervisors and co-workers"). Thus, the evidence relevant to this factor also supports defendant's contention that Ms. Valdivia has failed to present adequate support for her claim that she was subjected to discriminatory conduct that was severe or pervasive.

E.

Lastly, we consider whether the alleged comments at issue were directed at Ms. Valdivia. *Nichols*, 755 F.3d at 601. "When harassing statements are directed at someone other than the plaintiff, the impact of such second hand harassment is obviously not as great as the impact of harassment directed at the plaintiff." *Id.* at 602 (internal quotations omitted). Plaintiff argues that Ms. Miller's and Ms. Heinol's alleged comments were directed at her because Ms. Miller directly told her not to speak Spanish, and Ms. Heinol's comments suggesting that Latinos do not deserve a bilingual secretary "were, in fact, directed toward her" because she was the bilingual secretary in the office (Pl.'s Resp. at 8).

While some of the comments were directed at Ms. Valdivia, the record shows that Ms. Valdivia primarily complains about comments that her co-workers made about Latinos and illegal immigrants in general, or Latino families at Elk Grove. Regardless, even if Ms. Valdivia could show that the alleged discriminatory conduct was directed at her, the totality of circumstances shows that Ms. Valdivia has not presented evidence upon which a reasonable jury could find that she was subjected to discriminatory conduct that was severe or pervasive, a necessary component of her hostile work environment claim. Therefore, the Court grants defendant's motion for summary judgment on this claim.

IV.

In Count II of her complaint, Ms. Valdivia contends that District 214 "interfered with her rights under the FMLA by failing to provide her with notice or information regarding her right to take job-protected leave pursuant to the FMLA when it became objectively clear that she was suffering from anxiety and emotional distress resulting from one or more psychological conditions" (Compl., ¶ 56). The FMLA entitles eligible employees to take twelve weeks of leave "[b]ecause of a serious health condition that makes the employee unable to perform the functions of the position of such employee."

29 U.S.C. § 2612(a)(1)(D). The FMLA defines a serious health condition as "an illness, injury, impairment or physical or mental condition that involves inpatient care ... or continuing treatment by a health care provider." 29 C.F.R. § 825.113(a). It is unlawful for an employer to interfere with, restrain or deny an employee's attempt to exercise the right to take leave under the FMLA. *Preddie v. Bartholomew Consol. Sch. Corp.*, 799 F.3d 806, 816 (7th Cir. 2015).

To survive summary judgment on an FMLA interference claim, plaintiff must offer evidence that "(1) he was eligible for the FMLA's protections, (2) his employer was covered by the FMLA, (3) he was entitled to leave under the FMLA, (4) he provided sufficient notice of his intent to take leave, and (5) his employer denied or interfered with ... FMLA benefits to which he was entitled." *Preddie*, 799 F.3d at 816 (internal citations and quotations omitted). Here, District 214 focuses its summary judgment motion on one of these elements; the district contends that Ms. Valdivia has not raised a genuine issue of material fact on her FMLA claim, because she has not presented evidence that would allow a reasonable jury to find that she provided sufficient notice of a serious health condition entitling her to FMLA leave (Def.'s Mem. at 9).

Construed in the light most favorable to Ms. Valdivia, the evidence shows that beginning in June or July 2016—about the time she began working at Wheeling—Ms. Valdivia began feeling overwhelmed and anxious, and she had difficulty eating and sleeping. Ms. Valdivia was confused by these feelings, and although she was only one month into her new job at Wheeling, she started looking for employment closer to her home as a way to cope with these issues. Ms. Valdivia did not know or understand what was happening to her because she had never before received mental health treatment. Ms. Valdivia was crying and emotional when she spoke to Ms. Sisi about leaving Wheeling, and she was crying and emotional when she showed up at Ms. Sisi's house early in the morning on August 9, 2016 to try (unsuccessfully) to rescind her resignation letter five days after presenting it. Eleven days after that, Ms. Valdivia was hospitalized for depression and anxiety.

The FMLA "notice requirement is not demanding: The employee's duty is merely to place the employer on notice of a probable basis for FMLA leave." *Stevenson v. Hyre Elec. Co.*, 505 F.3d 720, 724 (7th Cir. 2007) (internal quotations omitted). "It is enough under the FMLA if the employer knows of the employee's need for leave; the employee need not mention the statute or demand its benefits." *Byrne v. Avon Prods.*, 328 F.3d 379, 382 (7th Cir. 2003). The Seventh Circuit has held that an employee may meet the FMLA notice requirement with "constructive notice" of a serious health condition where an employee is unable to communicate his illness to his employer or there are "clear abnormalities in the employee's behavior." *Stevenson*, 505 F.3d at 726 (citing *Byrne*, 328 F.3d at 381–82). In those cases, "observable changes in an employee's condition" or "uncharacteristic conduct at work" may themselves provide an employer with adequate notice of a serious medical condition. *Burnett v. LFW Inc.*, 472 F.3d 471, 479–80 (7th Cir. 2006). Indeed, direct notice may not be possible if the plaintiff "herself was unaware that she was suffering from a serious medical condition." *Stevenson*, 505 F.3d at 725.[26]

In *Stevenson*, the Seventh Circuit held that a trier of fact could find that the employee's "behavior was so bizarre that it amounted to constructive notice of the need for leave" where she had been a "model employee" for years, before "[h]er behavior changed dramatically." *Stevenson*, 505 F.3d at 726. Likewise, in *Byrne*, the Seventh Circuit found constructive notice where an employee with four years of highly regarded service began to show "unusual behavior," such as sleeping on the job. *Byrne*, 328 F.3d at 382–83. *Compare Guzman v. Brown Cty.*, No. 16-3599, 2018 WL 1177592, at *4 (7th Cir. Mar. 7, 2018) (finding that employer did not have constructive notice of employee's need for FMLA leave because six episodes of oversleeping spread over eighteen months did not constitute the sort of "stark and abrupt change which is capable of providing constructive notice of a serious health condition").

Here, Ms. Valdivia contends that District 214 had constructive notice of a serious health condition under *Byrne*, either because her behavior was so unusual that Ms. Sisi should have been alerted to her condition, or because her severe depressive disorder and moderate to severe generalized anxiety disorder rendered her incapable of providing notice (Pl.'s Resp. at 14–15). Defendant responds that Ms. Sisi did not know Ms. Valdivia well enough to recognize her behavior as unusual, and denies that Ms. Sisi ever observed Ms. Valdivia acting so unusual that she was on notice that Ms. Valdivia had a serious health condition (Def.'s Mem. at 10).

While their time together was brief, Ms. Valdivia has presented sufficient evidence to create a triable fact issue as to whether she exhibited bizarre or unusual behavior sufficient to give Ms. Sisi constructive notice of her serious health condition. When Ms. Sisi hired Ms. Valdivia, she knew that Ms. Valdivia came highly recommended by Ms. Sisi's mother and others at Elk Grove, after six years of working there and receiving glowing reviews. By contrast, after Ms. Valdivia obtained a new position at Wheeling, she abruptly announced her resignation barely four weeks into the job. Then, four days after submitting her resignation, Ms. Valdivia surprised Ms. Sisi by showing up at her home at 7:00 a.m. and asking to rescind her resignation. In addition, Ms. Valdivia states that she was crying and distraught in front of Ms. Sisi each time she discussed her decision to leave Wheeling with her. Although defendant disputes this characterization

---

26. [6] The Eighth Circuit has called into question the validity of constructive notice in the FMLA context. In *Byrne*, in describing what the Seventh Circuit later termed the "constructive notice" exception under the FMLA, the Seventh Circuit relied on 29 C.F.R. § 825.303(a), an FMLA regulation that provided for an employee to give notice to his or her employer "except in extraordinary circumstances where such notice is not feasible." *Byrne*, 328 F.3d at 382. However, that regulation was amended in 2009, and the extraordinary circumstances language was deleted. 29 C.F.R. § 825.303(a). Thus, in *Scobey v. Nucor Steel-Arkansas*, 580 F.3d 781, 788 (8th Cir. 2009), the Eighth Circuit held that constructive notice is not sufficient to give an employer notice under the FMLA. *See also Miles v. Nashville Elec. Serv.*, 525 Fed.Appx. 382, 387 (6th Cir. 2013) (recognizing conflict between Seventh and Eighth Circuits). The Seventh Circuit recently acknowledged this conflict, but declined to address it because the parties did not present the issue on appeal. *Guzman v. Brown Cty.*, No. 16-3599, 2018 WL 1177592, at *4 n.3 (7th Cir. Mar. 7, 2018).

of Ms. Valdivia's "emotional" behavior, that is a fact dispute for the jury to resolve at trial and not for the Court to resolve on summary judgment.

We conclude that Ms. Valdivia's testimony regarding her repeated crying, combined with her actions in seeking to leave her job four weeks after starting it and showing up at her employer's house early in the morning, raise a genuine issue of material fact as to whether Ms. Sisi had constructive notice that Ms. Valdivia had a serious health condition. *See Pagel v. TIN Inc.*, 695 F.3d 622, 628–29 (7th Cir. 2012) (noting that notice inquiry was "best resolved by the trier of fact, particularly, where, as is the case here, the employer and employee dispute the quantity and nature of communications regarding the employee's illness") (internal quotations and citations omitted). As the adequacy of notice is the only issue defendant raises in its motion on Ms. Valdivia's FMLA interference claim, we deny defendant's motion for summary judgment on this claim.[27]

CONCLUSION

For the foregoing reasons, defendant's motion for summary judgment is granted in part and denied in part (doc. # 58). The Court grants defendant's motion for summary judgment as to plaintiff's Title VII claim, but denies the motion as to plaintiff's FMLA claim. We set the matter for a status hearing on April 3, 2018 at 9:00 a.m. We direct the parties to discuss with each other the possibility of settlement prior to that status hearing.

Issues for Consideration

- What are some lessons learned for Township High School District 214?
- Did the facts lend to a hostile work environment claim. Why or why not?
- Was Township High School District 214 put on notice of Noemi Valdivia's medical condition? If so, what obligations did the school have?
- What are some things employers can do to avoid the situation presented in this case?

Medina v. Berwyn South School District 100

2018 WL 1726424 (N.D. Illinois, April 10, 2018)

Ronald A. Guzmán, United States District Judge

For the reasons stated below, Defendant's motion for summary judgment is granted and Plaintiff's cross-motion for summary judgment is denied. All pending motions are denied as moot. Civil case terminated.

---

27. [7] Defendant also contends that Ms. Sisi could not have had notice that Ms. Valdivia had a serious health condition because plaintiff herself was confused by her behavior and could not identify her condition (Def.'s Mem. at 10). However, a situation where the plaintiff "herself was unaware that she was suffering from a serious medical condition" is one of the circumstances in which the Seventh Circuit has opined that constructive notice might apply. *See Stevenson*, 505 F.3d at 725.

STATEMENT

After she was terminated from her position as an administrative assistant with Berwyn School District 100 ("District"), Gloria Medina sued the District for discrimination in violation of the Americans with Disabilities Act, 42 U.S.C. 12101, *et seq.* ("ADA") and interference with her rights under the Family and Medical Leave Act, 29 U.S.C. § 2601, *et seq.* ("FMLA"). Both the District and Medina move for summary judgment on both claims. For the reasons set forth below, the District's motion is granted and Medina's motion is denied.

Facts

Medina was hired by the District on or about January 5, 1998 to serve as the secretary and receptionist for the Building and Grounds Department. (Pl.'s Resp. Def.'s Stmt. Facts, Dkt. # 56, ¶ 1.) In 2000, Medina became the secretary to the Director of Title VII Grants, and in July 2001, she assumed the additional role of Administrative Assistant to the Director of the Bilingual Grant Program. (*Id.* ¶¶ 2, 3.) The Director of Title VII Grants and the Director of the Bilingual Grant Program were the same individual. (*Id.* ¶ 3.) Medina's duties as Administrative Assistant to the Bilingual Department included, among other things, providing clerical support to the director, interpreting and translating documents as needed, monitoring and meeting scheduled program reports, and maintaining an accurate record-keeping system. (*Id.* ¶ 4.) Medina's job required organizational, communication, and computer skills, effective interpersonal skills, and proficiency in both written and oral Spanish and English. (*Id.* ¶ 5.) Medina reported to the Director of the Bilingual Grant Program/Bilingual Department and the Superintendent. (*Id.* ¶ 6.) Medina was approved for and took an FMLA leave between July 30, 2014 and August 18, 2014, which was subsequently extended to October 1, 2014. (*Id.* ¶ 7.) Medina was approved for a second FMLA leave from July 6, 2015 to October 6, 2015, but returned to work on August 31, 2015. (*Id.* ¶¶ 11, 12.)

Beatriz Maldonado, who was Principal of the District's Emerson Elementary School, also became Director of the Bilingual Department in July 2015. (*Id.* ¶ 8.) Around the time that Medina was returning to work after her second FMLA leave, the District was combining the offices of Heritage School and Emerson Elementary School into one main office in the Heritage School building. (*Id.* ¶ 13.) Medina moved with Maldonado to the new combined office in the Heritage Building, and her job title remained the same. (*Id.* ¶ 14.) A new database for tracking student information, PowerSchool, was being introduced prior to the start of Medina's FMLA leave in July 2015. (*Id.* ¶ 15.) In a July 1, 2015 email to Medina, Maldonado informed Medina that she had arranged for Medina to be trained on the PowerSchool system, explaining that "data accuracy is one of the biggest responsibilities in the department, thus the importance of this task is high." (*Id.* ¶ 16.) In her July 2, 2015 response, Medina agreed with Maldonado that "data accuracy is a major responsibility," but she did not receive the training prior to her taking the scheduled FMLA leave. (*Id.* ¶¶ 15, 18.) The PowerSchool program was "very different" from the previous program used by the District, and knowledge of the PowerSchool program was required for Medina's position. (*Id.* ¶ 19.)

In a meeting on the morning of August 31, 2015, Medina's first day back, Maldonado told Medina that her priorities were learning and familiarizing herself with the PowerSchool program and translating. (*Id.* ¶¶ 20, 21.) While the parties dispute whether Medina had a private office prior to the combination of the Emerson and Heritage Schools, and the record is unclear in this regard, it is undisputed that upon her return to work on August 31, 2015, Medina was placed in a newly-combined office with two other secretaries, which served both Emerson and Heritage Schools. (Def.'s Resp. Pl's Stmt. Facts, Dkt. # 59, ¶ 16.)

On August 31, 2015, at 2:42 p.m., Jean Suchy, Assistant Principal of Emerson School, sent Medina an email asking her to complete a translation of a Welcome Back to School letter by noon on September 1, 2015. (Pl.'s Resp. Def.'s Stmt. Facts, Dkt. # 56, ¶ 23.) At approximately 3:00 p.m. on September 1, 2015, Medina had a meeting with Maldonado in her office, at which Suchy was also present. (*Id.* ¶ 24.) Medina explained that "she couldn't do the translations" because she had trouble concentrating due to the noise and confusion in the office. (*Id.* ¶ 25.) Medina further stated that the translation would take more time because she had to answer phones, take care of parents, and help a colleague. (*Id.*) According to Medina, Maldonado became upset when Medina told her she needed more time, and Maldonado, after telling Medina that "she needed to multitask, or else," "lunged" toward Medina. (*Id.* ¶ 26.) When Medina responded "Or else, what?", Maldonado told Medina she was being insubordinate. (*Id.*) On September 2, 2015, Maldonado had a conversation with Medina at her desk regarding the translations, and Medina recorded the conversation with her cell phone. (*Id.* ¶¶ 28, 29.) Later that day, at approximately 3:00 p.m., Medina and Maldonado met in Maldonado's office, again with Suchy present, and Maldonado pointed out errors in Medina's translation of the Welcome Back letter. (*Id.* ¶¶ 30, 31.) During the meeting, Maldonado asked Medina why she was holding her cell phone, and Medina responded by twice asking, "Why can't I hold my phone?" (*Id.* ¶ 33.)

Maldonado told Medina she was being insubordinate and ended the meeting. (*Id.* ¶¶ 33, 34.) Medina, who described her anxiety level at that time as being "high," accused Maldonado of treating her like an animal and kicking her out of the office. (*Id.* ¶ 34.) Using her cell phone, Medina called her therapist, who instructed her to call an ambulance. (*Id.* ¶ 35.) Medina then went to the main office, which she described as "noisy" and "crowded" with parents and students. (*Id.* ¶ 36.) Using her desk phone in the main office, Medina called 911 and hung up, called 911 a second time and again hung up, and on the third call, told the dispatch operator that she was having a panic attack. (*Id.* ¶ 37.) After the hang ups, a 911 operator called the school back, and the Assistant Principal of Heritage School, Allison Boutet, who was in the main office at the time, told the operator that the person who had called and hung up was, at that moment, on the phone with a 911 operator. (*Id.* ¶ 38.) Boutet told Medina the address of the school to provide to the 911 operator, and then escorted Medina to the nurse's office, which is located right next to the main office. (*Id.* ¶¶ 38, 39.) A police officer and paramedics arrived and took Medina out on a gurney while Maldonado and Suchy were standing in the hallway. (*Id.* ¶ 41.) As she was being taken out, with students and parents present, Medina testified that she yelled, "[Y]ou caused it. You did this to me. You both—you—did this to me, Beatrice. You did this to me," and Maldonado smirked. (Medina Dep., Def.'s Ex. K, Dkt. # 41-12, at 74.)

Suchy believed that Medina's behavior toward Maldonado in the meetings on September 1 and 2, 2015, which included raising her voice and using an inappropriate tone, was disrespectful and unprofessional. (Pl.'s Resp. Def.'s Stmt. Facts, Dkt. # 56, ¶ 43.) While the District disputes the evidentiary support for certain of Medina's statements of fact, it appears uncontested that Medina was diagnosed with major depression and generalized anxiety disorder at least as of August 2014, and that there was no physical harm or property damage related to Medina's purported panic attack on September 2, 2015. (Def.'s Resp. Pl.'s Stmt. Facts, Dkt. # 59, ¶¶ 3, 8, 11.)

The District sent a letter dated September 3, 2015 to Medina stating that she was being placed on administrative leave, effective immediately, due to her unprofessional and insubordinate conduct towards her supervisor and her 911 hang-up calls. (Pl.'s Resp. Def.'s Stmt. Facts, Dkt. # 56, ¶ 44.) The letter indicated that an investigation was necessary, and she would be arrested if she set foot on District property. (*Id.*) In a letter to the District dated September 4, 2015, Medina's psychiatrist, Dr. Lee Weiss, and her therapist, David Hodgson, related that it was in Medina's best interests to be placed on medical leave under the FMLA due to her medical condition and her inability to function at work. (*Id.* ¶ 45.)[28]

In a letter dated September 10, 2015, the District informed Medina that after an investigation, Superintendent Stanley Fields was recommending to the Board of Education of Berwyn South School District 100 ("Board") that Medina be terminated because she engaged in misconduct. (*Id.* ¶ 49.) Specifically, the letter stated, in part, as follows:

> Your conduct on September 2, 2015, constitutes insubordination and misconduct. Specifically, yelling at Principal Maldonado and Assistant Principal Suchy; speaking on your cell phone in an unprofessional manner in the presence of students, parents, and other staff in the Emerson main office; calling and hanging up in 911 emergency dispatchers from a District school phone line; and failing to follow proper District procedures for requesting and taking a personal day, is conduct that disrupts the educational environment and violates Board Policies 5:120, 5:125 and 5:330. Accordingly, I will be recommending your termination from employment with the District to the [Board] at its Wednesday, September 23, 2015, regularly scheduled Board meeting.

(Def.'s Ex. DD, Dkt. # 41-31, at 2.)

The letter advised Medina that she had the right to address the Board and present evidence. (*Id.*) Although the District moves to strike the relevant statements of fact,

28. [1] Because the parties construe this September 4, 2015 letter as a request for FMLA leave, the Court does as well.

Medina purportedly related to her therapist, Hodgson, that she felt harassed by the administration and believed that Fields was looking to get rid of her. (Def.'s Resp. Pl's Stmt. Facts, Dkt. # 59, ¶¶ 29, 30.)[29]

Medina provided a Certification of Health Provider dated September 18, 2015 and signed by Weiss and Hodgson, indicating that Medina was unable to do her job due to her mental health condition. (Pl.'s Resp. Def.'s Stmt. Facts, Dkt. # 56, ¶ 46.) The District acknowledged receipt of the certification in a letter to Medina dated September 22, 2015, which stated: "Please be advised that because you are currently on paid administrative leave, pending the Board of Education's vote on Dr. Fields' September 10 2015, recommendation to terminate your employment, the District will consider your FMLA request after the Board of Education's September 23, 2015 meeting." (*Id.* ¶ 51.) On September 23, 2015, the Board dismissed Medina from her administrative assistant position. (*Id.* ¶ 52.)

Standard

"The court shall grant summary judgment if the movant shows that there is no genuine dispute as to any material fact and the movant is entitled to judgment as a matter of law." Fed. R. Civ. P. 56(a); *see also Shell v. Smith*, 789 F.3d 715, 717 (7th Cir. 2015). To survive summary judgment, the nonmoving party must "do more than simply show that there is some metaphysical doubt as to the material facts," *Matsushita Elec. Indus. Co. v. Zenith Radio Corp.*, 475 U.S. 574, 586 (1986), and instead must "establish some genuine issue for trial such that a reasonable jury could return a verdict in her favor." *Gordon v. FedEx Freight, Inc.*, 674 F.3d 769, 772–73 (7th Cir. 2012). The Court gives the nonmoving party "the benefit of conflicts in the evidence and reasonable inferences that could be drawn from it." *Grochocinski v. Mayer Brown Rowe & Maw, LLP*, 719 F.3d 785, 794 (7th Cir. 2013). The Court must not make credibility determinations or weigh conflicting evidence. *McCann v. Iroquois Mem'l Hosp.*, 622 F.3d 745, 752 (7th Cir. 2010).

Analysis

ADA Discrimination (Count I)

Medina alleges that she was terminated in violation of the ADA "as the result of conduct that was a manifestation of her disability, that is, severe work-related stress." (Compl., Dkt. # 1, ¶ 56.) "The ADA … prohibit[s] an employer from discriminating against a qualified individual with a disability." *Guzman v. Brown Cty.*, No. 16-3599, 2018 WL 1177592, at *6 (7th Cir. Mar. 7, 2018) (citing 42 U.S.C. § 12112; 29 U.S.C. § 794). "In order to defeat summary judgment on her disability discrimination claim, [Medina] must point to evidence capable of establishing that (1) she is a person with a disability within the meaning of the ADA …; (2) she is qualified to perform the essential functions of her job with or without a reasonable accommodation; and (3) she suffered from an adverse employment decision as a result of her disability." *Id.* Under current Seventh Circuit precedent, if the parties do not argue for a different

29. [2] The Court need not rule on the motion to strike these statements of facts as they are not material to resolution of the motions for summary judgment.

type of causation, the "but for" standard is appropriate. *Monroe v. Ind. Dep't of Transp.*, 871 F.3d 495, 504 (7th Cir. 2017) (noting that the ADA Amendments Act changed the language from prohibiting employers from discriminating 'because of' a disability to 'on the basis of' a disability, but stating that because "the parties ... have not argued that another causation standard should apply, ... we will continue to apply the 'but for' causation standard") (citations omitted). "To show that disability discrimination was the 'but for' reason for the termination, a plaintiff can use either direct or circumstantial evidence." *Id.* While direct evidence is essentially an admission that the defendant fired the plaintiff due to her disability, circumstantial evidence can include:

(1) suspicious timing;

(2) ambiguous statements or behavior towards other employees in the protected group;

(3) evidence, statistical or otherwise, that similarly situated employees outside of the protected group systematically receive better treatment; and

(4) evidence that the employer offered a pretextual reason for an adverse employment action.

Bunn v. Khoury Enters., Inc., 753 F.3d 676, 684 (7th Cir. 2014).

Pointing to the events of the day at issue, the District contends that regardless of whether Medina was disabled, "when an employee engages in behavior that is unacceptable in the workplace ..., the fact that the behavior is precipitated by her mental illness 'does not present an issue under the Americans with Disabilities Act'; the behavior itself disqualifies her from continued employment and justifies her discharge." *Felix v. Wis. Dep't of Transp.*, 828 F.3d 560, 571 (7th Cir. 2016) (citation omitted). Medina does not dispute that she engaged in the conduct for which she was terminated. She seeks instead to downplay its seriousness, calling it a "single day's strained conduct" (Pl.'s Resp., Dkt. # 54, at 7), and asserting that she was actually terminated because she had become a "challenge and an irritation to [Superintendent] Fields' authority." (*Id.* at 9.) In addition, she maintains that the violations cited by Fields as the basis for his recommendation that she be terminated are "ludicrous" and unreasonable. (*Id.* at 11.)

But these arguments miss the point; Medina was terminated for her unprofessional conduct, not because of her disability. At her deposition, Medina testified that her conversation with Maldonado on the afternoon of September 2, 2015 became somewhat tense after Medina admitted to recording their conversation earlier in the day. (Def.'s Ex. K, Medina Dep., Dkt. # 41-12, at 55–57.) When Maldonado asked Medina why she again was holding her phone at the afternoon meeting, Medina responded twice with "Why can't I hold my phone?" (*Id.* at 56–57.)[30]

After Maldonado told Medina she was being insubordinate and directed her to leave the office, Medina testified that she began to have a panic attack and accused

30. [3] Medina testified that "[i]t's vague, but I may have recorded [Maldonado]" at the afternoon meeting. (Def.'s Ex. K, Medina Dep., Dkt. # 41-12, at 57.)

Maldonado of treating her like an animal. (*Id.* at 59.) According to Medina, she was "probably" yelling. (*Id.* at 60.) As she was walking down the internal hallway back to the main office, Medina used her cell phone to call both her therapist, who directed her to call 911, and her father. (*Id.* at 65.) Upon reaching the main office, Medina stated out loud to no one in particular that she was not feeling well, and "struggl[ed] to cross the students ... and parents" in order to "make [her] way" to her desk to call 911. (*Id.* at 66–67.) After Medina called 911 and twice hung up before speaking with a dispatcher on the third call, paramedics and a police officer arrived at the school. (*Id.*) According to Medina, as she was taken out of the school on a gurney by paramedics in front of other staff, parents, and children, she was "going crazy" and "yelling" that "Principal Maldonado did this to me." (*Id.* at 73–74.)

Superintendent Fields determined that Medina's behavior violated at least District Policy 5:120, which provides, in part, that "[a]ll District employees are expected to maintain high standards in their school relationships, ... to be considerate and co-operative, and to maintain professional and appropriate relationships with students, parents, staff members, and others." (Def.'s Ex. PP, District Policy 5:120 Ethics & Conduct, Dkt. # 41-43.) At a time of significantly-heightened concerns regarding school security and the physical safety of students and staff, the Court cannot conclude that the District's decision to terminate Medina based on her unprofessional and disruptive behavior violates the ADA. *See Palmer v. Cir. Ct. of Cook Cty.*, 117 F.3d 351, 352 (7th Cir. 1997) ("The [ADA] does not require an employer to retain a potentially violent employee. Such a requirement would place the employer on a razor's edge—in jeopardy of violating the Act if it fired such an employee, yet in jeopardy of being deemed negligent if it retained him and he hurt someone.").

Medina's cross-motion for summary judgment on the ADA claim is denied for the same reason. In addition, to the extent that Medina seeks to rely on the indirect method of proof to show discrimination, she has failed to establish a *prima facie* case as she does not demonstrate that she was meeting the District's legitimate expectations or identify any similarly-situated non-disabled comparators who were treated more favorably. *See Aberman v. Bd. of Educ. of City of Chi.*, 242 F. Supp. 3d 672, 689 (N.D. Ill. 2017) ("[S]ince Plaintiff has not shown that she was meeting her employer's legitimate expectations and has not shown that a ... nondisabled similarly situated comparator received more favorable treatment, Plaintiff has not established a *prima facie* case of discrimination under the ADA...."). Even assuming she established a *prima facie* case of discrimination, Medina engages only in speculation and points to no record evidence demonstrating that the District's basis for terminating her was a lie. *See Ennin v. CNH Indus. Am., LLC*, 878 F.3d 590, 596 (7th Cir. 2017) ("Because [the defendant] has proffered legitimate, nondiscriminatory reasons for firing [the plaintiff], he must produce evidence that those reasons were actually pretext for discrimination," or in other words, a "lie.").

Accordingly, the District's motion for summary judgment as to the ADA claim is granted while Plaintiff's cross-motion is denied.

FMLA Interference (Count II)

Under the FMLA, an eligible employee is entitled to twelve workweeks of leave because of, among other reasons, "a serious health condition that makes the employee unable to perform the functions of [her] position...." 29 U.S.C. § 2612(a)(1)(D). "The FMLA ... makes it unlawful for an employer to interfere with an employee's attempt to exercise FMLA rights or to retaliate against employees who exercise their FMLA rights." *Guzman*, 2018 WL 1177592, at *3 (citing 29 U.S.C. § 2615). An employee who takes FMLA leave is entitled upon returning from the leave to be restored to the same or equivalent position she held at the time the leave commenced. 29 U.S.C. §§ 2614(1)(A), (B). "In order to prevail on a FMLA interference claim, an employee must establish that (1) she was eligible for the FMLA's protections, (2) her employer was covered by the FMLA, (3) she was entitled to leave under the FMLA, (4) she provided sufficient notice of her intent to take leave, and (5) her employer denied her FMLA benefits to which she was entitled." *Id.*

Medina contends that when she returned from FMLA leave on August 31, 2015, she returned to a non-equivalent position. Medina's brief argument as to this issue, without supporting citations to the record, is as follows:

> Plaintiff returned from FMLA leave, without training, to an unfamiliar computer database, was stationed in the schools' secretarial pool, and was denied a private office commensurate with her position. Plaintiff was presented with a new job description replete with clerical tasks regarding which she was without training or experience. Plaintiff, receiving little guidance from her superiors, was told to seek instruction from one of the clerks. At one point she found herself, to the mutual dismay of herself and the school Librarian, at the school library pursuing a project designed to keep track of the school's I-pads! Plaintiff was left to wonder what the future would hold for her in terms of job prospects as she gazed across ... the hallway to the private office occupied by Maria Anderson, whom she was told had taken over the translation duties in Plaintiff's absence.

(Pl.'s Resp., Dkt. # 54, at 13.)[31] Notably, while making general statements about a "new" job description, Medina fails to point to any record evidence specifically identifying

31. [5] Medina often fails to include citations to statements of fact in her response brief, and further does not discuss many of her statements of fact in her response. It is not this Court's role to sift through the statements of fact to determine which might be relevant to a party's argument, particularly when the party is represented by counsel. As noted by another court in this district:

> It is not the Court's responsibility to find arguments, facts, and supporting case law for the parties. Instead, it is the advocate's job to make it easy for the court to rule in his client's favor. Judges are not like pigs, hunting for truffles buried in briefs. Nor are they archaeologists searching for treasure.

In re Ace Track Co., Ltd., 556 B.R. 887, 903 (Bankr. N.D. Ill. 2016) (internal citations, quotation marks, and ellipses omitted).

how her duties purportedly changed upon her return from FMLA leave. Nor does Medina place her perceived demotion in context of the relevant circumstances, including the following:

- Her former school was consolidating space and operations with another one, thus necessitating the move to a new working space
- The transition to the PowerSchool computer system was occurring before and during her FMLA leave, and for reasons she fails to identify, Medina did not obtain training on the new system prior to her leave, despite Maldonado having scheduled training for her
- While complaining that she was required to perform clerical duties on her return, Medina's job description as Administrative Assistant to the Director of the Bilingual Department included clerical duties to support the Director
- Medina returned to her job on August 31, 2015 with, she admits, the same title and salary, and still reported to the Director of Bilingual Studies.

In light of these deficiencies, the Court finds that Medina has failed to establish that she was not restored to the same or equivalent position upon returning from FMLA leave on August 31, 2015.

Medina also contends that her September 4, 2015 application for FMLA leave was wrongly denied. Medina's only argument in this regard is that because she was terminated in violation of the ADA, her request for FMLA leave was also improperly denied. The Court, however, has concluded that she was not terminated in violation of the ADA, so this argument fails. Accordingly, the District's motion for summary judgment as to Medina's FMLA interference claim is granted, and Plaintiff's cross-motion is denied.

Conclusion

For the reasons stated above, Defendant's motion for summary judgment is granted and Plaintiff's cross-motion is denied.

Issues for Consideration

- The court noted that a plaintiff can show disability discrimination through "direct" or "circumstantial" evidence—what does this mean?
- What if an employee's unprofessional conduct can be tied to their disability? How would that have changed the outcome in this case?
- What kinds of things does an employee need to produce or show that their FMLA was interfered with?

Bowie v. West Rock Co.

2018 WL 5017762 (E.D. Wis. October 16, 2018)

DAVID E. JONES, United States Magistrate Judge.

Robert Lee Bowie worked at WestRock Services Inc.[32] for nearly seventeen years. Growing tired of his excessive absenteeism, in February 2016, WestRock placed Mr. Bowie on a last-chance agreement that required him to have perfect attendance for about six months. When Mr. Bowie failed to show up for a scheduled shift in August 2016, WestRock terminated his employment for violating the terms of the agreement.

Mr. Bowie claims that he was not scheduled to work on the day in question and that the real reason for his firing was because he is old, African-American, and disabled and he had taken several days of medical leave. After his administrative claim was dismissed, Mr. Bowie filed an employment-discrimination suit against WestRock in federal court. The Court subsequently dismissed Mr. Bowie's age-discrimination claim because it was not included in the administrative charge. WestRock has moved for summary judgment on Mr. Bowie's remaining claims. Because no reasonable jury could return a verdict in favor of Mr. Bowie on those claims, the Court will grant WestRock's motion.

I. Factual Background

WestRock Services Inc. operates a manufacturing facility in Germantown, Wisconsin, that produces corrugated cardboard packaging products. Def.'s Facts ¶ 1. Robert Lee Bowie began working at WestRock in September 1999. *See* Complaint 2, ECF No. 1. Over the course of his employment, Mr. Bowie performed several positions before settling in as a bander operator. *See* Plaintiff's Response, ECF No. 38; *see also* Def.'s Facts ¶ 9. As a bander operator, Mr. Bowie operated a machine that banded together corrugated boards. Def.'s Facts ¶ 10.

In the bander operator role, Mr. Bowie worked on the third shift. Def.'s Facts ¶ 11. He usually worked eight-hour shifts, although he would occasionally be required to work extended shifts, for example, to cover another employee's vacation or as mandatory overtime to meet production goals. *Id.* Third-shift employees typically started their shift one evening and completed it the following morning. Def.'s Facts ¶¶ 24–25. WestRock's work schedule for third-shift employees listed the date that employees were to start their shift. Def.'s Facts ¶ 23.

In early February 2016, WestRock placed Mr. Bowie on a Last Chance Agreement because of ongoing attendance issues. Def.'s Facts ¶ 19 (citing Exhibit A to Declaration of Cindy Nelson, 33-1); *see also* Nelson Decl. ¶ 13, ECF No. 33. The Agreement required Mr. Bowie to "maintain perfect attendance until 8/19/2016" and indicated that "[a]ny absence must be approved in advance by the Production Supervisor or Superin-

32. [1] Mr. Bowie incorrectly identified his former employer as West Rock Co. is his complaints. *See* Defendant's Proposed Findings of Fact 1 n.1, ECF No. 30.

tendent." Nelson Decl., Ex. A. The Agreement further indicated that "[f]ailure to make improvement or recurrence of inappropriate behavior or conduct within the specified time period ... will result in immediate termination." *Id.* Mr. Bowie understood this to mean that he would automatically be fired if he incurred an attendance violation before August 19. Def.'s Facts ¶ 22. He signed the Agreement on February 2, 2016; the Agreement also was signed by WestRock's plant supervisor (Darrin Dohman), WestRock's human resources representative (Cindy Nelson), and Mr. Bowie's union representative. *See* Nelson Decl., Ex. A.

On February 11, 2016, Mr. Bowie was approved for intermittent medical leave under the Family and Medical Leave Act based on a range of health issues. *See* Exhibit 1 to Pl.'s Resp., ECF No. 38-1 at 2–4. The certification was to begin on March 1, 2016, and last for one year. *Id.* Mr. Bowie claims he used four days of FMLA leave: February 29, 2016; March 2, 2016; July 28, 2016; and July 29, 2016. *See* Pl.'s Resp. 1.

WestRock's longstanding practice is to post its overtime work schedules in its employee break room. Def.'s Facts ¶ 29. Mr. Bowie was aware of this practice. Def.'s Facts ¶ 30. Indeed, he checked the overtime schedule before leaving work each day. Def.'s Facts ¶ 31.

The overtime schedule for the week of July 31, 2016, indicated that Mr. Bowie was scheduled "7PM TO 7AM 8/4-6/16." *See* Exhibit B to Nelson Decl., ECF No. 33-2. In other words, he was scheduled to work from 7:00 p.m. to 7:00 a.m. on August 4, 5, and 6. Def.'s Facts ¶¶ 32–33. Mr. Bowie saw the schedule, Def.'s Facts ¶ 34, but he didn't think it required him to work on the evening of August 6, *see* Compl. 2–3; *see also* Def.'s Facts ¶ 42. Mr. Bowie worked his shifts on August 4 and 5. Def.'s Facts ¶¶ 36–37. However, he did not show up for work on the evening of August 6. Def.'s Facts ¶ 40. Mr. Bowie never called WestRock to clarify the schedule or report that he would not be working on the 6th. Def.'s Facts ¶¶ 41, 43.

On Monday, August 8, Mr. Bowie's immediate supervisor, Jon Hein, informed Mr. Dohman that Mr. Bowie had not shown up for his last-scheduled shift. Def.'s Facts ¶ 44. Mr. Dohman reviewed the Last Chance Agreement and determined that Mr. Bowie's unexcused absence on August 6 constituted a violation of the Agreement and warranted termination. Def.'s Facts ¶¶ 45–48. Rather than immediately fire him, Mr. Dohman waited a week to see if Mr. Bowie would report the absence as FMLA leave. Def.'s Facts ¶¶ 49–51. He failed to do so. Def.'s Facts ¶¶ 52–53. Consequently, on August 11, 2016, Mr. Dohman instructed Mr. Hein to inform Mr. Bowie that WestRock was terminating his employment because he violated the terms of the Last Chance Agreement. Def.'s Facts ¶ 54. Mr. Dohman asked Matthew Schoenbeck, the third-shift corrugator supervisor, to sit in on the termination meeting. Def.'s Facts ¶ 55.

Later that day, Mr. Bowie and his union rep met with Mr. Hein and Mr. Schoenbeck. Mr. Hein informed Mr. Bowie that WestRock was terminating his employment because his unexcused absence on August 6 constituted a violation of the Last Chance Agreement. Def.'s Facts ¶¶ 56–57.

Thereafter, Mr. Bowie filed a Charge of Discrimination with the Wisconsin Equal Rights Division, alleging that WestRock discriminated against him on the basis of his race and disability. *See* Exhibit A to Defendant's Brief in Support of Its Partial Motion to Dismiss, ECF No. 16. Specifically, Mr. Bowie alleged that he was discharged in violation of Title VII of the Civil Rights Act of 1964 and Title I of the Americans with Disabilities Act of 1990, as amended. *Id.* The U.S. Equal Employment Opportunity Commission was unable to conclude that the information obtained through its investigation established a violation of Title VII or the ADA. *See* Exhibit 1 to Amended Complaint, ECF No. 5-1. Thus, on May 26, 2017, it dismissed the Charge and issued Mr. Bowie a right-to-sue letter. *Id.*

On August 25, 2017, Mr. Bowie sued WestRock in federal court, alleging that the company discriminated against him on the basis of his age, race, and disability, and retaliated against him for using medical leave. *See* Compl. 2–3; *see also* Am. Compl., ECF No. 5. The matter was randomly assigned to this Court, and all parties consented to magistrate judge jurisdiction. *See* Consent to Proceed Before a Magistrate Judge, ECF Nos. 3, 9 (citing 28 U.S.C. § 636(c) and Fed. R. Civ. P. 73(b)). On December 29, 2017, the Court granted WestRock's motion to dismiss the age-discrimination claim for failure to exhaust administrative remedies. *See* Decision and Order Granting Defendant's Partial Motion to Dismiss, ECF No. 21.

On May 24, 2018, WestRock moved for summary judgment on Mr. Bowie's remaining claims. *See* Defendant's Motion for Summary Judgment, ECF No. 28; Defendant's Memorandum in Support of Its Motion for Summary Judgment, ECF No. 29. After Mr. Bowie failed to respond to the Motion within the time required by Local Rules, the Court issued a show-cause order directing him to explain why the Court should not rule in WestRock's favor. *See* Order to Show Cause, ECF No. 37. On July 30, 2018, Mr. Bowie submitted a letter in response to the Court's show-cause order. *See* Pl.'s Resp. WestRock filed its reply brief in August 15, 2018. *See* Defendant's Reply Brief in Support of Its Motion for Summary Judgment, ECF No. 41. At Mr. Bowie's request, the Court held a status conference with the parties on September 13, 2018. *See* Minute Sheet for Telephonic Pre-Motion Conference, ECF No. 42. Mr. Bowie addressed several arguments WestRock had made in its summary-judgment briefs, and the Court expressed its intent to rule on the Motion in short time.

II. Summary Judgment Standard

"The court shall grant summary judgment if the movant shows that there is no genuine dispute as to any material fact and the movant is entitled to judgment as a matter of law." Fed. R. Civ. P. 56(a). "Material facts" are those that, under the applicable substantive law, "might affect the outcome of the suit." *See Anderson v. Liberty Lobby, Inc.*, 477 U.S. 242, 248 (1986). A dispute over a material fact is "genuine" "if the evidence is such that a reasonable jury could return a verdict for the nonmoving party." *Id.*

A moving party "is 'entitled to a judgment as a matter of law'" when "the nonmoving party has failed to make a sufficient showing on an essential element of [its] case with respect to which [it] has the burden of proof." *Celotex Corp. v. Catrett*, 477 U.S. 317, 323 (1986). Still,

> a party seeking summary judgment always bears the initial responsibility of informing the district court of the basis for its motion, and identifying those portions of the pleadings, depositions, answers to interrogatories, and admissions on file, together with the affidavits, if any, which it believes demonstrate the absence of a genuine issue of material fact.

Id. (internal quotation marks omitted).

To determine whether a genuine issue of material fact exists, the court must review the record, construing all facts in the light most favorable to the nonmoving party and drawing all reasonable inferences in that party's favor. *See Heft v. Moore*, 351 F.3d 278, 282 (7th Cir. 2003) (citing *Liberty Lobby*, 477 U.S. at 255). "However, [the court's] favor toward the nonmoving party does not extend to drawing inferences that are supported by only speculation or conjecture." *Fitzgerald v. Santoro*, 707 F.3d 725, 730 (7th Cir. 2013) (quoting *Harper v. C.R. Eng., Inc.*, 687 F.3d 297, 306 (7th Cir. 2012)). That is, "to survive summary judgment, the non-moving party must establish some genuine issue for trial 'such that a reasonable jury could return a verdict' in [his] favor." *Fitzgerald*, 707 F.3d at 730 (quoting *Makowski v. SmithAmundsen LLC*, 662 F.3d 818, 822 (7th Cir. 2011)).

III. Discussion

WestRock argues that it is entitled to summary judgment on Mr. Bowie's remaining discrimination claims and FMLA retaliation claim.

A. Discrimination claims

In *Ortiz v. Werner Enterprises, Inc.*, 834 F.3d 760 (7th Cir. 2016), the Seventh Circuit shifted away from the traditional direct/indirect methods of analyzing employment-discrimination cases. Subsequent to *Ortiz*, the appropriate inquiry in such cases "is simply whether the evidence would permit a reasonable factfinder to conclude that the plaintiff's race, ethnicity, sex, religion, or other proscribed factor caused the discharge or other adverse employment action." *Ortiz*, 834 F.3d at 765. "Evidence must be considered as a whole, rather than asking whether any particular piece of evidence proves the case by itself—or whether just the 'direct' evidence does so, or the 'indirect' evidence." *Id.*

WestRock maintains that it fired Mr. Bowie for a legitimate, non-discriminatory reason: he violated the terms of the Last Chance Agreement when he failed to show up as scheduled on August 6, 2016. Mr. Bowie disputes whether he was in fact required to work on the evening of the 6th. From the Court's view, the schedule for the week of July 31—which indicated that Mr. Bowie had to work "7PM TO 7AM 8/4-6/16," *see* Nelson Decl., Ex. B—is ambiguous, and Mr. Bowie's reading is a reasonable one. But that interpretation does not help Mr. Bowie here. As long as WestRock honestly believed that Mr. Bowie had violated the terms of the Agreement, Mr. Bowie cannot demonstrate that the stated reason for his firing was a pretext for discrimination. *See Jordan v. Summers*, 205 F.3d 337, 343 (7th Cir. 2000) (noting that an employee in a discrimination action must present evidence to suggest not that the employer was mistaken in firing him but that it was lying to cover up the true reason) (citations omitted). The record here establishes that WestRock honestly believed that Mr. Bowie was scheduled to work on August 6 and that his failure to show up for work that day constituted a violation of the Last Chance Agreement, which required perfect attendance. *See* Def.'s Facts ¶¶ 32–33, 39–57; *see also* Exhibit B to Declaration of Jon Hein, ECF No. 32-2. The fact that this all occurred just prior to the expiration of the Agreement on August 19 appears to be coincidence rather than suspicious timing.

Moreover, Mr. Bowie has not presented any evidence from which a reasonable factfinder could conclude that WestRock fired him because he is African-American or disabled. Mr. Bowie admitted during his deposition that he had no proof of a discriminatory animus; his claims were based simply on his "feeling." *See* Exhibit B to Declaration of Tony H. McGrath, ECF No. 31-2. Unfortunately for Mr. Bowie, his feelings—no matter how sincerely held—are not alone sufficient to defeat summary judgment. Missing here is any evidence of racial animus, such as derogatory comments or disparate impact. Instead, the record simply contains no evidence to suggest that WestRock's decision to fire of Mr. Bowie was motivated by anything other than its belief that he had violated the Last Chance Agreement. Accordingly, WestRock is entitled to summary judgment on Mr. Bowie's discrimination claims.

B. FMLA retaliation claim

It is unlawful for employers to discriminate against an employee who has exercised his FMLA rights. *See* 29 U.S.C. § 2615(a)(2). To make out a claim of retaliation under the FMLA, the employee must show that (1) he engaged in protected activity; (2) he suffered an adverse employment action; and (3) a causal connection exists between the two. *King v. Ford Motor Co.*, 872 F.3d 833, 841 (7th Cir. 2017) (citations omitted). WestRock does not appear to dispute the first two elements. *See* Def.'s Mem. 15–17. Thus, the issue is whether Mr. Bowie has provided sufficient evidence to support a causal connection between his use of intermittent FMLA leave and his termination. In deciding that question, the Court must "consider the evidence as a whole and ask whether a reasonable jury could draw an inference of retaliation." *King*, 872 F.3d at 842 (citing *Ortiz*, 834 F.3d at 764–66).

Mr. Bowie has failed to present sufficient evidence from which a reasonable factfinder could infer that WestRock fired him for taking FMLA leave. WestRock didn't immediately fire Mr. Bowie after he failed to show up for work on August 6. Instead, the company waited a week to see if Mr. Bowie would claim the absence as FMLA leave. Despite successfully exercising his FMLA rights throughout 2016, Mr. Bowie did not submit a claim for the 6th, and so WestRock terminated his employment for violating the Last Chance Agreement. Mr. Bowie has not at any time in this action claimed to have been on FMLA leave on the 6th.

Furthermore, the record shows that WestRock did not consider an FMLA absence to be a violation of the Last Chance Agreement. Mr. Bowie acknowledges that he was out on FMLA leave on four occasions from February to July 2016. *See* Pl.'s Resp. 1. WestRock did not fire Mr. Bowie when he returned to work after those approved absences. And there is no evidence to suggest that WestRock waited until August 6—after Mr. Bowie's non-FMLA related, unexcused absence—to retaliate against him for his previous uses of FMLA leave. Accordingly, WestRock also is entitled to summary judgment on Mr. Bowie's FMLA retaliation claim.

IV. Conclusion

For all the foregoing reasons, the Court finds that no reasonable jury could return a verdict in favor of Mr. Bowie on any of his remaining claims. The Court will therefore grant WestRock's summary judgment motion.

NOW, THEREFORE, IT IS HEREBY ORDERED that Defendant's Motion for Summary Judgment, ECF No. 28, is GRANTED.

IT IS FURTHER ORDERED that this action is DISMISSED.

FINALLY, IT IS ORDERED that the Clerk of Court enter judgment that Mr. Bowie take nothing from the Complaint or Amended Complaint.

Issues for Consideration

- This case involved a number of claims by the plaintiff. Why did they fail?
- On the FMLA retaliation claim, what additional steps could West Rock Company have taken to validate any absences in question making their case even stronger?

Chapter IV

The Emergence of State Paid Family and Medical Leave

With FMLA in place at the federal level and applicable to a wide variety of businesses and industries, eligible employees were granted a bucket of leave that enabled them to care for themselves or immediate family members. This was a major breakthrough for employee advocates and created a new workplace dynamic where employees were given additional support to handle responsibilities outside of the workplace without fear of losing their job. More importantly, the law essentially locked in employee recourse through the courts if adverse employment actions were taken as a result of requesting, pursuing or taking the federally mandated leave.

It is important to remember that outside of federal FMLA, workers in the United States are not guaranteed a single paid day off through federal law. And private employers are not mandated to even provide paid time off.[1]

The glaring gap with leave under the FMLA is that it is unpaid. Although the concept of job protection remains a key aspect of leave under the FMLA, the fact that it has always been unpaid remains contentious. Despite the efforts of advocacy groups and industry trade organizations, efforts at the federal level to create a paid component of FMLA have been unsuccessful. At the same time, there has been a growing desire for a better leave experience in addition to the workplace flexibility created by a leave allowance. More specifically, taking a leave of absence while also getting paid is the type of experience employees were seeking.

California was the first state in the US to enact a Paid Family Leave (PFL) program in 2002. Financed through a payroll tax levied on employees, this revolutionary law was added to California's pre-existing Temporary Disability Insurance (TDI) program which provided partial compensation to individuals that met the criteria for disability. California's new PFL program ushered in a state mandate that allowed new parents to

1. Molly Weston Williamson, "The State of Paid Family and Medical Leave in the U.S. in 2025," The Center for American Progress (January 15, 2025), https://www.americanprogress.org/article/the-state-of-paid-family-and-medical-leave-in-the-u-s-in-2025/#:~:text=Thirteen%20states%20have%20passed%20paid,has%20taken%20a%20similar%20approach.

take up to 6 weeks of paid leave to bond with their child, as well as using the leave to care for a sick child, spouse (including domestic partner) or parent.[2]

Since the inception of California's PFL program, there have been changes, modifications, enhancements and a variety of updates over the years. These changes included things like expanded eligibility, coverage distinctions (beyond parent, child, spouse), wage replacement increases and even how the program is funded. While advantageous for employees who were now able to take leave with some kind of paid component, this also created strict requirements for employers to maintain compliance before, during and after an employee utilizes this leave. As of September 2025, there are over 15 states (including Washington DC) with individual and voluntary paid family leave programs.

In the years that followed California's passing of their PFL law, state legislatures across the country have grappled with the concept of enhancing medical and family leave through ancillary legislative measures that would provide leave with a paid component. Note that prior to California's PFL law, there were a handful of states that did offer state disability insurance covering employees who were unable to work due to their own injury or illness. But the concept of paid leave to care for a loved one was a new development that gained immense popularity over the years.

To better understand state paid family leave and how it differs from other leave types, let's address some fundamental questions about these relatively new state leaves.

What Is State Paid Family and Medical Leave?

State paid family leave is a type of wage replacement, with potential job protection, that an employee can receive to be away from work to care for a family member or to bond with a newborn, newly adopted child or in many cases, foster children. Some states have enacted "paid family and medical leave" laws where they provide benefits and coverage to both the employee and to care for their family member in one single law (referred to as paid family leave and medical leave, or PFML). These laws are essentially insurance schemes where employees can utilize the program if they need it. The funding of these programs will vary by state but is commonly done through either employee contributions, an employer tax or a hybrid model.

These state laws may operate separate and apart, or in conjunction, with the federal FMLA (run concurrently). Some states have chosen to align to federal FMLA standards (but include a pay component) and many states have chosen to go well beyond minimum standards for eligibility and with respect to who is covered. State PFL laws vary by state, and each program has distinguishing features.

What made these PFL laws so unique is that they only covered employees that worked in that specific state (and in some states, they require certain employees like

---

2. United States Department of Labor, "California's Paid Family Leave Law: Lessons from the First Decade Final Report" (June 1, 2014), https://www.dol.gov/resource-library/californias-paid-family-leave-law-lessons-first-decade-final-report.

contractors or sole proprietors to live in the state). So, while it provided a new set of leave protections for employees in that specific state, multistate employers were forced to comply with a variety of leave laws depending on where they had operations. The requirement of work location has also raised questions of remote workers and whether they may be entitled to state PFL if they work out of a specific location in addition to their remote (or virtual) status. This issue was also magnified during the COVID-19 pandemic.

What Are the Distinguishing Features of State Paid Family and Medical Leave Laws?

FMLA laid the groundwork for employee eligibility, qualifying reasons to take the leave, employee rights and prohibited actions by employers (among a long list of sections). With the influx of state paid family laws since 2000, the paid component was the biggest difference with FMLA, but many states went well beyond FMLA standards and expanded qualifying reasons, employee eligibility and even the definition of family member to enable more employees to utilize the leave.

Below is a list of distinguishing aspects of state paid family and medical leave laws (not an exhaustive list as individual states continue to develop new features aimed to provide more flexibility to employees).

Eligibility criteria/standards. States have leveraged several indicators here to determine eligibility. Remember that for federal FMLA, assuming the employer has 50 or more employees within 75 miles, employee eligibility requires 1 year of service and the employee must have worked 1,250 hours in the last year (approximately 25 hours per week, for 50 weeks, taking 2 weeks of vacation into account). Similar to FMLA, some states have implemented employee service for eligibility, but drastically reduced the service period. For example, when New York launched their PFL law, the employee needed to be employed for 26 weeks (6 months) or 175 days of employment for part-time employees.

Another unique way that states determined eligibility was through payroll. California introduced this concept with their PFL law enabling employee eligibility if they were paid $300 in taxable wages during the "base period" (previous 12 months). This aligned with California's already established state disability insurance program. Lastly, some states leveraged their unemployment benefit rate or state "average weekly wage" (AWW) to determine eligibility. In 2021, Massachusetts launched their PFL program where employee eligibility required that the employee must have earned $4,700 in the last calendar year and at least 30 times the weekly unemployment benefit amount.

To recap eligibility for state PFL programs, there is quite a lot of variance. States have not taken a unified approach to these laws and following the launch of their programs, they have updated, changed and modified their requirements. As with any other law, states have adjusted their requirements to align with workforce shifts and employee demands.

Reasons for taking the leave. Federal FMLA set the bar with providing eligible employees the right to take up to 12 workweeks of unpaid leave for: a serious health condition of an employee; care for a family member with a serious health condition; and birth, bonding, and placement of a child for adoption or foster care. FMLA also allowed for qualifying exigencies through military deployment or military caregiver leave. All the state paid family leave laws that have been passed after 2000 mirrored these allowances and some states went further to allow for "safe leave," which covers various needs when an employee of their loved one is a victim of sexual or domestic violence. This would include seeking legal assistance (restraining order) or relocating.[3] Interestingly enough, this is actually the one area where the majority of state paid family leave programs most closely resemble FMLA. Although similar, the passing of these state laws enabled even more employees to have access to paid leave whether they were entitled to federal FML or not. It guaranteed protections for those employees that may not have been eligible for leave under the FMLA. The variance of these laws can be seen mostly in the following sections.

Length of benefit. With FMLA providing up to 12 weeks for covered leave (26 weeks for military exigency), some state PFL programs introduced a new concept for mandated leave where each reason for taking leave has its own leave duration and typically has a maximum, total amount of leave to be taken in 1 year. For example, the state of Washington allows up to 12 weeks for a single qualifying event like parental leave, but also allows up to 16 weeks for a combination of medical and family leave. Washington also allows employees to take up to 18 weeks if they experience both a personal and family caregiving event.[4] Many states went beyond the standard 12 weeks of leave that FMLA put in place likely in recognition that employees may experience multiple qualifying events throughout the year (i.e., parental leave, own medical reasons, caregiving).

Definition of "family member." This is one of the most significant aspects of state PFL programs where states distinguished their programs from federal law. Under the FMLA, a family member is narrowly defined as spouse, child or parent and limiting caregiving coverage to these designations. Many states took an opportunity to greatly expand the definition of family member for purposes of their state law and included domestic partners, siblings, grandparents, grandchildren and parent in-laws. Like the FMLA, most states included the concept of *in loco parentis* where employees are standing in the place of a parent to be eligible for paid leave.

An example of a broad definition of family member can be seen through Colorado's Family and Medical Leave Insurance program. The law defines a family member as a spouse, parent, child, sibling, grandparent, grandchild, domestic partners and "indi-

---

3. Molly Weston Williamson, "The State of Paid Family and Medical Leave in the U.S. in 2025" (January 15, 2025) https://www.americanprogress.org/article/the-state-of-paid-family-and-medical-leave-in-the-u-s-in-2025/#:~:text=Thirteen%20states%20have%20passed%20paid,has%20taken%20a%20similar%20approach.

4. Washington Paid Family & Medical Leave, "How Paid Leave Works," accessed 2025, https://paidleave.wa.gov/how-paid-leave-works/.

viduals in your care" (referencing those who stand in for parents and children).[5] This designation of "individuals in your care" could span well beyond familial relationships and could conceivably include friends, neighbors and other relationships where care is provided. Colorado's definition of family member is a good example of how certain states leveraged the definition of family member to ensure paid family leave for as many employees as possible while keeping less stringent parameters in place.

Benefit rate and compensation levels. This is undoubtedly the most complex aspect of state paid family leave laws and lawmakers had to determine how—and how much—employees would be compensated when they utilized this leave. In theory, it would be relatively easy to mandate full-pay, or a simple salary/hourly rate continuation, for those who took leave, state legislators recognized that not only would these laws be difficult to pass, but it would potentially harm smaller employers needing to manage their workforce. Most states engaged in setting up formulas that factored in an employee's "average weekly wage" (AWW) as well as the state AWW (SAWW) to figure out how an employee would be compensated. And the majority of states utilized a maximum weekly benefit to ensure the sustainability of their program.

For example, when New York launched their paid family leave program in 2018 with the benefit going live in 2019, the benefit rate was 55% of the employee's AWW. By 2021, New York increased the benefit rate to 67% of the employee's AWW with a maximum weekly benefit of $1,177.32, which was equivalent to (0.67x the SAWW). In this example, you can see how New York leveraged an employee's AWW and factored in the SAWW for the maximum benefit rate. In the spirit of providing employees with some form of compensation while on leave, states have tapped into several calculations and formulas in an effort to balance employee needs, program sustainability and employer solvency concerns (i.e., backfilling roles, use of contractors when employees took leave).

While state lawmakers had good intentions with these compensation rates, there have been a few unintended consequences that have arisen. Mostly notably, the use of AWW and SAWW are not easy for the average employee to fully understand what they will be paid while on leave (other than recognizing that they would not be paid at 100%). And lastly, depending on the design of the program, employers, or their insurance carriers, had to stand up the infrastructure for paying employees. For multistate employers, this involved a complex scheme of systems, tracking and even sporadic audits to ensure they were in compliance with state laws.

Funding mechanisms. Unlike FMLA, where the federal government simply mandated unpaid leave, states had to figure out how these programs would be funded and in turn, how the employee would be compensated under the program. With most states following a traditional insurance scheme where premium payments ultimately fund a benefit amount, state lawmakers looked at two primary ways for funding this

5. Colorado Family and Medical Leave Insurance Program (FAMLI): Colorado Department of Labor and Employment, accessed 2025, https://famli.colorado.gov/.

benefit: (1) employee contributions through payroll deductions and (2) a payroll tax on employers dependent on size of employer. It is important to note that not every state leveraged both the employee and employer in funding these benefits. In fact, in many states, like New Jersey, the PFL program is funded entirely by employee payroll deductions. For example, New Jersey's current payroll deduction rate is 0.33% with a cap on income of up to $165,400. This translates into a maximum employee contribution of $545.82.[6] For an employee earning $50,000 in the state of New Jersey, the 0.33% deduction rate translates into a employee contribution of $165 spread out over the course of the year (through payroll deductions).

In some states, the PFL program is funded by both the employee and employer. In these arrangements, the state will dictate a required contribution rate and then determine the split between employee and employer. Oregon's PFL program requires a total contribution rate of 1% of the employee's wages, but with the employee contributing 60% of the required rate and the employer contributing 40%. In Oregon—and other states that have a shared funding model—"employers can also choose to pay the employee contribution, in full, or in part, as a benefit for their employees.[7]"

Claim administration. A major component of all PFL programs is how each claim is managed, adjudicated and ultimately approved or denied. This requires an infrastructure of claims examiners and systems to review, assess and collect the required documentation so that employees can utilize the leave. Traditionally, this has been through the submission of medical documentation or in the case of parental leave or bonding, a birth certificate or legal documentation of an adoption or foster care. Over the years, advances in technology have helped employees leverage electronic submissions through web portals, email and most recently, mobile applications.

It should be noted that the administration of these claims can be a major point of contention and employee frustration. Where claims need to be processed and medical records are required for approval, employees often struggle with obtaining these records which can cause delays in processing. The claims industry has evolved over time, but as new state laws are passed with new and sometimes unique requirements, claims administrators need to pivot and align to new requirements. Lastly, medical providers are not typically compensated for completing PFL or disability-related paperwork, so they are not incentivized to provide opinions or expedite the submission of their opinions. Again, this can cause delays in claim approvals which dictate the pay piece of the leave.

How the benefit is paid. With variance on funding the actual benefit for PFL, there is also variance with how the employee is compensated when they take leave under their respective PFL program. Some states that handle the claims administration of the benefit will also pay the employee through a check or direct deposit.

---

6. This maximum employee contribution is specific to 2025. Employee contributions and taxable wage caps are all subject to state legislative measures.

7. Paid Leave Oregon, "Common questions about Paid Leave," accessed 2025, https://paidleave.oregon.gov/resources/common-questions.html.

In some states, like New York, employers are required to obtain insurance coverage for PFL benefits through a commercial insurance carrier or through New York's disability insurance fund. This is typically done through a rider on an employer's existing disability insurance policy and for employers that are self-insured, New York will assist those employers to ensure they are providing a benefit that is "at least as favorable" to the statutory minimum.[8] This insurance model has become widely accepted as an efficient way to align with employer disability programs to offer some level of consistency when compensating employees for disability or PFL.

Job protection. FMLA guarantees eligible employees unpaid, job-protected leave that prohibits employers from discriminating and retaliating against, as well as interfering with that employee's leave. Some states chose to address—and expand—job protection as part of their program and other states decided that job protection was a function of federal law (FMLA). States that include job protection as part of their state PFL law include: Rhode Island, New York, Washington, Massachusetts and Maryland (not an exhaustive list). Some states added a caveat to the job protection piece and required a minimum amount of service before it kicked in. Colorado includes job protection in their law as long as the employee has at least 180 days of service.

In contrast, state PFL programs that don't have job protection include: Connecticut, New Hampshire, Vermont, California and DC (not an exhaustive list). Note that these states may have other ancillary laws that address job protection if the employee is not eligible for FMLA.

Remember that job protection in the context of leave is not absolute. Job protection under the FMLA guarantees protection from discrimination, retaliation and interference. The FMLA also requires employers to return the employee to the same, or similar job function with similar pay/benefits (unless they are a key employee). State PFL laws essentially followed the same parameters here and this ultimately protected employees from adverse employment decisions based solely on their usage of leave. Simply put, employers are prohibited from firing employees because they took this leave. But this does not protect against a large-scale reorganization or a reduction-in-force by an employer. The circumstances surrounding the job elimination and whether it was part of a larger workforce change is critical in determining whether the employee is rightfully entitled to job protection under state or federal law.

Voluntary PFL programs. For employees, state PFL programs meant even more workplace flexibility to handle responsibilities outside work. Although these programs came with automatic payroll tax deductions, they closely resembled the funding of federal social security benefits. Focusing on social security disability benefits (which we'll cover later in this text), an employee's payroll tax provides them with eligibility to be considered for the benefit if they are rendered disabled by the Social Security Administration.

8. New York State, "Paid Family Leave, Obtaining and Funding a Policy," https://paidfamilyleave.ny.gov/obtaining-and-funding-policy.

On the employer side, a payroll tax to fund a PFL program is not always unanimously accepted. This additional cost to fund a benefit that enables employees to take leave has workforce implications so not every business supported these legislative measures. As a result, a new type of program emerged allowing employers to "opt-in" to a state-sponsored PFL program. These voluntary PFL programs gave employers the choice of offering PFL insurance to their employees and it works like buying insurance on the private market. In states like New Hampshire and Vermont, they play an active role in establishing the private market and actually participate in selecting the insurance carrier that will provide the PFL. With these programs, the contracting, negotiations and program parameters are set by the states and employers are simply electing to opt-in. The primary distinction with voluntary plans is that the employer has the choice of offering this benefit to their employees.

Here is an example of Colorado's paid family and medical leave program:

Colorado Family and Medical Leave Insurance Program (CO FAMLI)[9]

State website: https://famli.colorado.gov/

Background: employer contributions began on January 1, 2023, and the benefit effective date was January 1, 2024.

Coverage: Can be provided through CO or a private plan that is either self-funded or fully-insured. Private plans must offer the same rights, protections and benefits as the state program.

Eligibility

Covered Employers	Employers with 1 or more employees Local governments, independent contractors, sole proprietors, partners and joint ventures can opt in
Covered Family Members	Child, parent, spouse, domestic partner, grandparent, grandchild, sibling, *in loco parentis** and "any other individual with whom the covered individual has a significant personal bond that is or is like a family relationship, regardless of biological or legal relationship"
Employee Eligibility	An eligible employee is one who has: • Earned at least $2,500 in wages within the state in the past four calendar quarters • For self-employed (1099 or contract workers) eligibility, they must live and work in Colorado, as well as opted into coverage

9. Much of this information was obtained from Colorado's Family and Medical Leave Insurance program home page listed and the Paid Statutory Leave Guide, Aflac Life, Absence and Disability Solutions; dated November 2024.

Eligible Leave Reasons	• Employee's own serious health condition • Bonding with a newly born, adopted, or fostered child • Care for a family member with serious health condition • Caring for military servicemember when deployed or on active military service (military exigency) Colorado also provides safe leave for an employee experiencing issues related to domestic violence, harassment, sexual assault or stalking

**In loco parentis* is a Latin phrase meaning "in the place of a parent." For purposes of paid leave eligibility, it refers to an employee being in a parental capacity for someone.

Benefits

Maximum Benefit	$1,324.21 per week in 2025
Wage Replacement Rate	90% of an employee's average weekly wage for the portion of their wages equal to or less than 50% of the state average weekly wage; and 50% of the portion of their wages that exceeds the state average weekly wage
Benefit Duration	12 weeks / Benefits are payable up to an additional four weeks to a covered individual with a serious health condition related to pregnancy complications or childbirth complications
Waiting Period	None
Miscellaneous Information	For public plans, appeals may be filed with Colorado's Family and Medical Leave Insurance division within 45 days of a denial

Colorado is just one example of a paid leave law passed since 2020. Like other paid leave laws, it is much more expansive than federal FML with respect to covered family members, leave eligibility reasons and of course, the pay component. While this law has been in place for a few years, Colorado legislators may review, revise and expand provisions as they see fit.

State PFL programs continue to ride a wave of momentum that started well before the COVID-19 pandemic. As workforce demographics have shifted, employees have prioritized things like paid time off, parental leave programs and workplace flexibility options including the ability to work outside of the traditional office. State lawmakers had to balance the needs of employees with the impact to employers in crafting these laws. What has transpired with the 15+ state PFL laws on the books is a complex patchwork of state laws that have a variety of differences within the law. For multistate employers with operations across the United States, this has created a high degree of complexity to ensure compliance with all of these laws. It also creates variance in terms of the leave that is available for employees. Employees working in one state may be entitled to more leave than employees working in a neighboring state. Simply put, unlike federal FMLA, there is no unified approach to state PFL programs.

COVID-19 Impact on State Paid Family and Medical Leave Programs

The COVID-19 pandemic highlighted and emphasized the importance of paid leave to care for themselves or a loved one. As the virus impacted each person and their family members differently, the need for leave and treatment varied. What was relatively consistent during the early stages of the pandemic was the acknowledgment that having the security of paid leave meant that an employee could step away from the workplace to handle their own care or family needs. At a time when employees were at their most vulnerable, state PFL programs and similar employer-sponsored initiatives were proven to be critical lifelines for employees.

Another consequence of the COVID-19 pandemic was the closure of schools and childcare centers when states implemented shelter-in-place mandates. This created an additional need for employee leave that would fall outside of traditional coverage under the FMLA or state leave. In these scenarios, the child was not experiencing a serious health condition, but due to state mandates, had to be home and ultimately cared for. For employees that did not have the luxury of working from home, this meant needing to find childcare coverage for their child.

In March of 2020, Congress passed the Families First Coronavirus Act (FFCRA), an emergency piece of legislation that established COVID-19 testing provisions, paid sick leave and most notably, expanded family and medical leave. The FFCRA was a significant piece of legislation for purposes of family and medical leave because it essentially expanded FMLA leave to care for a child whose school or place of care was closed due to the COVID-19 pandemic. Although the FFCRA only applied to employers with 500 or less employees, this type of coverage would go on to be influential with some state PFL programs. The concept of covering an employee for something outside of injury, illness or bonding began to take shape with state lawmakers.

The expansion of the FMLA under the FFCRA was a temporary one and expired in 2021, but the need for paid leave under this scenario was yet again highlighted for employees.

Chapter V

Parental Leave and New Employer Sponsored Programs

FMLA introduced unpaid leave to employees to care for their own serious health condition, to care for a loved one and military servicemember or to bond with a new child. Focusing on the bonding piece, FMLA ushered in new, important protections that enabled an employee to utilize leave to start or expand their family without fear of repercussions at their workplace. But the FMLA did not address the pay gap. In the years that followed the passage of the FMLA in 1993, leave advocates and employees began to vocalize the need for pay continuation while on any kind of leave. Unfortunately, those efforts were not successful at the federal level. And that remains to be the case today.

Remember that by the time FMLA was passed in the mid-90s, short and long-term disability programs were fairly common, so many employees had the opportunity for wage replacement if they met the disability criteria established by their employer-sponsored policies. Additionally, most short-term disability policies recognized pregnancy as a qualifying reason for disability, but non-birthing mothers were generally overlooked for any type of wage replacement related to the pregnancy or becoming a new parent.

The Evolution of Paid Parental Leave Programs

Traditional maternity leave. Historically speaking, it was quite common for employer-sponsored maternity leave to fall within a short-term disability program with added protections under the FMLA. For this to even take place, the employer needed to provide short-term disability as a benefit and be a covered employer under the FMLA. Under this arrangement, birthing mothers would be eligible to receive wage replacement under their short-term disability program depending on the type of delivery they had (i.e., vaginal birth or cesarian section) and if eligible, FMLA would run concurrently with the short-term disability leave for the 12 weeks of bonding time. Depending on the pregnancy, recovery time and whether there were complications, the birthing mother could leverage their short-term disability benefits under the employer's typical process of providing medical documentation to substantiate the leave.

As an example of many employer-sponsored short-term disability policies, birthing mothers were typically approved for 6 weeks of disability benefits for a vaginal birth and 8 weeks for a cesarian section. This was more of an industry standard, rather than a traditional offering by employers. Birthing mothers also had the option of leveraging short-term disability benefits prior to delivery if they experienced complications that rendered them unable to work. Lastly, if after their approved period of disability benefits based on the type of delivery they had, they could similarly apply for an extension of their short-term disability benefits if they had complications later on.

These types of programs focused squarely on the birthing mother and other than unpaid FMLA bonding time being available to all covered employees, non-birthing mothers were not provided with paid leave options under a traditional short-term disability program. It should also be noted that employers were not required to offer short-term disability programs so for many employees, the prospect of wage replacement when taking leave to deliver a child was not available to everyone.

Employer-sponsored programs. Beginning in the early 2000s, many employers began to embrace the concept of an all-encompassing "parental benefit" that included all parents, rather than focus on the birthing mother. This meant that non-birthing mothers and dads would be eligible to receive wage replacement and covered leave as part of an employer-sponsored parental leave benefit. This shift away from the concept of "maternity leave" was an enormous change that enabled employers to provide a generous paid leave package to all employees, not just birthing mothers. These employer-sponsored programs typically involved salary/pay continuation and covered leave for a specified period of time. They varied in shape and size and typically had unique components to them at the discretion of the employer. Over the years, private employers have launched a multitude of paid parental leave programs that have now become a staple in most benefit portfolios.

Corporate stigmas. One of the biggest challenges to rolling out a new, expansive paid parental leave program is overcoming the stigma when taking leave. Many employees have real concerns about leaving their job, their team and open projects. Although temporary—and with intentions to return to their job—corporate stigmas have discouraged employees from utilizing a program like parental leave even though it's offered to them. A workplace culture that prioritizes constant productivity and disregards the idea of a work-life balance may not be so keen to offer a generous parental leave program. And even with employers that do choose to offer one, employees may feel guilty taking the leave if they are concerned that it will negatively impact their career growth.

That said, the advent of paid parental leave programs ushered in a wave of change within employers to embrace the idea of taking leave to start, or expand, one's family. Rolling out a program of this magnitude has the ability to shift a corporate culture and in many ways, legitimize the employee desire to prioritize things outside of the workplace. This does not happen overnight and can take several years for a company's culture to accept a lengthy leave or to embrace an employee's familial aspirations. A formal program can be the lynchpin of cultural change with respect to a parental benefit, but there are many other factors that can impact the overall environment and whether an employee decides to utilize the leave.

Parental leave as a corporate recruitment tool. An employer's benefits portfolio has gained a tremendous amount of popularity in the last two decades. With baby-boomers exiting the labor force and new generations making up the majority of it, employees have looked beyond compensation and traditional perks like healthcare and dental and vision benefits. Things such as vacation time, paid-time-off, mental health support and paid parental leave have not only become popular among employees, but have also become key components of an employer's talent acquisition and retention strategy.

A paid parental leave program incorporates both a compensation component and a time off piece making it a highly attractive benefit for prospective employees.

The integration of parental leave with other leave and benefit programs. Employer-sponsored paid parental leave programs are unique in that they offer both wage replacement as well as a covered leave from the workplace. This creates opportunities for employers to weave in—and promote—existing benefit programs across physical, emotional and financial wellbeing.

Focusing on the leave aspect, birthing mothers may experience complications with their pregnancy so short-term disability might be an option if they are unable to work in the weeks/months before delivery. If the employer-sponsored parental leave program is a completely separate salary-continuation scheme, it is important to remember that for short-term disability benefits, an employee may have to provide medical documentation to substantiate their need for leave prior to utilizing parental leave. Once the child is delivered, employers typically allow the employee to transition into their parental leave. Once this transition takes place, the employee no longer needs to provide medical documentation to support their disability claim.

Illustrating the above example where a birthing mother experiences complications before her delivery, she could utilize short-term disability benefits as well as FMLA, before transitioning to her parental leave upon delivery.

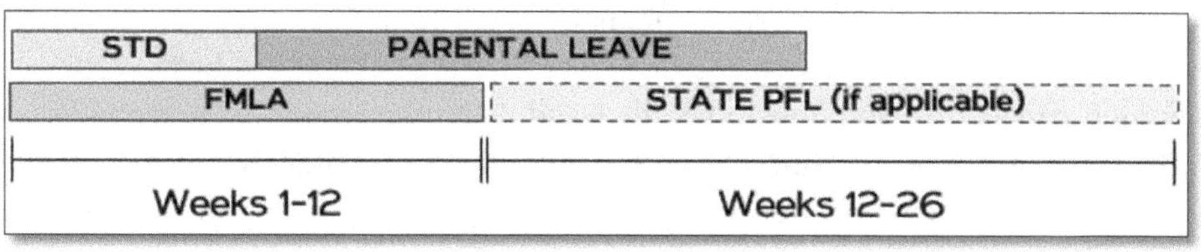

The above example shows a short-term disability claim running for 6 weeks before transitioning over to parental leave. If the employee is eligible and has not used any FMLA prior to this claim, the FMLA claim would run parallel to the STD claim and 6 weeks of the parental leave claim before it exhausts. If there is any applicable state leave protection, that would also run parallel. This example highlights the complexity of a single leave event with multiple entitlements.

Other benefit programs that can be weaved into a parental leave offering include maternity management (where employees are incentivized to engage with their health plan before, during and after a pregnancy); retirement programs (i.e., 401K) and college savings plans; and a variety of voluntary benefits including life insurance, supplemental disability insurance, hospital indemnity and accident insurance (not an exhaustive list).

Components of a Paid Parental Leave Program

Parental leave has become a highly desirable benefit over the years and one that employees have prioritized when choosing an employer. Employers have a lot of discretion in crafting their programs and have used ancillary benefits like cash and rich fertility programs to bolster their packages for employees. Acknowledging that "leave" is a major focus of a paid parental program, employers must recognize that FMLA and the variety of new state paid family leave laws will inevitably overlap with these programs. In many cases, this overlap is advantageous to an employee because it will likely provide them with either more leave or job protection overall.

Below are some core components of a paid parental leave program as well as some of the more unique offerings that employers have launched:

Eligibility. As more employers began to embrace this concept of "parental leave" rather than just provide short-term disability benefits for maternity leave, the notion that this benefit would be available to all parents—regardless of gender—was a large shift. Notably, this meant that non-birthing mothers would be eligible for a period of paid leave. Dads for example, who were previously only entitled to federal FMLA (if they were eligible) and maybe state paid family leave, could now utilize a parental leave benefit directly through their employer. Ultimately, this more inclusive offering meant that more employees would be taking a leave of absence through their employer-sponsored parental leave programs.

This did trigger several employer considerations like whether to offer this benefit to employees on day 1 of their employment or require a probationary period, whether to require any kind of documentation to receive the benefit (i.e., birth certificate, adoption paperwork) and how to handle fraud. With the advent of "parental leave," many employers took a holistic approach in offering this program to all employees. It also enabled them to publicize the launch of their programs in efforts to recruit and retain talent.

Length of paid leave. This is typically the most important piece of a parental leave program and dictates how much time off an employee will be entitled to receive. In crafting a program, employers must balance the needs of an employee bringing a child into their home with impacts to staffing and workforce management. Employers have a lot of discretion here if their program will entail a salary continuation scheme where the employee will just continue to get paid their salary, or hourly rate, even on leave.

Generally speaking, over the last decade, employers have launched programs ranging from paid leave up to 2 weeks all the way up to 52 weeks of paid parental leave.[1] There are no parameters or even mandates on the amount of leave employers can offer at the private level. There are, however, mandates at the federal level with FMLA, as well as state paid family leave laws that cover parental leave and typically run in parallel, or in conjunction with, to these offerings. It is best practice for an employer to recognize both the FMLA and any relevant state laws in crafting their program so they can make it easier for an employer to navigate an often complex web of leave and pay entitlement. See the below example for how an employer can offer a parental leave program in conjunction with federal and state law:

> *Example*—ABC store, a large hardware store in New York with over 5,000 employees, launches a Paid Parental Leave Program to all of its employees providing up to 10 weeks of paid parental leave. ABC is a covered employee for purposes of the FMLA. Employees who utilize this program will receive 10 weeks of paid leave and if eligible for federal FMLA leave, will be able to take advantage of an additional 2 weeks of unpaid leave. In this example, the first 10 weeks will include pay from the employer and unpaid job protection through the FMLA. The employee can also take advantage of the remaining unpaid leave under the FMLA or use it at a later date.
>
> *Note that this is just an example of how a private program interacts with the FMLA. This example also highlights how an employee may be available for paid leave benefits through the state of New York.

Compensation. The pay piece for the majority of modern parental leave programs is simple. Using what's known as a "payroll practice," employers will provide 100% pay for the duration of the parental leave. Alternatively, while it's quite rare, but certainly not out of the question, employers may choose to offer a parental leave program that provides for partial pay. Again, since most of these programs are private, employers have discretion to design something that provides partial pay, but it's quite rare. Partial pay structures are somewhat common with parental leave benefits found in state paid family leave laws. Lastly, like other employer-sponsored benefit programs, employers need to be mindful that their program design does discriminate in any way.

One unique way that some employers have chosen to design their parental leave programs is to leverage a current short-term disability program for birthing mothers, then provide a window of 100% paid leave for all employees. For instance, this window could be 2 weeks of paid parental leave to all employees. With this design, a birthing mother would receive either 6 or 8 weeks depending on the birth of the child (vaginal,

1. This range of time for the length of paid leave is just an example. Employers have the discretion to go beyond 52 weeks if they desire.

c-section), then could utilize the paid parental leave, giving them either 8 or 10 weeks of paid leave. Here is an example of how this would work:

> XYZ Company offers up to 2 weeks of paid parental leave. Under their program, birthing mothers can apply for short-term disability before their delivery date. XYZ Company allows birthing mothers to being their short-term disability 1 week prior to their delivery (which is very common).
>
> Mary, an employee of XYZ Company, is scheduled to deliver her child via c-section and applies for short-term disability well in advance of her delivery. She begins her leave for short-term disability and receives 8 weeks of disability benefits (per her policy) before transitioning to paid parental leave for 2 weeks. Under this example, Mary will receive 10 weeks of paid leave between short-term disability and XYZ Company's paid parental leave program.

There is nothing discriminatory about this practice, but it technically provides more paid leave to a birthing mother than other parents. It is undisputed that birthing mothers require recovery time following the delivery of a child and leveraging short-term disability for this is completely within the confines of all disability policies. That said, if a short-term disability policy only offers a percentage of one's pay, birthing mothers could be looking at partial pay for 6–8 weeks before moving to full pay under a parental leave program.[2] This type of program is often leveraged to save costs associated with 100% pay while a person is on leave. While this may be advantageous from a cost perspective, it's not indicative of a best-in-class program that truly provides the employee with flexibility to start or expand their family without concern about leaving their workplace for extended periods of time.

Caregiver status designations. One of the more modern features of a paid parental leave program is an employer's requirement for employees to designate themselves as either a primary or non-primary caregiver. This delineation is significant because it dictates how much paid leave an employee is entitled to. For example, an employer could provide up to 10 weeks of paid parental leave for "primary caregivers" and up to 2 weeks for "non-primary caregivers." From a legal standpoint, employers need to be extra careful that if they choose to deploy a program like this, they do not make assumptions as to caregiver status. To avoid a sex, or gender, based discrimination claim, the caregiver designation decision must come from the employee. Therefore, if an employer pre-designates male employees as "non-primary caregivers," thereby only making them eligible for the lesser amount of paid leave, this could be perceived as discriminatory since it favors non-male employees.

Any guardrails or additional requirements for fathers, or non-birthing mothers, will likely be perceived as discriminatory. Again, there is nothing illegal about deploying a program that requires an employee to designate their caregiver status, but it is an

2. Companies that have sophisticated payroll infrastructures can allow employees to use any available paid time off or vacation time to "top off" any partial pay from a short-term disability benefit.

absolute best practice to define each type of caregiver under the program and allow employees to choose and designate their status (often through an affidavit).

This is purely an option for employers and is often utilized as a cost-containment measure. By offering two options, there is at least a probability that some employees will elect the non-primary caregiver leave creating less exposure for the employer. That said, assuming an employer provides this choice to employees, they could all conceivably select the primary caregiver status.

Job protection. While employers can voluntarily decide to include job protection as part of their private program, federal and state leave mandates will also apply in conjunction with any employer-sponsored program. This means that if an employee is covered by the FMLA and/or any state paid family leave laws that include parental leave, they will be able to take advantage of the protected job status contained in those laws. But it is important to remember that job protection is not absolute. FMLA protects an employee from discrimination, retaliation and interference with respect to their leave. This means that employers cannot fire an employee or take an adverse employment action against an employee because their look leave.[3] State paid leave laws have similar protections.

Alternatively, job protection through the FMLA or state law generally does not protect employees from company reorganizations or large-scale reductions-in-force. Employers need to show that the job elimination, or firing, was not the result of, or in response to, the employee taking leave under the FMLA, state law or private parental leave program.

Other benefits related to parental leave programs. Some employers have gotten creative with their paid parental leave programs in efforts to bolster their program's value proposition and further amplify their commitment to family planning and workplace flexibility. A few examples include:

- **Fertility and women's health benefit**—in general, these programs can be very costly and fertility treatments alone can be financially steep. A number of versatile solutions have entered the market enabling employers to remove a large financial barrier for all of their employees. Some of the specific benefits include in-vitro fertilization, egg freezing, male fertility treatment and menopause support. Note that while these benefits are very specific, there could be implications to leave if an employee requires in-patient treatment or needs recovery time.
- **Cash for parental related expenses**—some employers have taken a more personalized approach to bolster their parental leave programs and include cash, or reimbursement, for parental-related expenses. Since these expenses are rather vague, it is critical that employers spell out eligible expenses.

3. Adverse employment actions could include a variety of things, but common ones include: a demotion, not providing growth opportunities for an employee or isolating them in meetings. These are just a few examples.

- **Transition-back-to-work programs**—Recognizing that returning to work following the birth, or placement, of a child into the home, can be difficult for a variety of reasons, some employers have embraced this with offering the option of easing, or transitioning, back into the workforce with a reduced schedule. This could also include the option of working from home or even an additional set of unpaid leave following the paid parental leave portion. With more employers making the decision to bring their employees back into the physical office, the prospect of allowing an employee to work-from-home in a transition period has become much more difficult.
- **Adoption and surrogacy assistance**. Employers have also recognized that starting or expanding a family can happen in different ways. Adoption and/or surrogacy can be costly so employers have addressed this by providing reimbursements for expenses tied to each process. This could include legal expenses, medical expenses, transportation, lodging, etc. These specific benefits can be incredibly significant for employees seeking either adoption or surrogacy.

Employers and states continue to modify, tweak and add to their parental leave programs in efforts to enhance the employee experience when starting or expanding their family. I anticipate this trend to continue as more employers embrace workplace flexibility.

Chapter VI

Workplace Accommodations under the Americans with Disabilities Act (ADA)

The Americans with Disabilities Act (ADA) became law in 1990 and served as a landmark law that guaranteed equal opportunity for individuals with disabilities in public areas, employment and transportation.

Eighteen years later in 2008, the ADA was amended to broaden employee protections under the law. Under these amendments, lawmakers focused on the definition of disability and made it easier for individuals seeking protection under the ADA to establish that they had a disability. The Equal Employment Opportunity Commission (EEOC) is the federal governmental agency tasked with enforcing title I of the ADA. The EEOC will investigate employment discrimination charges and will attempt to resolve charges with employers. They also produce legal guidance related to common situations involving all aspects of the ADA. Not that this guidance is not law, but rather a formal position on handling specific scenarios. In certain instances when they believe a violation has occurred, the EEOC will file lawsuits to have a court of law address the legal issue.

Title I of the ADA, which covers workplace accommodations, protects qualified individuals with disabilities from employment discrimination.[1] Under the ADA, discrimination must be construed broadly and prohibits employers from retaliation and interference. Employees are ultimately protected from discrimination or retaliation for asserting their rights under the ADA.[2] According to the EEOC, "speaking out about or exercising rights related to workplace discrimination is called 'protected activity' and can take many forms, including complaining to a supervisor about harassment.[3]

The ADA is quite a large body of law covering five areas of public life. These areas include: Employment (Title 1), State and Local Government Services (Title 2), Public

1. United States Equal Employment Opportunity Commission, "The ADA: Your Responsibilities as an Employer," accessed 2025, https://www.eeoc.gov/publications/ada-your-responsibilities-employer.

2. United States Equal Employment Opportunity Commission, "Disability Discrimination and Employment Decisions," accessed 2025, https://www.eeoc.gov/disability-discrimination-and-employment-decisions.

3. *Id.*

Accommodations and Commercial Facilities (Title 3), Telecommunications (Title 4) and miscellaneous provisions (Title 5). Our focus for this section will be workplace accommodations for employees under title 1 of the ADA.

Over the last 35 years, the courts have tackled a variety of issues under the ADA, but the law itself has remained intact. The amendments in 2008 unquestionably expanded employee protections under the law and in doing so, lawmakers created a sense of ambiguity when interpreting these provisions. Whether deliberate or not, the law is structured in ways that open the door to interpretation around things like disability discrimination, whether an employer satisfied their obligations under the ADA, whether an employee is a "qualified individual" under the law or whether an employee's ask for an accommodation is reasonable (not an exhaustive list). As a result, workplace accommodations under the ADA have become incredibly difficult for employers to maintain compliance in the wake of new case law, evolving workforce demographics, unique employee requests and the ability to perform core job responsibilities from anywhere due to rapidly changing advancements with technology.

Lastly, the COVID-19 pandemic had a significant impact on how workplace accommodations are evaluated. With large chunks of the workforce operating from home for approximately 1–2 years, the question of whether some jobs could be performed outside of a traditional office became a trending topic that still exists today. Telecommuting, or working from home, has emerged as the most popularizing accommodation request that employers continue to grapple with.

Workplace Accommodations and the ADA— Key Components of the Act

The ADA of 1990, including amendments made in 2008, can be found in title 42 of United States Code. Subchapter 1, Employment, contains key provisions outlining reasonable accommodations, covered individuals, the definition of disability, undue hardships and what constitutes discrimination[4] (not an exhaustive list).

Here is a list of the key components of the act:

- Employers with 15 or more workers are "covered entities"
- Employers cannot discriminate against a "qualified individual" on the basis of disability
- A "qualified individual" is one who meets the requirements of a position and who can perform the essential functions of the position with or without a reasonable accommodation

---

4. US Department of Justice: American Disabilities Act, "Americans with Disabilities Act of 1990, As Amended," accessed 2025, https://www.ada.gov/law-and-regs/ada/#subchapter-i---employment-title-i.

- Applies to employees and to applicants[5]
- Employers must provide a reasonable accommodation to a disabled worker
- A covered disability is defined as a "physical or mental impairment that substantially limits a major life activity[6]

The ADA, under title 42, Section 12102[7] (The Public Health and Welfare), defines disability, with respect to an individual as:

(1) A physical or mental impairment that substantially limits one or more major life activities or such individual.

Under this section, "major life activities include, but are not limited to, caring for oneself, performing manual tasks, seeing, hearing, eating, sleeping, walking, standing, lifting, bending, speaking, breathing, learning, reading, concentrating, thinking, communicating and working."[8] The Act goes on to say that a major life activity also includes the operation of major bodily functions like immune system, digestive or neurological systems. It is clear that lawmakers intended to broaden coverage with a far-reaching definition of disability and a low threshold for meeting the criteria of major life activities.

Per the ADA.gov website, "the term 'substantially limits' is interpreted broadly and is not meant to be a demanding standard." Although vague, this standard will vary depending on the condition and individual. It is difficult to generalize this standard or even classify a condition's severity as substantially limiting without additional facts around the impact to the individual. The following is needed:

(2) A record of such an impairment; or

(3) Being regarded as having such an impairment.

An individual meets this requirement if they "establish that they have been subjected to an action prohibited under this chapter because of an actual or perceived physical or mental impairment whether or not the impairment limits or is perceived to limit a major life activity."[9]

The ADA's definition of disability is quite different than other standards for programs like short and long-term disability, FMLA and state paid family and medical leave. As a quick recap, here is a snapshot of how the ADA's definition of disability differs from other standards (generally speaking):

---

5. The ADA makes it unlawful to discriminate in employment practices such as: recruitment, pay, hiring, firing, promotion, job assignments, training, leave, layoff, benefits (EEOC Guidance, "The ADA: Your Responsibilities as an Employer").

6. US Department of Justice: American Disabilities Act, "Americans with Disabilities Act of 1990, As Amended," accessed 2025, https://www.ada.gov/law-and-regs/ada/#subchapter-i---employment-title-i.

7. US Department of Justice: American Disabilities Act, "Americans with Disabilities Act of 1990, As Amended," accessed 2025, https://www.ada.gov/law-and-regs/ada/#subchapter-i---employment-title-i#section5.

8. *Id.*

9. *Id.*

Leave Type	Disability Standard
ADA (Workplace accommodations)	***Physical or mental impairment that substantially limits a major life activity***
Short / Long-term disability	Unable to perform own and/or any job; Totally incapacitated
FMLA	Serious health condition
State Paid FMLA	Serious health condition
Social Security Disability	Unable to perform own job and unable to perform any other job (in most cases)

The ADA is unique in that even if a person meets the criteria for having a disability, they must be a "qualified" individual, which means that in the context of workplace accommodations, they must be able to perform the essential functions of the job with or without an accommodation. This concept is very important because if an employee receives an accommodation that doesn't enable them to perform the essential functions of their job, they are not a qualified individual for purposes of the Act.

As we delve further into reasonable accommodations, we'll look at the significance of essential job functions, the interactive process, the importance of medical documentation, employer and employee obligations and the significance of undue hardships.

What Is a Reasonable Accommodation under the ADA?

The ADA expressly states that "a reasonable accommodation" may include:

(a) Making existing facilities used by employees readily accessible to and usable by individuals with disabilities; and

(b) Job restructuring, part-time or modified work schedules, reassignment to a vacant position, acquisition or modification of equipment or devices, appropriate adjustment or modifications of examinations, training materials or policies, the provision of qualified readers or interpreters, and other similar accommodations for individuals with disabilities."[10]

To summarize, reasonable accommodations are modifications or adjustments made to a job or work environment that enable employees with disabilities to perform the essential functions of the job. The ADA defines an accommodation as reasonable when it does not place an undue financial, administrative or operational burden on an employer. The specific facts and circumstances with each accommodation request will dictate whether the accommodation, or accommodation ask, was reasonable.

10. US Department of Justice: American Disabilities Act, "Americans with Disabilities Act of 1990, As Amended," accessed 2025, https://www.ada.gov/law-and-regs/ada/#inPageResult3.

The Act also defines an undue hardship as "an action requiring significant difficulty or expense, when considered in light of the [following factors]:

(i) The nature and cost of the accommodation under this chapter;

(ii) The overall financial resources of the facility or facilities involved in the provision of the reasonable accommodation; the number of persons employed at such facility; the effect on expenses and resources, or the impact otherwise of such accommodation upon the operation of facility;

(iii) The overall financial resources of the covered entity; the overall size of the business of a covered entity with respect to the number of its employees; the number, type, and location of its facilities; and

(iv) The type of operation or operations of the covered entity, including the composition, structure and functions of the workforce of such entity; the geographic separateness, administrative, or fiscal relationship of the facility or facilities in question to the covered entity."[11]

Undue hardships effectively operate as a defense to providing a reasonable accommodation. While the ADA is fairly clear that an accommodation is deemed unreasonable if it poses an undue hardship on an employer, the analysis of—and the relationship between—a reasonable accommodation and an undue hardship, is rather complex. Cost is objective and relatively easy to assess when determining whether it poses a hardship for an employer. But the operational impact to an employer can be unclear and even ambiguous as to whether it amounts to an undue hardship. When analyzing an undue hardship, one must take all factors into account to fully determine whether the reasonable accommodation at issue could have been made (or should have been made). And ultimately, this determination of whether something amounts to an undue hardship is decided by the courts if an employee brings a lawsuit.

For companies with significant revenue streams, the undue hardship argument becomes more difficult on cost alone. When the costs are straightforward—like the request for a piece of furniture—the analysis will hinge on whether the specific cost will cause a significant impact to the employer. For other accommodation requests that don't have an objective price tag, an employer must produce justification for why the specific accommodation request is an undue hardship to their business operations.

To better understand undue hardships, here are a few hypotheticals to consider:

> **Example 1:** Bob is an IT support specialist for a small company that generates $200,000 per year in revenue. He performs his job sitting at a desk for most of the day. Despite having a sit-stand workstation which gives Bob the ability to switch between sitting and standing during the day, Bob develops severe lower back pain that begins to interfere with his ability to do his job. Bob proceeds with an accommodation request for a special chair that his doctor recommends. The chair Bob is requesting costs $125,000.

---

11. *Id.*

Even though Bob's company may be able to acquire this chair, would this be considered an undue hardship? Discuss both sides.

Example 2: Sara is a marketing director for ABC Corporation, a global producer of mobile telephones. Sara's job consists of meetings and video calls throughout the day with customers across the globe. Sara's struggle with depression and anxiety begins to interfere with her work inside of the office. Sara proceeds with an accommodation request to work from home 2 days per week so that she can attempt to treat her condition. ABC Corporation is concerned if Sara is not performing her job onsite, the marketing efforts will suffer as a result.

Does ABC Corporation have an undue hardship argument? Discuss both sides.

The above hypotheticals represent two distinctly different analyses tied to whether an accommodation request may amount to an undue hardship. The first one illustrates a pure cost analysis with hard dollars associated with a request. The direct correlation between the cost of the chair and his company's revenue is enough to determine that it would be unreasonable to spend half of the company's revenue on a single piece of furniture as an accommodation. Alternatively, in the second hypothetical, the request to work from home raises questions about productivity and whether that employee can still perform the essential functions of the job at home. Specific costs are less clear and whether this would be an undue hardship would depend on several factors associated with overall impact to operations, ABC's resources, the significance of Sara's role and much more.

It is important to emphasize that employers have every opportunity to offer alternative solutions in the accommodations process and that is part of the discussions between the employer and the employee. This engagement is more commonly known as the interactive process.

Employee Accommodation Requests and Interactive Process

Requests for a workplace accommodation can take shape a few ways. The most common way is for an employee to expressly ask their employer for an accommodation or support with their job. Note that employees do not have to use specific language or even use the word "accommodation" in their request. Employees traditionally raise these requests with their manager or human resource contact and this will trigger an employer's obligation to engage in the interactive process. The ADA does not contain specific requirements for how employees should request an accommodation but employees have traditionally done this verbally or in writing. If an employer has chosen an external vendor to administer their workplace accommodation requests, employees will be directed to the external vendor.

In addition to employee requests, accommodation consideration by employers may be required if the employer "knows" or "has reason to know" that a disability exists and is impacting the employee's ability to perform their job. For this reason, managers, leaders and human resources must be always on the lookout for the potential of discussing a possible accommodation request with an employee. Here are a few examples of where it would be prudent for an employer to broach the possibility of an accommodation request with an employer:

> **Example 1:** In a meeting with his manager, Tim divulges that he's been having difficulties interpreting emails, concentrating on work tasks and figuring out what next steps are after team meetings. Time doesn't expressly ask for any kind of support or even use the word accommodation in his discussion with his manager.
>
> *Employer obligation*—The ADA is clear in that "an employer's obligation to provide a reasonable accommodation applies to known physical or mental limitations."[12] In this example, Tim has shed light on some challenges at work and made his manager aware of the possible need for an accommodation. Tim's manager should inquire about what kind of support could help him with his workplace challenges. The interactive process will flesh out whether Tim needs an accommodation and what kind of support is available. Even if this discussion does not result in an accommodation, this proactive identification of a possible accommodation will satisfy the ADA's requirements of properly vetting the need.
>
> **Example 2:** Mary is a line cook at a restaurant where she is standing and walking around the kitchen during her shifts. Mary's supervisor notices her leaning frequently and appears to be struggling while walking around the kitchen. Mary has not mentioned the need for any kind of accommodation.
>
> *Employer obligation*—although Mary has not brought up the need for any kind of support or a specific accommodation, her struggles while working could be enough for her employer to "know" or "have reason" to know that she has a disability where an accommodation could be appropriate. It would be prudent for Mary's supervisor, or the restaurant's human resources person, to engage Mary and discuss whether an accommodation (i.e., breaks, stool) could help Mary perform her job.

Often times, identifying the need for an accommodation will not be readily apparent. Outside of the employee expressly asking for one, employers need to be on the lookout for potential accommodation needs. While this may sound obvious, it is the employer's efforts to identify an accommodation, or lack thereof, that will dictate employer liability in failure to accommodate or a disability discrimination claim. It has long been a best practice for employers to take the necessary steps to ensure their leaders, supervisors and human resource departments are trained to identify possible

---

12. United States Equal Employment Opportunity Commission, "The ADA: Your responsibilities as an Employer," accessed 2025, https://www.eeoc.gov/publications/ada-your-responsibilities-employer.

accommodation needs and to engage the employee in a discussion about support. Even if the end result is not an accommodation, the employer has satisfied their obligation of vetting whether a possible accommodation would help the employee perform their job.

Essential Functions of the Job

Another critical component of determining whether a reasonable accommodation is appropriate—or even feasible—is the analysis of the employee's essential job functions. To be clear, a qualified individual under the ADA must be able to perform the essential functions of their job, with or without an accommodation. Essential functions are the core, fundamental job duties for the specific position. Essential functions must be distinguished from marginal responsibilities, but this will hinge on several factors including, but not limited to, the job description and how the employee actually performed the job on a daily basis. Employer job descriptions provide a solid foundation of essential functions but employees are often performing the job differently than what is described in their job description.

In addition to a job description, there are several other factors that the courts have used to determine whether a job function is essential. These factors are used in conjunction with a job description to ascertain whether the function is core to the job or marginal. If it is deemed to be essential, a failure to accommodate a claim may be successful if the employee can successfully show that (1) their accommodation request was reasonable and (2) they would've been able to perform the "essential functions" of their job with the requested accommodation.

To flesh this concept of essential functions out a bit more, the United States Courts for the Ninth Circuit developed a set of guidelines[13] for analyzing essential functions for civil claims under the ADA. Below are their instructions for the consideration of essential functions and some factors to help determine whether a function is essential (along with a few cases as examples):

12.8 ADA—Ability to Perform Essential Functions—Factors

> An essential function of an employment position means the fundamental job duties of the employment position that the plaintiff holds or desires. It does not include the marginal functions that may occur through the course of a job.
>
> You must consider the employer's judgment as to what functions of a job are essential. If any employer has prepared a written description before advertising or interviewing applicants for the job, this description is evidence of the essential functions of the job.
>
> Other factors that may bear upon whether a job function is essential include, but are not limited to:

13. United States Courts For the Ninth Circuit, "Manual of Model Civil Jury Instructions, Section 12.8 ADA, Ability to Perform Essential Functions—Factors," Revised March 2024; https://www.ce9.uscourts.gov/jury-instructions/node/216.

(1) Whether the reason the position exists is to perform that function;

(2) Whether there are a limited number of employees available among whom the performance of that job function can be distributed;

(3) Whether the job function is highly specialized, and the person in that particular position is hired for their expertise or ability to perform the particular function;

(4) The amount of time spent performing the job function;

(5) The consequences of not requiring the individual holding the position to perform the function;

(6) The terms of any collective bargaining agreement;

(7) The work experience of past employees who have held the position; and

(8) The work experience of current employees who hold similar positions.[14]

Within these instructions, the Ninth Circuit included the following cases to illustrate the essential functions analysis:

> In *Kaplan v. City of North Las Vegas*, 323 F.3d 1226, 1232–33 (9th Cir. 2003), the court held that an employer had no duty to accommodate a deputy marshal when it was undisputed that he could not perform the essential function of restraining prisoners through hand-to-hand combat, even though the cause of hand pain had been misdiagnosed.[15]
>
> In *Cripe v. City of San Jose*, 261 F.3d 877, 877 (9th Cir. 2001), the court observed that an employer may not turn every condition of employment which it elects to adopt into a job function, let alone as essential job function, merely by including it in a job description (quoting *Echazabal v. Chevron USA, Inc.*, 226 F.3d 1063, 1071 (9th Cir. 2000)). In *Cripe*, the 9th Circuit held that the issue of whether the ability of all specialized police officers to make a forcible arrest constituted as essential function of the job presented a factual question under the circumstances of that case.[16]

Generally speaking, employers are not required to eliminate or remove an essential function, or fundamental duty, of the job. Per EEOC guidance, "this is because a person with a disability who is unable to perform the essential functions, with or without [a] reasonable accommodation, is not a 'qualified' individual with a disability within the meaning of the ADA."[17] The EEOC goes on to add that employers are not required to lower production, or productivity, standards either. While they may agree to do so, there is no requirement for employers to do this. To reiterate, reasonable accommoda-

14. *Id.*

15. *Id.*

16. *Id.*

17. United States Equal Employment Opportunity Commission, "Enforcement Guidance on Reasonable Accommodation and Undue Hardship under the ADA," dated October 17, 2002, https://www.eeoc.gov/laws/guidance/enforcement-guidance-reasonable-accommodation-and-undue-hardship-under-ada.

tions should be considered that enable employees to perform the essential functions of the job and/or meet productivity standards. If you strip the core fundamentals of the role as well as expected productivity standards, an accommodation here would in many respects, change the job function, which is not a requirement under the ADA.

There is an exception to the general rule that employers are not required to eliminate or remove an essential function of the job. Under the Pregnant Workers Fairness Act (PWFA), which went into effect on June 27, 2003, employers are required to provide a reasonable accommodation to an employee's known limitations related to, affected by, or arising out of pregnancy, childbirth or related medical conditions, unless the accommodation will cause an undue hardship.

Under the PWFA, the EEOC has interpreted a "qualified" employee to be:

(1) Employee or applicant who can perform the essential functions of the job with or without a reasonable accommodation (no different than the general ADA standard), or

(2) Employee or applicant that cannot perform the essential functions of the job with or without a reasonable accommodation, as long as:

a. The inability is temporary;

b. The employee could perform the functions "in the near future;" and

c. The inability to perform the essential functions can be reasonably accommodated.[18]

Per the EEOC—and looking at the second section above—"an employee who is temporarily unable to perform one or more essential functions of their job, and who therefore needs light duty or a change in their work assignments, may be able to get such a change as a reasonable accommodation." [19] The PWFA ultimately protects birthing mothers through these regulations and broadens the responsibilities of employers with respect to accommodations. Under the ADA, employers are generally not required to eliminate an essential function but under the PWFA, they need to proceed with caution if they meet the elements above.

The PWFA is rather unique law that also includes an exception to an employer's fundamental right under the ADA to seek additional information from an employee's healthcare provider to better understand workplace challenges and/or limitations to consider a reasonable accommodation. To summarize the EEOC's guidance around seeking documentation, the PWFA states that a request is unreasonable if:

(1) The limitation and need for accommodation is obvious;

(2) The employer is aware of the limitation and accommodation;

---

18. United States Equal Employment Opportunity Commission, "What You Should Know About the Pregnant Workers Fairness Act, dated 2024, https://www.eeoc.gov/wysk/what-you-should-know-about-pregnant-workers-fairness-act.

19. *Id.*

(3) The employee is pregnant needs breaks for the bathroom or to eat or drink, needs to carry water with them, or needs to the ability to sit and stand while on the job;

(4) The employee needs to pump during work hours;

(5) The employer would not ask an employee for documentation in that situation normally.[20]

This means that employers can ask a qualified employee (pregnant woman or person who has returned to work post-delivery) for documentation only in limited circumstances. The PWFA has essentially made it even easier for pregnant workers to obtain an accommodation without the traditional hurdles associated with accommodations in general.

Most recently, the PWFA has come under some scrutiny. In October 2025, the state of Texas has asked the Fifth Circuit Court of Appeals to reconsider its decision validating the law (Texas previously filed suit claiming the PWFA was unconstitutional). In August 2025, the Fifth Circuit ruled that the PWFA was constitutional.

Leave as an Accommodation

Over the last decade, leave has become one of the most divisive and challenging accommodations for employers to provide for a variety of reasons. To distinguish leave from other accommodations, this entails providing the employee with time away from their workplace to heal, recover or receive treatment in advance of returning to their job. Unlike other, traditional accommodations that incorporate some kind of adjustment, or modification, to enable the employee to perform their job, leave as an accommodation is fundamentally different in that an outright leave request does not include the continuation of performing their job. Rather, it is the leave from their work that will ultimately enable them to perform their job when they return.

Employers are faced with several issues when considering leave as the accommodation. These include:

- How much leave time is appropriate?
- How should employees handle intermittent leave accommodation requests?
- Can employers offer an alternative solution to leave?
- When is too much leave considered to be an undue hardship?
- Can an employee request leave for an indefinite period of time?
- Do employers have to hold the employee's job open while they are out on leave?

The EEOC has been very clear with their guidance that employers should consider leave as an accommodation requests the same way they consider other accommodation requests. In guidance issued in May of 2016, the EEOC states, "Leave as a reasonable

20. *Id.*

accommodation is consistent with this purpose when it enables an employee to return to work following the period of leave."[21] Generally speaking, the EEOC's position on leave is that employer's cannot unilaterally reject a leave request and should engage in the interactive process to learn more about the employee's restrictions and limitations. As with other accommodation requests, employers may come up with alternative accommodations that are reasonable and enable to employee to perform their job. The EEOC has also said that employers are not obligated to provide the accommodation selected by the employee, but do need to ensure they provide an effective one that is both reasonable and meets the needs of the employee so they can perform the essential functions of the job.

It is important to remember that the EEOC's commentary here, as well as other related areas tied to the ADA, is guidance and not law. While they are definitively the agency that enforces the ADA employment provisions and investigates employee complaints, their guidance to employers is not a legal mandate. This is highlighted in some of the caselaw contained in this section where the courts may disagree with the EEOC's position (referencing *Severson v. Heartland Woodcraft, Inc.*, 872 F.3d 476, 7th Cir. 2017).

Focusing on the EEOC's 2016 guidance around leave and the interactive process, the EEOC states:

> As a general rule, the individual with a disability—who has the most knowledge about the need for reasonable accommodation—must inform the employer that an accommodation is needed. When an employee requests leave, or additional leave, for a medical condition, the employer must treat the request as one for a reasonable accommodation under the ADA. However, if the request for leave can be addressed by employer's leave program, the FMLA (or a similar state or local law), or the workers compensation program, the employer may provide leave under those programs. But if the leave cannot be granted under any other program, then an employer should promptly engage in an 'interactive process' with the employee—a process designed to enable the employer to obtain relevant information to determine the feasibility of providing the leave as a reasonable accommodation without causing an undue hardship.[22]

The EEOC further adds that employers may request additional information to substantiate the need for an accommodation. With respect to leave specifically, the EEOC identified some common focus areas, such as:

- The specific reason for leave (i.e., recovery, medication management, training of a new service animal)

---

21. United States Equal Employment Opportunity Commission, "Employer-Provided Leave and the Americans with Disabilities Act, dated May 9, 2016, https://www.eeoc.gov/laws/guidance/employer-provided-leave-and-americans-disabilities-act.

22. *Id.*

- Whether the leave will be continuous or intermittent (i.e., 3 consecutive weeks or 5 days per month sporadically depending on symptoms)
- When the need for leave will end

The information obtained by the employer will help to determine whether leave under the circumstances is reasonable and will also help the employer to make a decision as to whether the leave requested would create an undue hardship. Answers to both reasonableness and whether something is an undue hardship can be quite difficult and employers are forced to make judgment calls when considering something like leave as an accommodation.

To delve further into some of the considerations with leave as an accommodation, the topics below represent some of the more common issues associated with these requests.

How much leave is reasonable? There is no set amount of time that represents a reasonable accommodation. It will depend greatly on the specific facts and circumstances, as well as the fiscal and operational impact to the employer (undue hardship analysis). The ADA is silent on an exact period of time, but the EEOC has indicated that if employees provide a rationale for the leave along with an estimated return-to-work date, that *could* be considered reasonable. The EEOC's guidance is clear that employers are not required to provide an employee with an indefinite amount of leave. The courts are mixed on this issue with sporadic uniformity at the circuit level.

Employers need to carefully consider the reasons why leave may be a suitable accommodation and can inquire when the leave is expected to end. If an employee, or their health provider, is unsure of the duration, employers can come to an agreement with the employee on a specific period of time where a reassessment can be done. This will certainly vary depending on the circumstances and some employers have even engaged physicians or clinicians to help with determining what a reasonable leave period would be. With no formal mandate or guidance as to how much leave is appropriate, employers are ultimately making a judgment call depending on their risk tolerance.

The ADA does not require an employer to provide a specific period of leave. This will depend entirely on the specific facts surrounding the accommodation request. The Job Accommodation Network (JAN), a service of the US Department of Labor's Office of Disability Employment Policy (ODEP), explains this issue of leave duration in detail. Below is a section, copied in full, from JAN's website:[23]

What duration of leave is required under the ADA?

> Unlike the FMLA, the ADA does not require an employer to provide leave for a specified duration of time. It is up to the employer to determine, on a case-by-case basis, what duration of leave is reasonable as an ADA accommodation. This determination must be fact-specific and will often depend on whether a

23. Job Accommodation Network, "A to Z: Leave: Introduction," accessed 2025, https://askjan.org/topics/leave.cfm.

particular duration of leave causes an undue hardship for the employer. Determination of whether providing leave would result in undue hardship may involve consideration of various factors, including the amount and/or length of leave required, the frequency of the leave, whether the need for intermittent leave is predictable or unpredictable, the impact of the employee's absence on coworkers and on whether specific job duties are being performed in an appropriate and timely manner, and the impact on the employer's operations, among other factors.

How does leave enable an employee to perform the job? Workplace accommodations under the ADA are intended to remove barriers so that employees can perform the essential functions of their job. While this is traditionally done through an adjustment or workplace modification, the employee is typically able to remain working with some sort of assistance or support. Leave is an entirely different concept that removes the employee from their position completely. The EEOC provides a few examples of where this may be appropriate (recovery, medication management, training a service-dog), but there is no definitive list where leave would apply. This presents a level of complexity for employers because leave may need to be considered in a variety of situations.

Relevant to this question of how leave may enable an employee to perform their job is whether the request is for continuous or intermittent leave. With the latter, intermittent leave doesn't totally remove an employee from their job. Rather, an employee is seeking leave sporadically (i.e., 5 times per month) based on the frequency and duration of their symptoms—which, for almost all medical conditions is unpredictable. So the question for employers is whether an intermittent leave accommodation request will rise to the level of an undue hardship or whether it can withstand the reduction in days/hours by that employee. This will always depend on an array of facts and circumstances mostly tied to the impact on the operations of the employer.

When the leave request is for a continuous period, employers can ask for an estimated end date and are under no obligation to approve leave for an indefinite period. In many cases, an employee's return-to-work date can be a moving target and this is precisely why it's so critical for employers to maintain engagement with employees around their anticipated return-to-work date. Although an employee's recovery can be difficult to predict, the EEOC typically looks to whether they've indicated a return date and how often that date may have shifted. Remember that while the EEOC is the governmental agency that enforces the provisions of the ADA, they provide guidance, not law. So while they will take a position in a case involving disability discrimination or a failure to accommodate a claim, the court may not always agree.

Maximum leave policies. Employers will often have overarching limitations around how much leave an employee is entitled to take before any kind of disciplinary action—up to and including termination. These are sometimes referred to as "no fault" leave policies and are separate and apart from medical leave under the FMLA and any disability program they may have. One of the more common forms here would be an attendance policy where an employee is subject to discipline after exceeding a specific amount of unplanned, or unaccounted for, absences. Per EEOC guidance, "employees with disabilities are not exempt from these policies [referring to maximum leave policies] as a general rule ... but such policies may have to be modified as a reasonable accommodation for absences related to a disability, unless the employer can show that doing so would cause an undue hardship."[24]

While maximum leave policies are legal and frequently used by employers to help with workforce management, it is critical for employers to ensure they've vetted any potential accommodation needs or medical leave with the employee before making any kind of adverse employment decision. Communication with the employee to gain an explanation of the absence and a better understanding of a potential return-to-work date will ensure compliance with ADA obligations regardless of the maximum leave policy in place. The EEOC guidance here calls on employers to use caution when an employee's absence exceeds a general leave policy and they should engage in the interactive process to gain a full understanding of the need for leave and ultimately, an anticipated return-to-work date. If an employer fails to engage in this way, or an employer chooses to discipline an employee without engaging in the interactive process, this could be deemed a violation of the ADA for failure to accommodate.[25]

Disability Discrimination under the ADA

The primary purpose of the ADA is to prohibit discrimination against individuals with disabilities. Focusing on the employer space, the ADA acknowledged that an individual's disability would often cause unfair treatment so lawmakers were deliberate when drafting the provisions of the ADA to not only prohibit discrimination, but ensure that employers took steps to mitigate unfair treatment across all of their practices.

Under the ADA of 1990, as amended, title 42, chapter 126, congressional findings (when developing the law) expressly laid out the purpose of the Act:

It is the purpose of this chapter—

(1) To provide a clear comprehensive national mandate for the elimination of discrimination against individuals with disabilities;

(2) To provide clear, strong, consistent, enforceable standards addressing discrimination against individuals with disabilities;

(3) To ensure that the Federal Government plays a central role in enforcing the standards established in this chapter on behalf of individuals with disabilities; and

24. United States Equal Employment Opportunity Commission, "Employer-Provided Leave and American with Disabilities Act," dated May 9, 2016, https://www.eeoc.gov/laws/guidance/employer-provided-leave-and-americans-disabilities-act.

25. *Id.*

(4) To invoke the sweep of congressional authority, including the power to enforce the fourteenth amendment and to regulate commerce, in order to address the major areas of discrimination faced day-to-day by people with disabilities.[26]

In addition to the specific provisions of the ADA, the EEOC has offered a variety of guidance indicating that disability discrimination occurs when an employer treats a qualified individual with a disability who is an employee or applicant unfavorably because of their disability. This applies to employment, hiring, firing, pay, job assignments, promotions, layoffs, trainings, benefits and other conditions of employment.

To further cement this concept of disability discrimination, here are some examples of where disability discrimination could occur in the workplace.

Dismissing an employee for disability-related absences. This occurs when an employer terminates an employee because they have used, or sought, some kind of medical leave. This could be categorized as retaliation and the ADA was put in place to protect employees from these adverse employment actions.

A more frequent occurrence of these situations takes place if an employee is terminated following a lengthy period of leave where an employer may have engaged in the interactive process throughout the leave. Whether there is a claim for disability discrimination will depend heavily on the facts and circumstances around the extended leave. A court will look at the communication between employer and employee (interactive process), the overall reasonableness of the extended leave, the impact to the employer and whether the continued leave would amount to an undue hardship (not an exhaustive list of factors). If an employer can show they acted in good faith in their communications with the employee to come up with an effective accommodation, an ultimate termination does not automatically amount to disability discrimination. Remember, the ADA does not require an employer to provide permanent accommodations so employer are under no obligation to provide an indefinite amount of leave. The legal review of these cases must always be done on a case-by-case basis.

If an employer terminates an employee for violating their maximum leave policy without engaging the employee to ascertain whether they might need a medical accommodation or potentially leave, this could also be perceived as disability discrimination. A common example of this occurs if an employee uses their 12 weeks of federal FMLA leave and subsequently requests additional leave. The ADA does not require employers to automatically approve an employee's additional leave, but unlike the FMLA, the ADA does require an employer to engage in the interactive process to better understand the employee's need more additional leave—this time as an accommodation rather than leave allotted under the FMLA (i.e., serious health condition). To be clear, the obligation of an employer in this situation is to engage the employee and potentially gather additional information around their work limitations in coming up

---

26. US Department of Justice: Americans with Disabilities Act, "Americans with Disabilities Act of 1990, As Amended: Title 42, Chapter 126—Equal Opportunity for Individuals with Disabilities, Sec. 12101. Findings and purpose," https://www.ada.gov/law-and-regs/ada/#subchapter-i---employment-title-i.

with a prospective accommodation. Employers that have maximum leave policies in place must ensure they engage with employees requesting an accommodation—even if that ask would exceed the leave amount stated in their policy.

100% healed policies. Often times, employees diagnosed with a medical condition or returning to work after a period of time may be "released" to return to their job but with restrictions. For physical impairments, this could come in the form of lifting restrictions or needing the ability to sit down during the day. For mental impairments, common restrictions include a reduced schedule or increased breaks. This may also come in the form of a health care provider letter or narrative report indicating that an employee is at 80% capacity or is not quite fully recovered from their injuries/illness but can work in some capacity. Prohibiting an employee from returning to work without restrictions is a violation of the ADA.

Here is EEOC guidance around this:[27]

> An employer will violate the ADA if it requires an employee with a disability to have no medical restrictions—that is, to be "100%" healed or recovered.... Similarly, an employer will violate the ADA if it claims an employee with medical restrictions poses a safety risk but it cannot show that the individual is a "direct threat."
>
> Direct threat is the ADA standard for determining whether an employee's disability poses a direct threat, an employer must consider whether reasonable accommodation will eliminate or diminish the direct threat.

This notion that an employee must be completely healed, or recovered, before they can return to work is a blatant violation of the ADA. An employee's release to work with restrictions actually helps with identifying what their workplace restrictions are in a collaborative effort to consider an effective, reasonable accommodation. Leave as an accommodation here should only be sought as a last resort.

Additionally, the "direct threat" concept became quite relevant during the COVID-19 pandemic when some employers began to reopen their office spaces for their employees. The novel issues for employers at the time included whether a positive COVID-19 diagnosis or even symptoms indicative of COVID-19 should be considered a disability. At the outset of the pandemic, we knew very little about the illness, symptoms and just how contagious it was. For this primary reason, most employers erred on the side of caution and recommended that employees with a confirmed diagnosis or were experiencing symptoms were encouraged to stay home (or in many cases, encouraged to work-from-home) for a specified period of time. The "direct threat" standard was not necessarily expressly leveraged during this time, but the spirit of the rule was applied where an employee's COVID-19 infection, or possibly infection, posed a threat to other employees at a job site.

---

27. United States Equal Employment Opportunity Commission, "Employer-Provided Leave and the Americans with Disabilities Act," dated May 9, 2016, https://www.eeoc.gov/laws/guidance/employer-provided-leave-and-americans-disabilities-act.

Many employers essentially approved leave—or allowed work-from-home—for employees who may have been infected with the COVID-19 virus. While this was primarily executed through company policy rather than a formal accommodations process, blanket company policies enabling employees to use their discretion about coming into the worksite mitigated the risk of employers for potentially failing to accommodate each and every one of these instances (which were high-volume at the outset of the pandemic).

Another issue related to the question of whether a confirmed COVID-19 diagnosis would amount to a disability under the ADA was the shortage of tests on the market. Between 2020–2022, the availability of tests greatly depended on a spotty supply chain across the country so for many employees, obtaining COVID-19 tests was a major challenge. For this reason, many employers chose not to use a positive test as proof that someone could be accommodated through leave or allowed to work-from-home. Again, most employers leveraged a blanket policy that allowed for sick leave, or administrative leave, to allow for recovery.

Looking at these issues within the context of "100% healed policies" which the ADA seeks to prohibit, the COVID-19 pandemic raised new considerations for employers but effectively limited adverse employment decisions where employees were permitted to stay home and recover or if feasible with their specific job, work-from-home while recovering.

Failing to consider suitable alternative employment. The ADA's requirements for employers to consider and provide reasonable accommodations also include the consideration of transferring, or reassigning, the employee to an entirely new position if the employee is unable to perform the essential functions of their current position with an agreed-upon modification or adjustment. This concept of "job-reassignment" is widely considered an accommodation of last resort and enables an employee to remain with their employer but with a different job. Like accommodations, the employee must be able to perform the essential functions of this new job with or without a reasonable accommodation. Failing to even consider a new position following a thorough accommodations process by an employer could be considered discriminatory especially with larger employers that have a variety of business units performing different functions.

There are a few distinguishing aspects of job reassignment for an employee unable to perform their current job. First, there must be job availability for consideration to be made for the employee. Employers are not required to create a new position or even a vacancy by moving another employee out. In guidance provided by the EEOC about job reassignment, the agency expressly states:

> When must I consider reassigning an employee with a disability to another job as a reasonable accommodation?
>
> When an employee with a disability is unable to perform her present job even with the provision of a reasonable accommodation, you must consider reassigning the employee to an existing position that [they] can perform with or without a reasonable accommodation. The requirement to consider reassign-

ment applies only to employees and not candidates. You are not required to create a position or to bump another employee in order to create vacancy. Nor are you required to promote an employee with a disability to a higher level position.[28]

The next distinguishing factor with job reassignment is if the employee is minimally qualified for the new role, they do not have to go through the competitive hiring process. Minimally qualified is different from the most qualified in that the employee does need to possess the skills necessary to perform the essential functions of the new job, with or without an accommodation. It should also be called out this does not necessarily mean employees vying for a vacant position do not have to go through an interview process. Often times with vacant positions, an interview process allows an employer to gain critical information about an employee's ability to perform the essential functions of the job.

Lastly, employees do need to apply for any vacant position and the availability of these positions will certainly depend on a number of factors. The EEOC encourages employers to have a process in place to help employees identify any vacant positions that might work for an employee. Depending on the employer, there may be internal teams that help the employee drill down on potential jobs leading to interviews or an expedited reassignment. It is critical for employers to remember that in these situations, the job reassignment is considered a component of the reasonable accommodation process so the traditional requirements of the ADA still apply. For example, an employer cannot force an employee to switch jobs just like they cannot force an employee to take a specific accommodation in their current job. If a different position is not identified within a reasonable period, or it is determined that the employee is unable to perform the essential functions of any new jobs identified, the employer will have satisfied their obligations to consider reassignment as an accommodation.

Hostile work environments. In the context of disability discrimination, this can take many shapes. Hostile work environments stemming from a disability could come in the form of verbal remarks like jokes or offensive comments about an employee's disability. It can include exclusion from team meetings, gatherings or even email communications where an inference of isolation due to a disability could be made. Other examples of creating a hostile work environment include intimidation, bullying and retaliation based on an employee's disability. These situations are very fact specific and often involve a pattern of conduct that would lead a reasonable person to conclude that the compilation of hostility towards the employee created an unwelcome or abusive workplace atmosphere.

Historically, courts have evaluated hostile work environment claims differently but have used similar principles in determining whether an employee could prevail under these claims. In *Flowers v. Southern Regional Physician Services, Inc.*, 247 F.3d 229 (5th

28. United States Equal Employment Opportunity Commission, "The ADA: Your Responsibilities as an Employer," https://www.eeoc.gov/publications/ada-your-responsibilities-employer.

Cir. 2001), the plaintiff was allegedly terminated from her physician as a medical assistant after her supervisor discovered that she was diagnosed with the Human Immunodeficiency Virus (HIV). The plaintiff further alleged discrimination based on her disability through a pattern of harassment that ultimately led to her termination. The Fifth Circuit in *Flowers* applied a five-factor test to specify what a plaintiff must show to prevail under a hostile work environment claim under the ADA:[29]

1. [They] are a qualified individual with a disability;
2. [They] were subject to unwelcome harassment;
3. The harassment was based on their disability;
4. The harassment was sufficiently severe or pervasive to alter a team, condition, or privilege or employment; and
5. Some factual basis exists to impute liability for the harassment to the employer (the employer knew or should have known of the harassment and failed to take prompt, remedial action).

In *Flowers*, the plaintiff produced evidence of a solid working relationship with her immediate supervisor and strong performance prior to the discovery of her HIV diagnosis. Following this discovery, plaintiff detailed how her working and personal relationship soured with her supervisor but she also laid out how she was subjected to four random drug tests in one week (where before, she was only subjected to one), she received a negative performance review after several positive ones (prior to the discovery of her HIV diagnosis), she received a significantly reduced year-end raise and was written up numerous times. Leveraging the five-prong test in *Flowers*, the court found both subjective and objective evidence to validate that a hostile working environment did in fact exist and justified the plaintiff's claim for relief.

Another example confirming how a hostile work environment cause of action can exist under the ADA can be seen in ***Shaver v. Independent Stave Co.***, 350 F.3d 716 *(8th Cir. Dec. 1, 2003)*. Here the plaintiff was terminated from his job and alleged harassment and retaliation stemming from his diagnosis of nocturnal epilepsy that required him to undergo a cranial operation. His allegations comprised of verbal abuse where he was called "plate-head" and regarded as "stupid" before he was terminated. The 8th Circuit Court of Appeals provided some insight into their analysis of hostile work environment claims through these findings:[30]

- Harassment must be both subjectively hostile or abusive to the victim and "severe and pervasive enough to create an objectively hostile or abusive work environment—an environment that a reasonable person would find hostile or abusive."

29. Southwest ADA Center, "Disability Law Index—Employment: Hostile Work Environment; citing *Flowers v. Southern Regional Physician Services, Inc.*, 247 F.3d 229 (5th Cir. 2001), accessed 2025, http://www.southwestada.org/html/topical/employment/emp_hostile.html.

30. *Id.* Citing *Shaver v. Independent Stave Co.*, 350 F.3d 716 (8th Cir. 2003).

- Anti-discrimination laws do not create a general civility code. Conduct that is merely rude, abusive, unkind, or insensitive does not come within the scope of the law.

The Eighth Circuit here provided a justification for a hostile work environment claim through a reasonableness standard that would enable a juror to assess the specific allegations and facts within the case and then form a conclusion as to whether the employer's conduct created an environment that was hostile towards the plaintiff. While the Eighth Circuit did not find that a hostile work environment existed in this claim, it did allow the retaliation to proceed.

Disability discrimination claims arise through a bevy of circumstances but they will all consistently involve allegations tied to one's disability. An employer's knowledge of the disability, or appropriate knowledge, will always be a critical piece of determining whether discriminatory conduct existed. Beyond knowledge of a disability, the employer's conduct, typically by way of an employee's supervisor or human resource professional, will often dictate whether a plaintiff can succeed with a disability discrimination claim. And lastly, an adverse employment action must always be present for a plaintiff to allege damages resulting from any discriminatory conduct.

The following caselaw helps to flesh out and illustrate common issues within disability discrimination claims.

Equal Employment Opportunity Commission, Linda K. Atkins v. Dolgencorp, LLC, dba Dollar General Corporation

899 F.3d 428 (6th Cir. 2018)

SUTTON, Circuit Judge.

Linda Atkins, once a sales associate at Dollar General, is a type II diabetic who occasionally suffers from low blood sugar. She must respond to these episodes by quickly consuming glucose to avoid the risk of seizing or passing out. When she asked her manager if she could keep orange juice at her register in case of an emergency, the manager refused. Atkins' fears came to fruition. In late 2011 and early 2012, she suffered two episodes while working alone. Each time she responded by drinking orange juice from the checkout cooler, paying for it immediately after the episode, and reporting the incident to her supervisor. Dollar General fired Atkins. And the Equal Employment Opportunity Commission filed this lawsuit. Because a jury permissibly found that Dollar General had "discriminate[d] ... on the basis of disability," we affirm.

I.

Diabetes is a chronic, sometimes life-long, condition caused by dysfunction of the endocrine system. Linda Atkins must monitor her blood sugar level daily to ensure that it is sufficiently high. Even when she does, Atkins occasionally experiences low blood sugar episodes (hypoglycemia), prompting her to shake and have difficulty seeing and thinking clearly. These episodes can cause Atkins to seize or pass out and, left untreated, can be fatal. Twice before, severe episodes required Atkins to be hospitalized.

To minimize the number of hypoglycemic episodes, Atkins takes insulin daily and monitors her diet closely. When an episode occurs, Atkins must ingest 100 calories of glucose but no more. As a remedy, Atkins prefers to drink orange juice because it acts quickly and is easy to measure.

Atkins began working at Dollar General as a sales associate in August 2009. Between then and March 2012, Dollar General gave Atkins annual raises and promoted her to lead sales associate, a position that put her in charge of handling the cash in the store during the day, depositing the cash at night, and closing the store. The store's assistant manager considered Atkins a "good supervisor," a "hard worker," and "trustworthy." R. 151 at 78.

When Atkins experienced hypoglycemic episodes at work, she typically excused herself to the break room, where she kept her orange juice in a cooler. Her new role often required her to work alone, however. Atkins spoke to the store manager, Wanda Shown, about keeping orange juice at her register. But Shown told her that store policy prohibited it.

After the promotion, Atkins suffered two hypoglycemic episodes, one in late 2011, the other in early 2012. Because Atkins worked alone each time and because there were eight to ten customers in the store each time, she could not retreat to the break room. Instead she took a bottle of orange juice from the store cooler and drank it. After each episode ended, she paid the $1.69 she owed for each bottle of juice. Both times, Atkins told the store manager what had happened.

In March 2012, District Manager Scott Strange and Regional Loss Prevention Manager Matt Irwin conducted an audit of the store to address employee-theft and other merchandise "shrinkage" issues. They interviewed Atkins, telling her they had heard she eats Little Debbie cakes behind the counter. Atkins denied the accusation but admitted that she had twice taken orange juice from the store cooler during a medical emergency and paid for it each time.

Strange and Irwin thought that these two events violated Dollar General's "grazing policy," which forbids employees from consuming merchandise in the store before paying for it. They fired Atkins at the end of the meeting.

Atkins filed a discrimination complaint with the Equal Employment Opportunity Commission. After investigating the charge, the Commission filed this lawsuit against Dollar General under the Americans with Disabilities Act. Atkins intervened in the lawsuit as a plaintiff. Atkins' reasonable accommodation and discriminatory discharge claims proceeded to trial, and the jury found in her favor on both. The jury awarded Atkins $27,565 in back pay and $250,000 in compensatory damages. The court awarded Atkins' lawyers $445,322 in attorney's fees and $1,677 in expenses.

II.

Dollar General challenges this judgment on four grounds: (1) Atkins waited too long to file her complaint; (2) Dollar General should win as a matter of law on the plaintiffs' reasonable accommodation claim; (3) Dollar General should win as a matter of law on the discriminatory discharge claim; and (4) the district court miscalculated the attorney's fees.

Timeliness. A claimant under the Americans with Disabilities Act must file her charge with the Commission within 180 days of the "alleged unlawful employment practice." 42 U.S.C. § 2000e-5(e)(1). But in a "deferral state"—one that has a "law prohibiting the unlawful employment practice alleged and establishing or authorizing a State or local authority to grant or seek relief from such practice"—she also must exhaust her claim by filing it with the state or local agency. *Id.* § 2000e-5(c). Filing a claim with the state or local agency extends the time for filing a claim with the Commission to 300 days. *Id.* § 2000e-5(e)(1). All agree that Atkins filed her claim more than 180 days, but fewer than 300 days, after Dollar General fired her. The question is whether she "initially instituted proceedings with a State or local agency with authority to grant or seek relief from such practice." *Id.*

The Tennessee Human Rights Commission administers the Tennessee Disability Act, which says: "There shall be no discrimination in the hiring, firing and other terms and conditions of employment ... of any private employer, against any applicant for employment based solely upon any physical, mental or visual disability...." Tenn. Code Ann. § 8-50-103(b). Filing a charge with the Tennessee Commission, as Atkins did here, thus entitled her to file the complaint with the federal Commission within 300 days of the discharge, and thus explains why the Equal Employment Opportunity Commission properly designated the Tennessee Human Rights Commission as a deferral agency. *See* 29 C.F.R. § 1601.80.

Dollar General counters that the Tennessee Commission does not qualify because some federal and state courts have refused to recognize a reasonable accommodations theory under the Tennessee Act. But the state Act need not map perfectly onto the federal Act in order to require exhaustion. Our federalist system assumes that there often will be more than one way to solve a policy problem. For that reason, the exhaustion statute speaks in terms of subject matter jurisdiction, referring to any state agency "with authority to grant or seek relief" from the employment practice at issue. 42 U.S.C. § 2000e-5(e)(1). The relevant question is whether the state agency has the power to entertain the claimant's disability discrimination claim, not whether state law recognizes the same theories of discrimination as federal law. *See Amini v. Oberlin Coll.*, 259 F.3d 493, 498 (6th Cir. 2001).

Whether Tennessee recognizes a reasonable accommodation theory of discrimination is neither here nor there. Atkins claims that Dollar General fired her because of her disability. The Tennessee statute prohibits "discrimination in the hiring, firing and other terms and conditions of employment," Tenn. Code Ann. § 8-50-103(b), just as the Americans with Disabilities Act prohibits "discriminat[ion] ... in regard to ... the hiring, advancement, or discharge of employees ... and other, terms, conditions, and privileges of employment," 42 U.S.C. § 12112(a). Because Atkins filed her disability discrimination charge with a state agency that had authority to entertain it, she receives the benefit of the 300-day limitations period.

That conclusion follows the U.S. Supreme Court's example of preferring easy-to-apply, bright-line rules for determining which clock to apply. *See EEOC v. Commercial Office Prods. Co.*, 486 U.S. 107, 124, 108 S.Ct. 1666, 100 L.Ed.2d 96 (1988). In a comparable setting, it rejected an interpretation that would "confuse lay complainants" and "embroil the EEOC in complicated issues of state law" because the "EEOC has neither the time nor the expertise to make such determinations under the varying laws of the many deferral States." *Id.* That remains sound advice today.

Reasonable Accommodation. Dollar General claims that the jury erred in finding that it discriminated against Atkins by failing to provide her with a reasonable accommodation for her disability. 42 U.S.C. § 12112(a), (b)(5)(A). The company faces a steep hill. We may grant judgment as a matter of law only if, after reading the evidence in the light most favorable to Atkins, there is no material fact issue for the jury to decide. *See* Fed. R. Civ. P. 50; *Garrison v. Cassens Transp. Co.*, 334 F.3d 528, 537–38 (6th Cir. 2003).

Dollar General claims that it had no duty to accommodate Atkins because Teresa Thayer, her nurse, testified that Atkins could treat hypoglycemia in other ways. Thayer mentioned several equally effective treatment options to address hypoglycemia, including glucose tablets or gels, honey, candy, and peanut butter crackers. Given these options, Dollar General maintains, it had no obligation to let Atkins keep orange juice at the register.

But these options do not make the jury's verdict unreasonable. The company's "Personal Appearance" policy states that employees "should not chew gum or eat/drink, except during breaks (which should not be taken on the sales floor, at registers, etc.)." R. 28-1 at 101. Just as a jury could find that the company prohibited employees from drinking orange juice at the register, so too could it find that it prohibited them from consuming glucose tablets, cough drops, candy, and honey packets at the register.

The policy's disclaimer, it is true, states that "[r]eligious and/or disability-related exceptions may be permitted depending on the circumstances." R. 28-1 at 101. But Atkins asked for such an exception and got nowhere. When she asked her store manager if she could keep orange juice at her register because of her diabetic condition, the manager told her "it's against company policy" and to "[b]e careful of the cameras." R. 154 at 16–17.

Once Atkins requested this reasonable accommodation, the employer had a duty to explore the nature of the employee's limitations, if and how those limitations affected her work, and what types of accommodations could be made. *See Kleiber v. Honda of Am. Mfg., Inc.*, 485 F.3d 862, 871 (6th Cir. 2007); 29 C.F.R. § 1630.2(o)(3). Had Dollar General followed this route, it might well have told Atkins that she could consume glucose pills at the register and perhaps that would have resolved the matter. But that's not what it did. The store manager categorically denied Atkins' request, failed to explore any alternatives, and never relayed the matter to a superior. That was Dollar General's problem, not Atkins'—or at least a reasonable jury could so conclude.

Even if the company's policy permitted alternative glucose sources, the plaintiffs presented evidence suggesting that those options, though medically equivalent in the abstract, were not practically equivalent in the concrete. Candy ran the risk of getting crushed or melting in Atkins' pocket, and it is more difficult to measure its sugar content anyway, creating the further risk of a "spike" in which her body would be "thrown from down here to up here." R. 151 at 160. Honey packets were hard to use because they required Atkins to "stick [her] tongue in there and get it out." R. 154 at 60. Nor could she imagine doing her job while "cramming peanut butter crackers in [her] mouth" at the same time. R. 154 at 155. She said that the glucose tablets were "useless" because she would have to take four or five pills, each the size of an Alka-Seltzer, all while under duress. R. 154 at 30.

Dollar General insists that glucose is glucose and thus its accommodate-thyself defense should have prevailed. But we need not decide whether Dollar General could have reasonably accommodated Atkins by permitting one of these alternatives because it did not do so. All that matters is whether the jury had a legally sufficient basis to conclude that Dollar General failed to provide Atkins reasonable alternatives to keeping orange juice at her register. Ample evidence supported that conclusion.

Discriminatory Discharge. Dollar General also claims that the jury went astray when it found that it discriminated against Atkins by terminating her because of her disability. 42 U.S.C. § 12112(a). Boiled to its essence, Dollar General's claim is that it had a legitimate, nondiscriminatory reason for firing Atkins, namely the company anti-grazing policy.

But a company may not illegitimately deny an employee a reasonable accommodation to a general policy and use that same policy as a neutral basis for firing him. Imagine a school that lacked an elevator to accommodate a teacher with mobility problems. It could not refuse to assign him to classrooms on the first floor, then turn around and fire him for being late to class after he took too long to climb the stairs between periods. In the same way, Atkins never would have had a reason to buy the store's orange juice during a medical emergency if Dollar General had allowed her to keep her own orange juice at the register or worked with her to find another solution.

Happily for us, doctrine lines up with common sense in this setting. A defendant may use a legitimate, nondiscriminatory rationale as a shield against *indirect* or *circumstantial* evidence of discrimination. *See Ferrari v. Ford Motor Co.*, 826 F.3d 885, 891–92 (6th Cir. 2016). But a neutral policy is of no moment when an employee presents *direct* evidence of discrimination. *See id.* And failing to provide a protected employee a reasonable accommodation constitutes direct evidence of discrimination. *See Kleiber*, 485 F.3d at 868. Hence "failure to consider the possibility of reasonable accommodation for known disabilities, if it leads to discharge for performance inadequacies resulting from the disabilities, amounts to a discharge solely because of the disabilities." *See McPherson v. Mich. High Sch. Athletic Ass'n, Inc.*, 119 F.3d 453, 460 (6th Cir. 1997) (en banc) (quotations omitted).

This insight disposes of several of Dollar General's arguments. The company maintains that the plaintiffs failed to demonstrate that similarly situated non-protected employees were treated more favorably than Atkins. But this showing is necessary only when there is no direct evidence of discrimination. *See Hopkins v. Elec. Data Sys. Corp.*, 196 F.3d 655, 660 (6th Cir. 1999). For good reason: The company cannot mask discrimination by firing able-bodied employees who need no accommodation. Any such comparison gives analogy a bad name.

Dollar General also challenges the district court's neutral-explanation jury instruction. But we may set aside jury instructions only if they prejudice someone. *See EEOC v. New Breed Logistics*, 783 F.3d 1057, 1074–75 (6th Cir. 2015). That did not happen in view of our earlier conclusion that Dollar General failed to provide Atkins a reasonable accommodation.

Dollar General adds that the verdict cannot stand because Atkins never produced evidence of *animus* towards the disabled. As support, it invokes this statement by Atkins' counsel at closing argument: "We're not claiming that Dollar General dislikes people with diabetes or that it fired her to get rid of people with diabetes." R. 156 at 129. But the Act speaks in terms of causation, not *animus*. *See Lewis v. Humboldt Acquisition Corp.*, 681 F.3d 312, 314–17 (6th Cir. 2012) (*en banc*). An employer violates the Act whenever it discharges an employee "on the basis of disability" (a necessary requirement for liability), not only when it harbors ill will (a sufficient way of establishing liability). 42 U.S.C. § 12112(a). Imagine a company that fired a visually impaired employee to save itself the minimal expense of buying special software for her. Without more, that would constitute termination "on the basis of disability," even if all of the evidence showed that cost-savings, not *animus* towards the blind, motivated the company.

Attorney's Fees. The Act entitles prevailing parties to a reasonable attorney's fee. *Id.* § 12205. We presume that the "lodestar amount"—the number of hours worked times a reasonable hourly rate—amounts to a reasonable fee. *See Perdue v. Kenny A. ex rel. Winn*, 559 U.S. 542, 546, 130 S.Ct. 1662, 176 L.Ed.2d 494 (2010). We review all such awards for an abuse of discretion. *Hensley v. Eckerhart*, 461 U.S. 424, 437, 103 S.Ct. 1933, 76 L.Ed.2d 40 (1983).

A magistrate judge prepared a report and recommendation on attorney's fees, which the district court adopted. The report considered the market rate in the Knoxville area, fee awards in similar cases, and the rate necessary to entice legal counsel to perform this kind of work.

Dollar General alleges that the magistrate overlooked *Perdue v. Kenny A. ex rel. Winn*, 559 U.S. 542, 130 S.Ct. 1662, 176 L.Ed.2d 494 (2010), when it considered the success and complexity of Atkins' case. In *Perdue*, the Supreme Court warned of double-counting, stressing that "factors subsumed in the lodestar calculation cannot be used as a ground for increasing an award above the lodestar." *Id.* at 546, 130 S.Ct.

1662. But the magistrate in this case did no such thing. He considered both success and complexity in his calculation of the lodestar amount, not as an enhancement to the lodestar.

Dollar General resists this conclusion on the ground that courts have awarded Atkins' attorneys, Jennifer Morton and Maha Ayesh, lower hourly rates in the past. Because that rate should be the same here, the argument goes, there must have been a double-counting, post-lodestar enhancement in violation of *Perdue*. But the company makes the mistake of assuming constant rates. The magistrate considered the prior awards and adequately explained why he deviated from them. Morton's past case was a discovery dispute, in which the court took no testimony about Morton's hourly rate. And in Ayesh's past case, the court adopted the amount that the plaintiff's counsel had billed. The magistrate found and applied more analogous cases, which led him to a higher reasonable hourly rate. But he did not further enhance the lodestar for success or complexity. That analysis respects *Perdue*.

On its last breath, Dollar General argues that the court failed to reduce the reward for duplicative work by Atkins' attorneys and the Commission's attorneys. But the magistrate reasonably relied on testimony that the two teams of lawyers worked cooperatively and avoided duplicative work by dividing up "briefs, jury instructions, motions *in limine*, trial witnesses, and arguments," among other tasks. R. 214 at 23. No abuse of discretion occurred.

We affirm.

Issues for Consideration

- Do you agree with the Sixth Circuit's decision? Why or why not?
- Was Linda Atkins's request to eat and/or drink at her register reasonable?
- Is Dollar General's "no grazing" policy a reasonable one?
- What could Dollar General have done to avoid this lawsuit?

Brien O. Hill v. Associates for Renewal in Education, Inc.

897 F.3d 232 (D.C. Cir. 2018)

Wilkins, Circuit Judge.

This is an Americans with Disabilities Act ("ADA") employment case. Plaintiff Brien Hill is a single-leg amputee who taught in defendant Associates for Renewal in Education's ("ARE's") afterschool program. The District Court granted partial summary judgment for ARE on two of Hill's claims, which he now appeals. Three other claims went to trial, where Hill was awarded damages for ARE's failure to accommodate his disability by refusing his request to teach on a lower floor. The primary issues on appeal are whether ARE also failed to reasonably accommodate Hill's disability by refusing his request for a classroom aide, and whether ARE's failures to accommodate Hill's disability created a hostile work environment. Hill proceeded pro se in the District Court and was represented by appointed counsel for this appeal.

We affirm the District Court's conclusion that Hill has not proffered sufficient undisputed facts for his hostile-work-environment claim to survive summary judgment. We reverse as to Hill's remaining failure-to-accommodate claim, however, because Hill's allegations present a triable issue of fact as to whether ARE violated the ADA when it refused his request for a classroom aide.

I.

A.

The following facts are taken from the parties' submissions on ARE's motion for summary judgment and are undisputed unless otherwise indicated. ARE is a nonprofit that provides care and educational programs to underserved children and adults in Washington, D.C. It is located in a three-story building with no elevator, requiring teachers to climb up and down the stairs "for fire and emergency evacuation drills, supervised outdoor play and scheduled student lavatory breaks located on the basement floor." Supplemental Brief for Plaintiff ("Pl. Supp.") 3, *Hill v. Assoc. for Renewal in Educ.*, No. 12-cv-823, ECF No. 41. Hill, who wears a leg prosthesis, was employed by ARE in various capacities until his employment was terminated in December 2008. As an ARE teacher and program aide, Hill's duties included "instructing participants in the classroom, on field trips or outside activities; prepar[ing] and administer[ing] overall classroom management; counsel[ing] participants on academic and behavioral challenges, as well as, provid[ing] administrative and/or clerical support to the administrative personnel." Affidavit of La'Troy Bailey ("Bailey Aff.") ¶ 5, ECF No. 32-1. Prior to 2007, Hill requested and was granted several accommodations for his disability, including a request for assignment to a lower-level classroom.

In May 2007, Hill fell while walking across the ARE playground, "severely injur[ing his] amputated stump and damag[ing his] prosthesis." Declaration of Brien Hill ¶ 5, ECF No. 33. Upon returning to work, he requested a classroom aide for himself and his pregnant co-teacher. Hill also requested that he be able to continue holding class on the second floor of the building. These requests were granted until August 27, 2007, when Hill was reassigned to a classroom by himself on the third floor and without a classroom aide. Hill alleged that he "expressed [his] concerns" about this reassignment verbally on August 31, 2007; that he made a written request to be "repositioned back to the lower level" and have "the accommodation of having an Aide assigned to [his] classroom;" and that he followed up with "daily verbal request[s]" for these two accommodations throughout the school year.

Declaration of Brien Hill ("Hill Decl.") ¶¶ 8–10, ECF No. 10. These accommodations were not provided. Hill was the only teacher in his program who was not assigned a classroom aide, and Hill taught more students than any of his colleagues.

Around the same period of time, Hill began to have disciplinary issues at work. On September 1, 2007, Hill's duties were changed to a part-time position due to a reduction in force and due to his "excessive tardiness and inconsistent call-ins." Bailey Aff. ¶ 4. His supervisor eventually recommended Hill's termination, and on that same day, Hill submitted a letter to ARE's Deputy Director of Education requesting review of the denial of his requests for a classroom aide and for assignment to a lower floor, among other issues. Hill was terminated effective December 15, 2008.

B.

Hill filed a *pro se* complaint against ARE asserting, among other things, a hostile work environment and several ADA claims, including failure to accommodate for denying his requests for a classroom aide and for denying his request to teach on a lower floor. Compl. ¶¶ 43–78, ECF No. 1. ARE moved for summary judgment on most of the ADA claims, arguing that Hill did not actually make the accommodation requests. ARE did not argue that the accommodations of a lower floor or a classroom aide were unreasonable or unnecessary for Hill to perform the essential functions of his job, nor did ARE argue that Hill was unqualified for his position by being physically unable to perform the essential functions of his job with or without accommodation.

After receiving the parties' filings, the District Court issued an order *sua sponte* stating that "[t]he record contains no evidence (or argument) on the third element of plaintiff's reasonable accommodation claim," *i.e.*, "whether or not plaintiff could perform [his job's essential] functions with or without reasonable accommodation." Order, ECF No. 40, at 1. The order directed the parties "to supplement the record" and "advised [Hill] that he should (1) clearly describe the essential functions of the part-time job he held in September 2007 when he allegedly began requesting the accommodations at issue and (2) explain why he needed 'the accommodation of an Aide' and a relocation to a lower level room to perform the essential functions of the job.'" *Id.* at 2. Hill responded with a fifteen-page supplemental submission explaining that "his physical disability substantially limited his ability to walk for long distances, stand for long periods of time (as required given that he supervised his classroom alone), ... [and] supervise[ ] outdoor play and scheduled student lavatory breaks on the basement floor ... without the hazard of pain and bruises." Pl. Supp. 3. Hill's supplemental submission also stated that "he worked alone and suffered a gradual decline in strength and energy due to injury and fatigue from August '07–December '08," *id.* at 4, and that he "performed all the DBA Program Aide job(s) ... alone, from August '07–December '08, and experienced grave hardships in doing so," *id.* at 12.

In response, ARE argued that Hill admitted he was able to perform the essential functions of his job without accommodation, "but not without pain." Supplemental Brief for Defendant ("Def. Supp.") at 3, ECF No. 42. ARE's supplemental submission did not argue that Hill was unqualified for his position or that the requested accommodations would cause ARE undue hardship. ARE, which was counseled, argued only that Hill did not make the accommodation requests and that he did not need the accommodations of a lower floor or classroom aide because he could perform the essential functions of his position, just with "pain."

The District Court granted summary judgment for ARE on Hill's claims for hostile work environment and failure to accommodate by refusing to assign him a classroom aide, and denied summary judgment on Hill's claim for failure to accommodate by refusing to assign him to a lower floor. *Hill v. Assoc. for Renewal in Educ.*, 69 F.Supp.3d 260, 267–68 (D.D.C. 2014). Regarding the claim for denial of a classroom aide, the District Court concluded Hill "ha[d] not adduced any evidence to show that an Aide would have been an effective means of addressing the limitations imposed by his amputated leg," and granted summary judgment because "when an employee seeks a workplace accommodation, the accommodation must be related to the limitation that rendered the person disabled." *Id.* at 268 (quoting *Adams v. Rice*, 531 F.3d 936, 944 (D.C. Cir. 2008)).

Three of Hill's ADA claims proceeded to trial. The jury found for Hill on his failure-to-accommodate claim for ARE's refusal to assign him to a classroom on a lower floor, awarding him compensatory and punitive damages. ARE and Hill both moved to set aside the verdict, and the District Court denied both motions. Hill now appeals the District Court's grant of summary judgment for ARE on his claims for hostile work environment and failure to accommodate by denying the request for a classroom aide.

II.

This Court reviews a grant of summary judgment de novo, viewing the "evidence in the light most favorable to the nonmoving party" and drawing all reasonable inferences in his or her favor. *Minter v. District of Columbia*, 809 F.3d 66, 68 (D.C. Cir. 2015) (quoting *Breen v. Dep't of Transp.*, 282 F.3d 839, 841 (D.C. Cir. 2002)). Summary judgment is appropriate only if "there is no genuine issue as to any material fact and that the movant is entitled to judgment as a matter of law," meaning that "the evidence is such that a reasonable jury could return a verdict for the nonmoving party," *Anderson v. Liberty Lobby*, Inc., 477 U.S. 242, 247–48, 106 S.Ct. 2505, 91 L.Ed.2d 202 (1986). We follow the general principle that "[a] document filed pro se is 'to be liberally construed.'" *Erickson v. Pardus*, 551 U.S. 89, 94, 127 S.Ct. 2197, 167 L.Ed.2d 1081 (2007) (quoting *Estelle v. Gamble*, 429 U.S. 97, 106, 97 S.Ct. 285, 50 L.Ed.2d 251 (1976)).

A.

ARE did not raise whether a hostile-work-environment claim is available under the ADA, a question that this Court has not yet decided and that we do not reach here. *Cf. Lanman v. Johnson Cty.*, 393 F.3d 1151, 1155–56 (10th Cir. 2004) (joining three other circuits in holding that the ADA's incorporation of language from Title VII shows Congress's intent to allow hostile-work-environment claims to proceed under the ADA). Even assuming that the ADA allows recovery for a hostile work environment, we affirm the entry of summary judgment for ARE on this claim. To prevail on a hostile-work-environment claim, "a plaintiff must show that his employer subjected him to 'discriminatory intimidation, ridicule, and insult' that is 'sufficiently severe or pervasive to alter the conditions of the victim's employment and create an abusive working environment.'" *Baloch v. Kempthorne*, 550 F.3d 1191, 1201 (D.C. Cir. 2008) (quoting *Harris v. Forklift Sys., Inc.*, 510 U.S. 17, 21, 114 S.Ct. 367, 126 L.Ed.2d 295 (1993)). The work environment must be both objectively and subjectively hostile, meaning that a "reasonable person would find [it] hostile or abusive," and that the victim must "subjectively perceive the environment to be abusive." *Harris*, 510 U.S. at 21–22, 114 S.Ct. 367. The "conduct must be extreme to amount to a change in the terms and conditions of employment." *Faragher v. City of Boca Raton*, 524 U.S. 775, 788, 118 S.Ct. 2275, 141 L.Ed.2d 662 (1998).

We affirm the dismissal of Hill's hostile-work-environment claim because he has not shown that "his employer subjected him to 'discriminatory intimidation, ridicule, and insult ... sufficiently severe or pervasive to alter the conditions of [his] employment and create an abusive working environment.'" *Baloch*, 550 F.3d at 1201. While a jury could find that assigning Hill to the third floor and denying him a classroom aide failed to reasonably accommodate his disability, these are not the kind of "extreme" conditions that this Court and the Supreme Court have found to constitute a hostile work environment. *See Faragher*, 524 U.S. at 788, 118 S.Ct. 2275; *cf. Singletary v. District of Columbia*, 351 F.3d 519, 528 (D.C. Cir. 2003) (concluding that a reasonable factfinder could find a hostile work environment when the plaintiff was assigned to a storage room containing brooms and boxes of debris that lacked heat, ventilation, proper lighting, and a working phone, and to which plaintiff lacked keys so he was at risk of getting locked in). The District Court therefore correctly concluded that a reasonable jury could not return a verdict for Hill on his hostile-work-environment claim.

B.

The ADA prohibits covered employers from "discriminat[ing] against a qualified individual on the basis of disability ... [in the] terms, conditions, and privileges of employment." 42 U.S.C. § 12112(a). Discrimination under the ADA includes "not making reasonable accommodations to the known physical or mental limitations of an otherwise qualified individual with a disability." *Id.* § 12112(b)(5)(A). The ADA defines "reasonable accommodation" to include, among other things, "making existing facilities used by employees readily accessible to and usable by individuals with disabilities," and "the provision of qualified readers or interpreters, and other similar accommodations for individuals with disabilities." *Id.* § 12111(9)(A), (B).

To prevail on a failure-to-accommodate claim, a plaintiff must show by a preponderance of the evidence (1) that he or she has a disability under the ADA; (2) that the employer had notice of the disability; (3) that the plaintiff could perform the essential functions of the position either with reasonable accommodation or without it; and (4) that the employer refused to make the accommodation. *See Solomon v. Vilsack*, 763 F.3d 1, 9 (D.C. Cir. 2014). The requested accommodation "must be related to the limitation that rendered the person disabled." Adams, 531 F.3d at 944 (quoting *Nuzum v. Ozark Auto. Distribs., Inc.*, 432 F.3d 839, 848 (8th Cir. 2005)). A plaintiff "need only show that an 'accommodation' seems reasonable on its face, i.e., ordinarily or in the run of cases. Once the plaintiff has made this showing, the defendant/employer then must show special (typically case-specific) circumstances that demonstrate undue hardship in the particular circumstances." *U.S. Airways v. Barnett*, 535 U.S. 391, 401–02, 122 S.Ct. 1516, 152 L.Ed.2d 589 (2002) (citations omitted).

We conclude Hill sufficiently alleged a connection between his disability and the assistance a classroom aide could provide while Hill supervised his students to present a triable issue of fact as to whether ARE's denial of an aide violated the ADA. The ADA's purpose in requiring reasonable accommodations is reducing barriers to employment for persons with disabilities. Therefore, to be "reasonable" under the ADA, an accommodation must be related to the disability that creates the employment barrier and must address that barrier; the ADA does not make employers responsible for alleviating any and all challenges presented by an employee's disability. *See Nuzum*, 432 F.3d at 848 ("[T]here must be a causal connection between the major life activity that is limited and the accommodation sought."); *Felix v. New York City Transit Auth.*, 324 F.3d 102, 107 (2d Cir. 2003) ("Adverse effects of disabilities and adverse or side effects from the medical treatment of disabilities arise 'because of the disability.' However, other impairments not caused by the disability need not be accommodated."); EEOC's Interpretive Guidance on Title I of the Americans with Disabilities Act, 29 C.F.R. Pt. 1630, App. (2016) ("[A]n employer [does not] have to provide as an accommodation any amenity or convenience that is not job-related" and "that is not provided to employees without disabilities."). Hill satisfied these requirements by alleging that he experienced a hazard of pain and bruising on his stump while standing for long periods of time, and by specifically connecting that hazard to supervising his class without assistance. Construing Hill's pro se submissions liberally and with all reasonable inferences drawn in his favor, a reasonable jury could find that if ARE provided Hill a classroom aide as it did for his colleagues, that aide could help Hill supervise students in the classroom and during outdoor activities, reducing his need for prolonged standing and mitigating the alleged "hazard of pain and bruising." Pl. Supp. 3.

ARE argues, for the first time on appeal, that a classroom aide would not be a reasonable accommodation. (Recall that ARE argued below that Hill did not request these accommodations, a losing argument on summary judgment because Hill introduced documentary and testimonial evidence of the request).

According to ARE, Hill feared only "falling while walking" or his prosthesis breaking while he was working, and provided "no evidence as to how an aide would alleviate this fear" once Hill was assigned to a lower floor. ARE Br. in Response to Amicus 10–11. ARE now asserts that "[i]t is unlikely an Aide could prevent a fall." *Id.* 11. ARE also emphasizes that an aide could not help with "problems arising from staircase climbing," and that in any event Hill "assured [his supervisor] that his disability did not affect him while he worked on the lower level of the facility and did not prevent him from performing essential job duties there." *Id.* 12. ARE uses some language from the complaint to suggest that Hill conceded that he did not need an aide if he was moved to a lower floor, ignoring that the complaint also alleged that Hill supplied ARE "with medical records attesting to his ability to perform the essential functions of his job with reasonable accommodation of his disability *(an aide assigned to his classroom)*." Compl. ¶ 32 (emphasis added).

ARE also fails to view the evidence in the light most favorable to Hill, as we must at this stage. *Keefe Co. v. Americable Int'l, Inc.*, 169 F.3d 34, 38 (D.C. Cir. 1999). Hill's evidence tended to show not only that he was at risk from falling while walking long distances or climbing stairs, but also that he would suffer "pain and bruises" from prolonged standing while supervising his classroom alone. Hill's submission in response to the District Court's order also stated that "he worked alone and suffered a gradual decline in strength and energy due to injury and fatigue from August '07–December '08," Pl. Supp. 4, and that he "performed all the DBA Program Aide job(s) ... alone, from August '07–December '08, and experienced grave hardships in doing so," *id.* at 12. Hill's documentary evidence showed that he requested an aide "to keep with [my] daily schedule, which requires both indoor and outdoor gross motor activities," Mem. from Brien Hill to Nykia Washington, ECF No. 22, at 22, thereby connecting the accommodation request to job functions that are made difficult and painful by his disability. Construing this evidence in the light most favorable to Hill, a reasonable jury could find that Hill's disability put him at risk of pain and bruises when standing for long periods of time, that he would have to stand for long periods of time while supervising his classroom or outdoor play without an aide to assist him, and that he did in fact suffer harm "due to injury and fatigue" during the time he was denied the accommodation of a classroom aide. *See Anderson*, 477 U.S. at 248, 106 S.Ct. 2505. A reasonable jury could also conclude that Hill suffered from prolonged standing on his stump regardless of the floor on which he taught; therefore, contrary to ARE's assertions, moving Hill to a lower floor would not necessarily have resolved his classroom-aide request.

ARE's assertion that Hill did not need the accommodation of a classroom aide because he could perform the essential functions of his job without accommodation, "but not without pain," Def. Supp. at 3, is unavailing. A reasonable jury could conclude that forcing Hill to work with pain when that pain could be alleviated by his requested accommodation violates the ADA. *See Marshall v. Fed. Exp. Corp.*, 130 F.3d 1095, 1099 (D.C. Cir. 1997) ("We assume without deciding that if working conditions inflict pain or hardship on a disabled employee, the employer fails to modify the conditions upon the employee's demand, and the employee simply bears the conditions, this could amount to a denial of reasonable accommodation, despite there being no job loss, pay loss, transfer, demotion, denial of advancement, or other adverse personnel action."); *Gleed v. AT & T Mobility Servs., LLC*, 613 F. App'x 535, 538–39 (6th Cir. 2015) (rejecting an employer's argument that providing a chair to an employee who experienced pain from prolonged standing was not a reasonable accommodation because "the ADA's implementing regulations require employers to provide reasonable accommodations not only to enable an employee to perform his job, but also to allow the employee to 'enjoy equal benefits and privileges of employment as are enjoyed by ... similarly situated employees without disabilities.'" (quoting 29 C.F.R. § 1630.2(o)(1)(iii))).

To be clear, we do not decide that the classroom aide should have been provided as a reasonable accommodation for Hill's disability; rather, we conclude only that on this record, a reasonable jury could have concluded as much. We also note that this is not a case where Hill's request for an aide can be dismissed, as a matter of law, as a request to have someone else perform one or more essential job functions for him. *See, e.g., Dark v. Curry Cty.*, 451 F.3d 1078, 1089 (9th Cir. 2006) ("The ADA does not require an employer to exempt an employee from performing essential functions or to reallocate essential functions to other employees."); LARSON, EMPLOYMENT DISCRIMINATION § 154.04[1] (2d ed. 2007) ("[A]n employer is not required to provide an 'assistant' to help an employee with a disability to perform his or her job" if that assistant is simply "reassign[ed] essential functions of a job.").

This is because an employer may be required to accommodate an employee's disability by "reallocating or redistributing nonessential, marginal job functions," or by providing an aide to enable the employee to perform an essential function without replacing the employee in performing that function. 29 C.F.R. Pt. 1630, App.; *see also* 42 U.S.C. § 12111(9)(B) (A reasonable accommodation may include "job restructuring," the "provision of qualified readers or interpreters," and "other similar accommodations for individuals with disabilities."); *see also Borkowski v. Valley Cent. Sch. Dist.*, 63 F.3d 131, 140 (2d Cir. 1995). Viewing the evidence regarding Hill's request for a classroom aide in the light most favorable to Hill, *Minter*, 809 F.3d at 68, we understand his request to be for assistance with class supervision so that he would not have to "stand for long periods of time (as required given that he supervised his classroom alone)," Pl. Supp. 3, not a request that an aide conduct all class supervision in Hill's stead, particularly since every teacher but Hill had a classroom aide and ARE had given Hill such an aide in the past.

* * *

We affirm the District Court's dismissal of Hill's hostile-work-environment claim, and we reverse, vacate, and remand the partial grant of summary judgment on the claim that Hill was denied the reasonable accommodation of a classroom aide for further proceedings consistent with this opinion.

So ordered.

Issues for Consideration

- Were Hill's accommodation requests reasonable? Why or why not?
- How could ARE have handled this situation differently?
- What is the significance of the court's "preponderance" of the evidence criteria?
- If you were to change the facts, how could ARE have shown the hiring of a classroom aid would have been an undue hardship?

Aaron Williams v. Maryland Department of Health

2024 WL 2746979 (4th Cir. May 29, 2024)

PER CURIAM.

Aaron Williams appeals the district court's order granting summary judgment in favor of his former employer, Maryland Department of Health, and denying his Federal Rule of Civil Procedure 56(d) motion to postpone ruling on summary judgment until the parties have the opportunity to engage in discovery regarding his claims under Section 504 of the Rehabilitation Act of 1973 for failure to accommodate his disability, discrimination, and retaliation. Our review of the record and the district court's opinion reveals no error. Accordingly, we affirm.

I.

"We review *de novo* a district court's decision to grant summary judgment, applying the same legal standards as the district court and viewing all facts and reasonable inferences in the light most favorable to the nonmoving party." *Ballengee v. CBS Broadcasting, Inc.*, 968 F.3d 344, 349 (4th Cir. 2020). This Court reviews a district court's denial of a Rule 56(d) motion under an abuse of discretion standard. *Pisano v. Strach*, 743 F.3d 927, 931 (4th Cir. 2014) (citing *Greater Baltimore Ctr. for Pregnancy Concerns, Inc. v. Mayor & City Council Baltimore*, 721 F.3d 264, 280 (4th Cir. 2013)).

II.

The Maryland Department of Health's ("MDH") Division of Cost Accounting Reimbursement ("DCAR") secures payment for services administered by MDH healthcare providers. S.J.A. 61. DCAR investigates who is responsible for payment related to the care provided to MDH patients and bills the responsible party once they are identified. S.J.A. 61–62. Williams began working as a full-time administrative aide within DCAR on January 29, 2020. S.J.A. 62, 70. Williams' tasks included, among other things, opening, date stamping, sorting, and distributing daily mail, handling daily cash receipts, managing and endorsing checks, and dealing with invoices. S.J.A. 71.

Williams suffers from asthma, pre-diabetes, and is moderately obese. J.A. 18. These physical impairments limit his ability to walk long distances, exercise, perform activities in high temperatures, and walk up and down stairs. *Id.* at 18–19.

Starting a month into his employment, Williams' supervisor began noticing performance issues from him, including returning checks to the wrong addressees, failing to make copies of important documents, and not following proper template form when drafting letters. S.J.A. 62–63, 78–81. In April, Williams' supervisor advised him to proofread his completed work and open mail before assisting with deposits to ensure checks are not missed or returned in error. S.J.A. 83.

Due to the COVID-19 pandemic, Williams first requested an accommodation to telework in May, which DCAR granted. S.J.A. 64. Williams began submitting monthly doctor's notes to DCAR requesting that he be allowed to telework for an additional month due to his heightened risk of COVID-19 exposure because of his disabilities.

S.J.A. 64–65, 84–87. DCAR granted his requests without question until October 2020, at which point MDH's American's with Disabilities Act Amendments Act ("ADAAA") Coordinator communicated to Williams that they could no longer grant this accommodation because it created an undue hardship on the company. S.J.A. 91. The Coordinator proposed three alternative accommodations for Williams to choose from, none of which required his presence in the office more than eight hours a week. *Id.* The Coordinator also requested that Williams propose alternative accommodations if her suggestions were not plausible. S.J.A. 92. Williams failed to select an alternative accommodation or engage in further discussion on this topic. S.J.A. 88–92. He continued to telework. J.A. 20, S.J.A. 66.

Williams continued to experience performance issues while teleworking. He, among other things, produced error-ridden work products, failed to make requested revisions to his work, continued to use the incorrect templates to draft letters, did not order supplies in accordance with procedure, and did not respond to emails or answer phone calls within an hour as required by company policy. S.J.A. 94–97. MDH also issued disciplinary action, in the form of a written reprimand, towards Williams for not following procedure regarding returning checks and for failing to complete requisitions to order supplies. S.J.A. 100–02. Williams received an "unsatisfactory" rating on his performance review in which his supervisor explained that Williams did not review examples and templates, as instructed, before completing tasks, became defensive and argumentative upon receiving constructive criticism, and used an improper tone when communicating with co-workers via e-mail. S.J.A. 103–07.

On December 7, 2020, Williams' supervisor notified him that he needs to start working in the office from 8:00 a.m. to 4:30 p.m. every Tuesday. S.J.A. 98. Then, on December 11, 2020, Williams submitted another doctor's note to DCAR. S.J.A. 99. This note, however, stated that Williams could return to work on January 11, 2021, without any mention of him teleworking in the meantime. *Id.* In response, MDH placed Williams on medical leave. J.A. 22. A human resources representative informed Williams that he is to return to the office on January 11, 2021, and that he is to enter sick leave on his timesheet until then. *Id.* Williams questioned why he needed to use his sick leave when he was teleworking due to his "heightened risk of covid exposure." *Id.* The representative explained that "[m]anagement is going off the information provided in your most recent note" and that employees on medical leave are required to input sick leave into their timesheets. *Id.*

Williams did not return to the office on January 11, 2021, as instructed. J.A. 21, 108, 111. His supervisor informed Williams that because he did not report to the office that day, that he is to return to the office Thursday, January 14 instead. S.J.A. 108. Williams responded after working hours by sending another doctor's note stating he could only telework until February 8, 2021. S.J.A. 108–11.

On January 12, 2021, Williams' supervisor sent him a letter stating that he failed to follow protocol by not returning to the office on January 11 without communicating with management about teleworking. S.J.A. 111.

On January 13, 2021, MDH informed Williams they were terminating his employment because he "lacked the technical skills as well as the judgment necessary for a satisfactory performance" as an administrative aide, failed to follow procedures, and because of his "high error rate" in completing tasks. S.J.A. 67–68, 114–18. MDH placed him on paid administrative leave with his termination effective January 27, 2021. S.J.A. 112, 118.

On August 6, 2021, Williams filed suit against MDH, alleging violations under Section 504 of the Rehabilitation Act of 1973 for failure to accommodate his disability, discrimination, and retaliation. J.A. 5. On September 17, 2021, prior to any discovery, MDH moved to dismiss the complaint, or in the alternative, for summary judgment. S.J.A. 56. In response, Williams filed a declaration pursuant to Rule 56(d), requesting that the court defer ruling on the motion to allow the parties to engage in discovery. J.A. 16–21. In considering the parties' exhibits and declarations, the district court treated MDH's motion as one for summary judgment. J.A. 40–41. The district court concluded that "it is simply not possible for [Williams] to sufficiently prove" his failure to accommodate claim because of the clear evidence that he could not perform the essential functions of his position even with his requested accommodation and because Williams failed to engage in the interactive process with MDH to identify an alternative accommodation. J.A. 49. In considering the discrimination and retaliation claims together, the district court determined that Williams failed to generate a genuine dispute of material fact because he did not "describe specific information not currently in his possession that would call into question any of the material facts" showing that his termination was due to his inadequate work performance. J.A. 50–51. As a result, the district court granted summary judgment and denied Williams' request for discovery. J.A. 53.

A.

"The Rehabilitation Act prohibits federal agencies from discriminating against its employees on the basis of disability." *Hannah P. v. Coats*, 916 F.3d 327, 336 (4th Cir. 2019). For the following reasons, we find no error as to the district court's order granting summary judgment on the Section 504 claims.

1.

To establish a *prima facie* claim for failure to accommodate under the Rehabilitation Act, the plaintiff must show that: "(1) [he] was a qualified person with a disability; (2) the employer had notice of the disability; (3) [he] could perform the essential functions of the position with a reasonable accommodation; and (4) the employer nonetheless refused to make the accommodation." *Id.* at 337. The parties agree that the first two factors are met.

Upon review of the record, we reach the same conclusions as the district court and find clear evidence that Williams could not perform the essential functions of his job even with a reasonable accommodation and that he failed to engage in the interactive process with MDH to identify a reasonable, alternative accommodation, thereby discharging MDH of any liability for its alleged failure to engage in the interactive process. Accordingly, we affirm the grant of summary judgment on this claim.

An employer is not obligated to provide an employee with the exact accommodation he requested, but instead may provide an alternative reasonable accommodation. *Reyazuddin v. Montgomery Cnty.*, 789 F.3d 407, 415 (4th Cir. 2015). Further, an employer need not provide an unreasonable accommodation, such as one that imposes undue financial or administrative hardship on the employer, is unlikely to allow the employee to successfully perform the functions of his job, or one that requires a fundamental modification of the position. *Class v. Townson Univ.*, 806 F.3d 236, 248 (4th Cir. 2015); *Elledge v. Lowe's Home Centers, LLC*, 979 F.3d 1004, 1013 (4th Cir. 2020).

Williams' position required in-office tasks including opening, sorting, and distributing mail; handling hard copies of checks; managing daily cash receipt operations and endorsing checks; and maintaining the card holder activity log. S.J.A. 65, 71–72. Clearly, these are tasks that require at least some presence in the office. For the period Williams teleworked full-time, other employees had to perform essential responsibilities of Williams' job. S.J.A. 65. Williams raises no inference that creates a dispute that he could in fact perform these tasks by teleworking. Thus, it is undisputed that MDH could not continue to grant his preferred accommodation without incurring administrative hardship and needing to allocate some of his essential tasks to other employees.

Moreover, MDH provided extensive documentation that, even with Williams' requested accommodation in place, he failed to perform in accordance with MDH's expectations. Such evidence is more than sufficient to demonstrate that he could not perform the essential functions of his position with a reasonable accommodation. *See Shin v. Univ. of Md. Med. Sys. Corp.*, 369 Fed. Appx. 472, 480–81 (4th Cir. 2020). To dispute this, Williams only offers self-serving statements that he "always performed [his] job duties in a competent manner and met the Division's reasonable expectations." J.A. 18. However, absent objective corroboration, self-serving statements cannot defeat summary judgment. *Williams v. Giant Food, Inc.*, 370 F.3d 423, 433 (4th Cir. 2004).

Lastly, Williams claims that MDH, by not engaging with him in the interactive process in response to his December and January accommodation requests, failed to reasonably accommodate him. J.A. 11; Opening Br. 12. It is true an employer must "engage ... in an interactive process to identify a reasonable accommodation" for an employee once the employee notifies them of their desire for an accommodation. *See Jacobs v. N.C. Admin. Office of the Courts*, 780 F.3d 562, 581 (4th Cir. 2015) (quoting *Wilson v. Dollar General Corp.*, 717 F.3d 337, 346 (4th Cir. 2013)). However, "an employer who fails to engage in the interactive process will not be held liable if the employee cannot identify a reasonable accommodation that would have been possible." *Wilson*, 717 F.3d at 347.

After MDH informed Williams it could no longer grant his request for 100% telework, Williams refused to engage in discussions about an alternative accommodation. Because of this, MDH had no obligation to continue to offer additional accommodations or grant his requested accommodation. *See Williams v. Va. Polytechnic Inst. & State Univ.*, 451 F. Supp. 3d 467, 477 (E.D. Va. Mar. 31, 2020) (quoting *Maubach v. City of Fairfax*, 2018 WL 2018552, at *5 (E.D. Va. Apr. 30, 2018)).

For these reasons, the district court did not err in granting summary judgment on Williams' failure to accommodate claim.

2.

Because the district court and the parties considered the discrimination and retaliation claims together, we will do the same.

To establish a *prima facie* case of discrimination under the Rehabilitation Act, a plaintiff has the burden of showing: "(1) [he] is disabled; (2) [he] was otherwise qualified for the position; and (3) [he] suffered an adverse employment action solely on the basis of [his] disability." *Hannah P.*, 916 F.3d at 342. Retaliation claims under the Rehabilitation Act require that a plaintiff demonstrate: (1) he engaged in a protected activity; (2) his employer took adverse action against him; and (3) there was a causal relationship between the protected activity and the adverse employment action. *Noonan v. Consol. Shoe Co.*, 84 F.4th 566, 574 (4th Cir. 2023) (quoting *Sempowich v. Tactile Sys. Tech., Inc.*, 19 F.4th 643, 653 (4th Cir. 2021)).

The parties both agree that Williams is disabled. MDH took an adverse action against Williams by terminating his employment. *See Jacobs*, 780 F.3d at 577. Further, Williams engaged in a protected activity by requesting an accommodation. *See Haulbrook v. Michelin N. Am., Inc.*, 252 F.3d 696, 706 (4th Cir. 2001).

Williams claims that MDH employees targeted him when he worked remotely. Specifically, he alleges that his supervisor reprimanded him for mistakes that were minor or a result of unclear instructions or another employee's refusal to respond to his requests for instructions or information. J.A. 20. Poor performance can certainly function as pretext for termination; however, Williams does not deny—but instead justifies—reasons for his mistakes. "[W]hen an employer gives a legitimate, nondiscriminatory reason for discharging the plaintiff, it is not our province to decide whether the reason was wise, fair, or even correct, ultimately, so long as it truly was the reason for the plaintiff's termination." *Laing v. Fed. Express Corp.*, 703 F.3d 713, 722 (4th Cir. 2013) (quoting *Hawkins v. PepsiCo, Inc.*, 203 F.3d 274, 279 (4th Cir. 2000)).

Williams' own perception that these mistakes were minor, or the result of another employees' unclear instructions, does nothing to undermine MDH's identified, and well-documented, reason for terminating Williams. For this reason, Williams fails to create a genuine dispute of material fact as to whether MDH terminated him solely for his disability, instead of his performance.

Regarding his retaliation claim, Williams argues that the district court did not properly consider how he requested an accommodation on January 11, 2021, and two days later MDH terminated him. While "close temporal proximity weighs heavily in favor of finding a genuine dispute as to causation," that alone cannot defeat summary judgment when an employer identifies a legitimate, nonretaliatory reason for its action. *Jacobs*, 780 F.3d at 575; *S.B. v. Bd. of Educ.*, 819 F.3d 69, 79 (4th Cir. 2016); *see Lewis v. Gibson*, 621 Fed. Appx. 163, 165–66 (4th Cir. 2015) (holding that even if the plaintiff could establish a *prima facie* case for his retaliation claim, "the temporal proximity between his protected activity and termination is, without more, insufficient to create a genuine issue of material fact"). We find that timing alone does not defeat summary judgment on this claim since MDH offered well-supported documentation that it had a non-retaliatory reason for terminating Williams, his poor performance.

Williams also claims that MDH placing him on unpaid medical leave was discriminatory and retaliatory. In reviewing the proffered evidence in the light most favorable to Williams, it shows, at best, a miscommunication between Williams and MDH, or that MDH misinterpreted the doctor's note. Further, Williams has not provided any proof sufficient to create a genuine dispute as to whether MDH placed Williams on medical leave for any reason other than to comply with the doctor's note and accommodate his disability.

For the forgoing reasons, we affirm the district court's order granting summary judgment on Williams' discrimination and retaliation claims.

B.

With respect to Williams' Rule 56(d) motion, we now consider whether the district court erred in ruling on the summary judgment motion before the parties had a chance to engage in discovery.

"Rule 56(d) mandates that summary judgment be denied when the nonmovant 'has not had the opportunity to discover information that is essential to his opposition.'" *Pisano*, 743 F.3d at 931 931 (quoting *Ingle ex rel. Estate of Ingle v. Yelton*, 439 F.3d 191, 195 (4th Cir. 2006)). However, a court need not allow discovery "when the information sought would not by itself create a genuine issue of material fact sufficient for the nonmovant to survive summary judgment." *Hodgin v. UTC Fire & Security Americas Corp.*, 885 F.3d 243, 250 (4th Cir. 2018) (quoting *Pisano*, 743 F.3d at 931).

According to Williams, the issues of whether MDH intentionally discriminated and retaliated against Williams due to his disability, whether he met the expectations of his job, and whether his supervisor targeted and acted aggressively toward him, are fact intensive. J.A. 17. Accordingly, Williams requested the opportunity to examine relevant MDH employees and to obtain discovery regarding his "job responsibilities, his requests for accommodations, MDH's responses to those requests, and MDH's supposed reasons for terminating [Williams'] employment." *Id.*

Regarding the failure to accommodate claim, the district court determined that "there is ample evidence that Plaintiff was not performing the essential functions of his position, and there is no specific and meaningful proffered evidence to the contrary as to justify discovery." J.A. 49. For the discrimination and retaliation claims, the district court concluded discovery is not necessary there either because Williams failed to describe documents or information not currently available to him which would call into question MDH's reason for terminating Williams. J.A. 51.

The district court did not abuse its discretion by denying Williams' Rule 56(d) motion because Williams failed to demonstrate that the discovery sought would create a genuine issue of material fact.

III.

Accordingly, we affirm the district court's order. We dispense with oral argument because the facts and legal contentions are adequately presented in the materials before this court and argument would not aid the decisional process.

AFFIRMED.

Issues for Consideration

- Can an employer claim an undue hardship after granting an accommodation to an employee?
- What is the significance of Williams continuing to experience performance issues while working from home?
- Do you think Williams has a valid claim for disability discrimination?

Huber v. Westar Foods

106 F.4th 725 (8th Cir. 2024)

MELLOY, Circuit Judge.

In December 2019, Tonya Huber experienced a diabetic episode that caused her to miss work. Days later, her employer, Westar Foods, Inc., fired her. Thereafter, Huber brought this action alleging disability discrimination under the Americans with Disabilities Act ("ADA") and Nebraska Fair Employment Practice Act ("NFEPA"), as well as interference with and retaliation for exercising her rights under the Family and Medical Leave Act ("FMLA"). Westar filed a motion for summary judgment, which the district court granted. Huber appeals. We reverse and remand for further proceedings consistent with this opinion.

I.

On appeal from a grant of summary judgment, we view the facts in the light most favorable to Huber as the nonmoving party and draw all reasonable inferences in her favor. *Lightner v. Catalent CTS (Kansas City), LLC*, 89 F.4th 648, 651 (8th Cir. 2023).

Westar Foods operates a number of Hardee's restaurants in the Midwest, employing more than 200 people. In December 2018, Westar hired Huber as a store manager for a Nebraska Hardee's location. Prior to employment with Westar, Huber had worked in the fast-food industry for fifteen years. Westar hired Huber to work full-time at fifty hours per week. Huber's ten-hour shifts typically began at 5 a.m. and ended at 3 p.m., while Huber's duties included managing restaurant staff, overseeing store operations, and ensuring the store was opened each day.

Soon after Huber started working at Westar, she was diagnosed with diabetes. In March 2019, Huber had to start taking insulin, including at work. Over the course of her employment, Huber's insulin dosage increased. To manage her diabetes, Huber needed a room temperature location where she could store her insulin. The restaurant's kitchen and office ran upwards of ninety degrees, and Huber struggled to find a room temperature place for insulin storage. As such, she asked her district manager at the time, Matt Thayer, for help finding suitable storage, but he responded, "That's a [you] problem, not a [me] problem." After Cindy Kelchen became Huber's district manager in September 2019, Huber renewed her request for help finding a room temperature location for her insulin, and Kelchen advised storing it in the freezer. When Huber pointed out that the freezer was not room temperature, Kelchen responded, "Then I don't know what to tell you."

In addition to insulin storage, Huber also needed to find time during her shift to eat a meal so she could take her insulin. Huber was often too busy to take meal breaks during her shifts, so she sought help from Kelchen. Kelchen responded by telling Huber to get better at time management.

In December 2019, Huber began to feel sick because of her diabetes. When Huber woke up for her shift on the morning of December 20, her blood glucose level was low, and she was experiencing symptoms consistent with hypoglycemia. Indeed, because of her blood glucose level, Huber "felt out of it" and did not know who or where she was. Huber realized she needed to go to work but then forgot and became confused as to what was happening or where she was supposed to be. Eventually, Huber was able to drive herself to a nearby doctor's office where she was given an IV and medications that sedated her.

Throughout the day of her stay at the doctor's office, Huber called her son and her boyfriend, Richard Grondin, on multiple occasions. One call to Grondin lasted 45 minutes. According to Grondin, Huber was groggy and incoherent when he spoke with her. Huber's son recalled that her communication was "all over the place" and difficult to comprehend. Huber does not remember these calls due to the impact of her diabetic episode.

On the day of the diabetic episode, Westar first discovered that Huber had not come into work when a customer notified Kelchen that Hardee's was not open. Kelchen tried calling Huber, who did not answer, so Kelchen called Huber's son, who was listed as her emergency contact. Huber's son told Kelchen that Huber was at the doctor's office, that her "levels were off," and that Huber would call back. Huber did not end up calling Kelchen that day.

The doctor's office kept Huber under its care until it closed for business. When Huber was discharged in the evening, the medical staff would not permit her to drive because of her condition, so she called Grondin for a ride. Because of her state, Huber was unable to convey to Grondin the directions to where she was, "so he had to use an app to locate her." When they eventually arrived at Huber's home, Huber was delirious, disoriented, and ill, so Grondin decided to stay overnight out of concern for her safety.

Huber slept until 7:45 a.m. the next day, December 21. She had been scheduled to work at 5 a.m. that morning, but she was still ill and recovering from the medications administered at the doctor's office the day before. Westar's attendance policy has a "call-in" requirement, which states that if a store manager is going to be late for work or if they are unable to work, they must call their district manager immediately and at least two hours prior to the start of their shift "when possible." Additionally, the attendance policy states that "[t]exting, emailing or leaving a message is not" an acceptable way to notify management of an absence or tardiness. Huber was aware of the call-in policy, so immediately upon awaking, she called Kelchen and emailed her a doctor's note excusing her from work through December 26. On the call, Huber conveyed her experience and the nature of the diabetic episode to Kelchen. Kelchen took notes of the conversation and wrote that Huber was at the doctor's office because "her levels of her diabetic [sic] was off." During the call, Kelchen was yelling at Huber; indeed, her voice was so loud that it woke Grondin, who was asleep in an adjacent room. When Kelchen asked Huber why she did not notify her in accordance with the call-in policy on either December 20 or 21, Huber explained how the diabetic episode made it extremely difficult to call, mentioning to Kelchen that she could do an internet search to understand the symptoms better. Kelchen did not understand or believe that Huber could not have called, especially when she was able to call her boyfriend and son and drive herself to the doctor's office. During the conversation, Kelchen asked Huber five times why she did not make a "simple phone call" to inform Westar about her absence.

Immediately following her call with Huber, Kelchen called Frank Westermajer, Westar's owner and president, to convey her conversation with Huber. It is undisputed that during the call, the decision was made to fire Huber when she returned from sick leave on December 26. The parties disagree as to whether Westermajer was the sole decision-maker, or whether Kelchen was also a decision-maker.

In the days following her diabetic episode, Huber continued to struggle with her health, experiencing fluctuating blood glucose levels that required hourly readings. On December 22, pursuant to her doctor's guidance, Huber emailed Kelchen and Amy Rowe, Westar's HR representative, requesting FMLA paperwork. Huber did not receive a response and followed up on December 23 to request FMLA forms ahead of a follow-up doctor's appointment that day. Rowe did not provide the paperwork but responded that she had the doctor's note excusing Huber from work and therefore needed nothing additional from Huber's doctor.

At the follow-up appointment, the doctor provided Huber with another note requiring her to be out of work through January 2 due to her diabetes. After the doctor's appointment, Huber once again requested FMLA paperwork, but received no response. The next morning, on December 24, Rowe responded, once again not providing paperwork, but instead requesting a meeting that afternoon despite her awareness of Huber's medical leave. Rowe planned to fire Huber at the meeting. Huber, whose condition was not stable, responded by declining the meeting, providing the new doctor's note, and asking once again for the FMLA paperwork.

Because Huber's sick leave was extended, the December 26 meeting did not occur, and Rowe instead sent Huber a termination letter. The letter stated that the reason for the termination was because Huber "failed to follow the Company's notice procedures for [her] absences on December 20, 2019 and on December 21, 2019."

The letter noted that Huber was "fully aware" of the company's notice procedures in part because the company had previously disciplined her for not abiding by them. The letter further explained that because Huber was "driving and in contact with [her] son" on the day of her diabetic episode, she "should have been able to provide notification of [her] absences to the Company ... or at the very least prior to [her] scheduled shift on Saturday, December 21."

In addition to providing a reason for termination, Westar's letter also addressed Huber's FMLA request, stating that "[b]ased on [her] explanation that [she] drove [herself] to the clinic on December 20th and the circumstances on December 21, 2019," and because she had "failed to provide notice as soon as possible and practical [and] did not request any need for an accommodation until after the unscheduled absences," her absences would not be covered under the FMLA.

Thereafter, Huber brought this lawsuit alleging Westar violated the ADA and NFEPA by discriminating against her on the basis of her diabetes. Huber also alleged that Westar interfered with her rights and retaliated against her in violation of the FMLA.

Westar moved for summary judgment on all claims. Huber then filed a partial motion for summary judgment on Westar's affirmative defenses. Subsequently, Huber also moved to strike two affidavits that Westar filed in opposition to her partial motion for summary judgment. The district court granted Westar's motion for summary judgment. Additionally, the district court denied both of Huber's motions without further discussion. Huber now appeals.

II.

The Court "review[s] a grant of summary judgment *de novo*." *Wages v. Stuart Mgmt. Corp.*, 798 F.3d 675, 679 (8th Cir. 2015). "Summary judgment is proper if, after viewing the evidence and drawing all reasonable inferences in the light most favorable to the nonmovant, no genuine issue of material fact exists and the movant is entitled to judgment as a matter of law." *Corkrean v. Drake Univ.*, 55 F.4th 623, 630 (8th Cir. 2022) (citation omitted); Fed. R. Civ. P. 56(a). "A court at this stage 'does not weigh the evidence, make credibility determinations, or attempt to discern the truth of any factual issue' but focuses on whether there are genuine disputes of material fact for trial." *Walz v. Randall*, 2 F.4th 1091, 1099 (8th Cir. 2021) (quoting *Morris v. City of Chillicothe*, 512 F.3d 1013, 1018 (8th Cir. 2008)).

III.

We first address Huber's disability discrimination claim. Under the ADA, employers are prohibited from discriminating against qualified individuals on the basis of their disability. *Gruttemeyer v. Transit Auth.*, 31 F.4th 638, 646 (8th Cir. 2022); 42 U.S.C. § 12112(a)–(b). To establish that an employer took an adverse employment action motivated by discriminatory animus, a plaintiff may present "evidence of disparate treatment or other proof that will vary according to the specific facts of the case." *Lipp v. Cargill Meat Solutions Corp.*, 911 F.3d 537, 543 (8th Cir. 2018). Such evidence can be "direct" or "indirect," terms that refer to the causal strength of the evidence, not necessarily whether evidence is circumstantial. *Id.*; *St. Martin v. City of St. Paul*, 680 F.3d 1027, 1033 (8th Cir. 2012). Direct evidence provides a strong causal "link between the alleged discriminatory animus and the challenged decision, sufficient to support a finding by a reasonable fact finder that an illegitimate criterion actually motivated the adverse employment action." *St. Martin*, 680 F.3d at 1033 (quoting *Griffith v. City of Des Moines*, 387 F.3d 733, 736 (8th Cir. 2004)). "Direct evidence includes 'evidence of conduct or statements by persons involved in the decisionmaking process that may be viewed as directly reflecting the alleged discriminatory attitude,' where it is sufficient to support an inference that discriminatory attitude more likely than not was a motivating factor." *Lipp*, 911 F.3d at 543 (quoting *Schierhoff v. GlaxoSmithKline Consumer Healthcare, L.P.*, 444 F.3d 961, 966 (8th Cir. 2006)). Direct evidence often, though not always, comes in the form of blatant statements expressing discriminatory animus.

Indirect evidence, on the other hand, provides a weaker causal connection but may nonetheless establish discrimination. Where a plaintiff puts forth indirect evidence, we apply the *McDonnell Douglas* burden-shifting framework. *St. Martin*, 680 F.3d at 1033. Under the *McDonnell Douglas* framework, the plaintiff must first make a *prima facie* showing of discrimination by establishing: "(1) that the plaintiff was disabled within the meaning of the ADA; (2) that the plaintiff was qualified to perform the essential functions of the job; and (3) a causal connection between an adverse employment action and the disability." *Oehmke v. Medtronic, Inc.*, 844 F.3d 748, 755 (8th Cir. 2016). After the plaintiff establishes their *prima facie* case, the burden then shifts to the employer to put forth "a legitimate, nondiscriminatory reason for the adverse action." *Id.* Finally, if the employer offers such a reason, the burden shifts back to the plaintiff, who must establish pretext, i.e., "that a [prohibited] reason more likely motivated the employer.'" *Torgerson v. City of Rochester*, 643 F.3d 1031, 1047 (8th Cir. 2011) (citation omitted) (alteration in original). Although the burden of production shifts, the burden of persuasion always remains with the plaintiff. *Donathan v. Oakley Grain, Inc.*, 861 F.3d 735, 740 (8th Cir. 2017).

The district court found that Huber did not present direct evidence, and we agree. Huber has offered no evidence with the causal strength to dispositively show disability discrimination; therefore, we apply the *McDonnell Douglas* burden-shifting framework. The burden for establishing a plaintiff's *prima facie* case is not onerous, and the district court assumed without determining that Huber met her *prima facie* burden. *Id.* The employer's burden is likewise not onerous, and the district court found that Westar offered a legitimate, nondiscriminatory reason for terminating Huber's employment. *Torgerson*, 643 F.3d at 1047. Finally, the district court found that Huber failed to show Westar's reason for firing her was pretextual.

Huber disputes the district court's conclusions. Specifically, Huber argues that genuine issues of fact exist as to whether Westar's reason for firing Huber was pretextual. When considering whether an employer's reason for firing is pretext, "the ultimate question is whether the plaintiff presents evidence of 'conduct or statements by persons involved in [the employer's] decision-making process reflective of a discriminatory attitude sufficient to allow a reasonable jury to infer that that attitude was a motivating factor in [the employer's] decision to fire [the plaintiff].'" *Kiel v. Select Artificials, Inc.*, 169 F.3d 1131, 1135 (8th Cir. 1999) (*en banc*) (alterations in original) (quoting *Feltmann v. Sieben*, 108 F.3d 970, 975 (8th Cir. 1997)). There are at least two ways a plaintiff may show a question of fact exists regarding pretext: a plaintiff may present evidence that (A) "the employer's explanation is unworthy of credence ... because it has no basis in fact" or (B) "a prohibited reason more likely motivated the employer." *Gardner v. Wal-Mart Stores, Inc.*, 2 F.4th 745, 748 (8th Cir. 2021) (alteration in original) (citations omitted).

A.

Huber first argues that Westar's reason for terminating her is "unworthy of credence" and "has no basis in fact." *Id.* Westar maintains that it terminated Huber because she violated the company call-in policy on December 20 and 21. Violation of company policies is a legitimate, nondiscriminatory reason for employment termination. *See, e.g., Miner v. Bi-State Dev. Agency*, 943 F.2d 912, 913–14 (8th Cir. 1991). Huber disputes that she violated company policy on the days she was experiencing a diabetic episode. In rejecting Huber's argument, the district court concluded that even assuming Huber did not violate the call-in policy, Westar presented evidence that it had a "good-faith belief that she violated the call-in policy on both occasions."

In reaching its decision, the district court cited *Pulczinski*, where we held that "[t]aken alone, that the employer's belief turns out to be wrong is not enough to prove discrimination." *Pulczinski v. Trinity Structural Towers, Inc.*, 691 F.3d 996, 1003 (8th Cir. 2012). Indeed, typically the "rule in discrimination cases is that if an employer honestly believes that an employee is terminated for misconduct, but it turns out later that the employer was mistaken about whether the employee violated a workplace rule, the employer cannot be liable for discrimination." *Richey v. City of Indep.*, 540 F.3d 779, 784 (8th Cir. 2008); *see also Pulczinski*, 691 F.3d at 1002. Therefore, "[i]f the employer takes an adverse action based on a good faith belief that an employee engaged in misconduct, then the employer has acted because of perceived misconduct, not because of protected status or activity." *Richey*, 540 F.3d at 784. "The relevant inquiry is whether the [employer] *believed* [the employee] was guilty of the conduct justifying discharge." *Id.* (quoting *Scroggins v. Univ. of Minn.*, 221 F.3d 1042, 1045 (8th Cir. 2000)) (alterations in original).

In *Pulczinski*, an employer had a genuine belief that the discharged employee had engaged in impermissible activity—specifically, activity that would slow down work. 691 F.3d at 1002. This activity was wholly unrelated to the employee's disability. *Id.* Following an unexcused absence, which the employee argued resulted from his disability, the employer, not believing the employee, conducted a formal investigation into the absence. *Id.* at 1001. During the investigation, the employer learned that the employee had planned to miss work that day to go gambling, encouraged his colleagues to come with him to the casino or to also skip work, and actively discouraged his colleagues from working overtime. *Id.* Based on uncontroverted evidence, the employer terminated the employee not for missing work, which the plaintiff maintained was due to his disability, but rather for "attempting to cause a slowdown in work by discouraging others from working overtime." *Id.* The plaintiff sued.

On an appeal from a motion for summary judgment, the *Pulczinski* employee argued that the district court's decision should be reversed because there was "a genuine issue of fact about whether he truly discouraged overtime work," which the plaintiff argued showed pretext. *Id.* at 1003. We held that even if the employer erred in coming to its conclusion that the plaintiff had sought to cause a work slowdown, the reasoning, like the justification for termination, was unrelated to the plaintiff's disability. *Id.* at 1003–04. *See also, e.g., Johnson v. Securitas Sec. Servs. USA, Inc.*, 769 F.3d 605, 612 (8th Cir. 2014) (applying good faith principle to age discrimination claim); *Liles v. C.S. McCrossan, Inc.*, 851 F.3d 810, 821–22 (8th Cir. 2017) (applying good faith principle to claim of sex discrimination); *Main v. Ozark Health, Inc.*, 959 F.3d 319, 324–26 (8th Cir. 2020) (same).

Notwithstanding the principle articulated in *Pulczinski*, an employer's argument of good faith will not always preclude a discrimination case from reaching a jury. Where an employer seeks to assert a good faith argument, the underlying "reasons for firing must be 'sufficiently independent from'" the protected status or activity. *Gilooly v. Missouri Dep't of Health & Senior Servs.*, 421 F.3d 734, 740 (8th Cir. 2005) (quoting *Womack v. Munson*, 619 F.2d 1292, 1297 (8th Cir. 1980)); *Richey*, 540 F.3d at 785. Thus, if the reason for an employer's adverse employment action is "so inextricably related to" the disability, "they cannot be considered independently of one another." *Womack*, 619 F.2d at 1297. Indeed, we recently explained that where "a disability caused missed work, and missed work caused termination, it [is not] much of a stretch to conclude that ... [the] disability caused [the] termination." *Weatherly v. Ford Motor Co.*, 994 F.3d 940, 946 (8th Cir. 2021).

Huber's case is distinguishable from *Pulczinski* because a reasonable jury could conclude her diabetic episode was not independent from her firing. *Gilooly*, 421 F.3d at 740. Here, Huber was fired because she failed to call in to work on days she was experiencing a diabetic episode. As such, Huber argues that her disability precluded her from calling in. Kelchen, on the other hand, did not believe Huber and assumed she was able to abide by the call-in policy on the days of her diabetic episode. Westar's decision to terminate Huber was based on this assumption. Although Westar argues that its termination decision was underscored by Huber's failure to follow the call-in policy on two prior occasions, a factfinder could determine this evidence weighs in favor of Huber. Indeed, a factfinder may conclude that Westar's decision not to terminate Huber on two prior occasions, where her failure to call in was unrelated to her disability, only bolsters Huber's pretext argument.

In these situations, whether the employee's disability caused the conduct that violated company policy and whether the employer acted in good faith are both questions of fact. *See Townsend v. Bayer Corp.*, 774 F.3d 446, 461 (8th Cir. 2014). Therefore, we cannot say as a matter of law that Huber was capable of calling in during her diabetic episode on December 20 and 21, and a jury must decide whether Westar's termination decision was made in good faith or supports a showing of pretext.

B.

Huber also argues that "a prohibited reason more likely motivated" Westar's termination decision as evidenced by the actions of her two district supervisors, Kelchen and Thayer. *Gardner*, 2 F.4th at 748. The district court determined that Kelchen and Thayer were not decision-makers, and therefore did not consider their actions as evidence of pretext. Because the issue of who qualifies as a decision-maker is critical to whether Huber presented evidence of pretext sufficient to survive a motion for summary judgment, we address that first.

1.

Where an employer "attempt[s] to confine decisionmaking power to a small number of individuals, those individuals will have a limited ability to exercise independent discretion when making decisions and will likely rely on other workers who actually interact with the affected employee." *Vance v. Ball State Univ.*, 570 U.S. 421, 447, 133 S.Ct. 2434, 186 L.Ed.2d 565 (2013). "Under those circumstances, the employer may be held to have effectively delegated the power to take tangible employment actions to the employees on whose recommendations it relies." *Id.* Thus, "[e]ven if an employer concentrates all decisionmaking authority in a few individuals, it likely will not isolate itself from ... liability." *Id.* at 446–47, 133 S.Ct. 2434. Moreover, one need not be a "decision-maker" for an employer to face liability: "Evidence of discriminatory *animus* among individuals with influence over decisionmaking can be sufficient for a reasonable jury to conclude discrimination was a motivating factor." *Gruttemeyer*, 31 F.4th at 648; *see also Kiel*, 169 F.3d at 1135 (explaining that a factfinder will consider evidence of discriminatory *animus* by "persons involved" in the adverse employment action).

Huber argues that Kelchen and Thayer were decision-makers or had influence over the decision-making process, and therefore their actions should be considered for evidence of discriminatory *animus*. The district court concluded that only Westar's CEO, Westermajer, was a decision-maker, and therefore did not consider Kelchen and Thayer's actions as evidence of discriminatory *animus*. But it is undisputed that Kelchen and Thayer were Huber's direct supervisors, and as such, Huber went to them when she requested accommodations for her diabetes. A factfinder could interpret their responses to Huber's accommodation requests as exercising delegated decision-making authority.

Moreover, Kelchen called Westermajer immediately after her call with Huber to convey the conversation about Huber's missed absence. During that call, Westermajer made the termination decision. A reasonable factfinder could determine that, at the very least, Kelchen wielded decision-making influence over Westermajer's termination decision. Accordingly, we conclude that Huber has presented sufficient evidence to raise a genuine issue as to whether Kelchen and Thayer were decision-makers or influenced the decision-making process.

2.

Because a factfinder could determine that Kelchen and Thayer were decision-makers or influenced the decision-making process, we consider whether their actions show that "a prohibited reason," i.e., discriminatory *animus*, more likely motivated Westar's termination decision. A plaintiff may raise a question of fact as to pretext by showing "'a specific link between the alleged discriminatory *animus* and the challenged decision, sufficient to support a finding ... that an illegitimate criterion actually motivated' the adverse employment action." *Othman v. City of Country Club Hills*, 671 F.3d 672, 675 (8th Cir. 2012) (quoting *Torgerson*, 643 F.3d at 1044).

To support her pretext argument, Huber first asserts that Kelchen's comments and conduct show discriminatory *animus*. Comments "uttered by individuals closely involved in employment decisions may" provide evidence of discriminatory *animus*. *Beshears v. Asbill*, 930 F.2d 1348, 1354 (8th Cir. 1991). Moreover, where conduct and actions indicate contempt toward an employee's disability, we have found a question of fact exists regarding discriminatory *animus*. *Kells v. Sinclair Buick-GMC Truck, Inc.*, 210 F.3d 827, 833–34 (8th Cir. 2000), *abrogated on other grounds by Torgerson*, 643 F.3d 1031 (2011). Huber alleges that Kelchen displayed contempt and anger toward her when explaining her absence from work on account of her diabetic episode. Huber alleges that Kelchen was angry over the phone, which is corroborated by Grondin, who stated that he was awoken by Kelchen "screaming" through the phone at Huber and observed that Kelchen was not "very receptive" to what Huber was explaining. A factfinder could infer discriminatory *animus* from Kelchen's actions and words.

Second, Huber asserts that the close temporal proximity between Kelchen's angry call and Westar's termination decision is further evidence of discriminatory *animus*. Indeed, close temporal proximity between an employer's discovery of the disability and the adverse employment action can contribute to an inference of discrimination, though on its own this is typically not sufficient to establish pretext. *See Sprenger v. Fed. Home Loan Bank of Des Moines*, 253 F.3d 1106, 1114 (8th Cir. 2001); *Smith v. Allen Health Sys., Inc.*, 302 F.3d 827, 833 (8th Cir. 2002). We have clarified that an interval of two months is likely not enough, but "a matter of weeks" could contribute to a finding of discrimination. *See Sprenger*, 253 F.3d at 1113–14; *see also Kipp v. Mo. Highway & Transp. Comm'n*, 280 F.3d 893, 897 (8th Cir. 2002); *Allen Health Sys., Inc.*, 302 F.3d at 833–34. On the other hand, "a 'mere coincidence of timing' can rarely be sufficient." *Kipp*, 280 F.3d at 897 (citation omitted). Here, according to Kelchen's notes, she learned of Huber's disability and the nature of her diabetic episode during their phone call. Immediately after ending the call, Kelchen spoke with Westermajer, during which time the decision was made to terminate Huber. On its face, this timing does not appear coincidental; rather, the timing of the call to Westermajer is strong evidence of pretext.

Huber also argues that Westar demonstrated discriminatory *animus* when it failed to help her with accommodations. We have held that "[f]ailing to provide an employee with reasonable accommodations can tend to prove that the employer also acted adversely against the employee because of the individual's disability." *Kells*, 210 F.3d at 834. As noted above, Huber presented evidence that Kelchen and Thayer were ambivalent toward Huber's insulin storage and meal break requests. Huber also provides evidence of Kelchen and Rowe's shared contempt toward accommodating her sick leave after the diabetic episode.

Moreover, Kelchen not only yelled at Huber over the phone on December 21, Kelchen equivocated on whether she expected Huber to find coverage for her shifts despite her sick leave. Kelchen stated that Huber was expected to find coverage for her shifts while on medical leave, then backtracked and explained that employees with doctor's notes are not expected to find coverage during leave. Kelchen's expectation that Huber work while sick is further suggested in Kelchen's disciplinary notes from December 23, where she wrote that Huber provided "[n]o communication to [Westar] for her store responsibilities and coverage." Moreover, on December 24, Rowe and Kelchen requested a meeting with Huber even though they were aware of Huber's doctor's note excusing her from work through December 26. Reviewing the facts in the light most favorable to Huber, a reasonable factfinder could interpret Westar as showing contempt toward Huber's disability accommodations.

For its part, Westar denies having ever known about Huber's diabetes until *after* the company had already decided to terminate her employment on December 21. Yet Westar's own records contradict this assertion. Both Kelchen's notes and the termination letter from Rowe suggest that the company knew about Huber's diabetes at least as early as Kelchen's call with Huber's son, who conveyed that Huber's "levels were low." Although "levels were low" did not explicitly say glucose or diabetes, a trier of fact could find that Westar knew nonetheless, especially since those exact words were used in the termination letter Westar sent Huber. Regardless, Westar's company notes confirm that immediately prior to Kelchen's call with Westermajer, Kelchen had learned from talking with Huber that the reason she missed work on December 20 and 21 was due to her diabetes. The fact that Westar was aware of Huber's disability yet continues to deny awareness is strong evidence of pretext. *Reeves v. Sanderson Plumbing Prods., Inc.*, 530 U.S. 133, 147, 120 S.Ct. 2097, 147 L.Ed.2d 105 (2000) (holding that a "trier of fact can reasonably infer from the falsity of the explanation that the employer is dissembling to cover up a discriminatory purpose"); *see also Ridout v. JBS USA, LLC*, 716 F.3d 1079, 1086 (8th Cir. 2013) (same).

In sum, viewed in the light most favorable to Huber, genuine issues of fact exist regarding whether Westar's termination decision was motivated by discriminatory *animus* and therefore whether its reason for firing Huber was pretext.

IV.

We next turn to Huber's FMLA claims. The FMLA requires employers to provide 12 weeks of unpaid leave to employees who experience "a serious health condition that makes the employee unable to perform the functions of the employee's job." 29 U.S.C. § 2612(a)(1)(D); 29 C.F.R. § 825.112; *Darby v. Bratch*, 287 F.3d 673, 679 (8th Cir. 2002).

Under the FMLA, an employee must notify their employer that they plan to take leave, while an employer is prohibited from "discriminating against employees for asserting rights under the Act." *Darby*, 287 F.3d at 679; 29 U.S.C. §§ 2612(e)(2), 2615(a)(2). Huber asserts two types of FMLA discrimination claims: interference and retaliation. 29 U.S.C. § 2615(a)(1)–(2). Huber argues that genuine issues of fact exist as to both her interference and retaliation claims against Westar. An interference claim "alleges that an employer denied or interfered with his substantive rights under the FMLA," while a retaliation claim "alleges that the employer discriminated against him for exercising his FMLA rights." *Stallings v. Hussmann Corp.*, 447 F.3d 1041, 1050 (8th Cir. 2006) (citing 29 U.S.C. § 2615(a)(1)–(2)). We address each of Huber's FMLA claims in turn.

A.

"An employer is prohibited from interfering with, restraining, or denying an employee's exercise of or attempted exercise[ ] of any right contained in the FMLA." *Stallings*, 447 F.3d at 1050 (8th Cir. 2006) (citing 29 U.S.C. § 2615(a)(1)). "An employer's action that deters an employee from participating in protected activities constitutes an 'interference' or 'restraint' of the employee's exercise of his rights." *Id.* "Interference includes ... 'manipulation by a covered employer to avoid responsibilities under FMLA.'" *Id.* (quoting 29 C.F.R. § 825.220(b)).

To succeed on an FMLA interference claim, an employee need only show they were "denied substantive rights under the FMLA for a reason connected with [their] FMLA leave." *Id.* Thus, to prevail on an FMLA interference claim the employee must establish (1) they were eligible for FMLA leave, (2) the employer was on notice of the need for FMLA leave, and (3) the employer denied the employee an FMLA benefit. *Smith v. AS Am., Inc.*, 829 F.3d 616, 621 (8th Cir. 2016). On appeal, Westar does not seriously contest that Huber became eligible for FMLA leave when her diabetic episode caused her to miss more than three days of work. *See Rankin v. Seagate Techs., Inc.*, 246 F.3d 1145, 1147–49 (8th Cir. 2001). Rather, the parties dispute whether Westar was on notice of Huber's eligibility for FMLA leave prior to the company's decision to terminate Huber's employment.

"An employee need not invoke the FMLA by name in order to put an employer on notice that the Act may have relevance to the employee's absence from work." *Thorson v. Gemini, Inc.*, 205 F.3d 370, 381 (8th Cir. 2000). "Under the FMLA, the employer's duties are triggered when the employee provides enough information to put the employer on notice that the employee may be in need of FMLA leave." *Spangler v. Fed. Home Loan Bank of Des Moines*, 278 F.3d 847, 852 (8th Cir. 2002) (citation omitted). For the employer to be on notice of the need for FMLA leave, they must be aware of a "serious health condition" and not simply that an employee is "sick." *Id.* at 852–53. A serious health condition would not typically include the common cold. *Rankin*, 246 F.3d at 1147. Instead, a serious health condition includes an "illness" or "impairment" that causes "[a] period of incapacity ... of more than three consecutive calendar days" or "[t]reatment two or more times by a health care provider." *Id.* (citing 29 C.F.R. § 825.114(a)(2)); *see also* 29 U.S.C. § 2611(11)(B).

If a factfinder determines that an employer was on notice of an employee's serious health condition, the inquiry does not end there. First, the employee must have notified the employer as "soon as practicable." *Spangler*, 278 F.3d at 852 (quoting 29 C.F.R. § 825.302(a)). "This ordinarily means at least verbal notification to the employer within one or two business days of when the need for leave becomes known to the employee." *Id.* (citation omitted) (alterations omitted). Moreover, there must be a causal connection between the termination and the employee's need for FMLA leave. *Stallings*, 447 F.3d at 1050–51.

Huber argues that she put Westar on notice of her need for FMLA leave at least as early as her December 21 call with Kelchen. Westar, on the other hand, asserts that Huber first notified them of her need for FMLA leave when she emailed her request for FMLA paperwork on December 22, after the decision to fire her had been made. As such, Westar argues that Huber failed to provide notification "as soon as practicable." Additionally, Westar argues that even if Huber had notified Westar as soon as practicable, Huber still could not establish FMLA interference because Westar terminated her "for reasons wholly unrelated" to her FMLA needs.

To resolve this issue, we find *Clinkscale v. St. Therese of New Hope* controls. 701 F.3d 825 (8th Cir. 2012). There, the employee was a nurse with undiagnosed situational anxiety disorder. *Id.* at 826. While at work one day, the employee had a panic attack. *Id.* During the attack, the employee spoke to her employer's HR department who instructed her to go home. *Id.* The next day, the employee met with her personal physician regarding the panic attack, after which, she was given a doctor's note requiring her to take sick leave. *Id.* The employee promptly provided the doctor's note to her HR department, who in turn provided FMLA forms for her physician to complete. *Id.* Later that day, the employer called and fired her on grounds of patient abandonment. *Id.* at 827. The employee sued alleging FMLA interference. The employer contended that it had not interfered with the employee's FMLA rights, because the termination occurred before she put the employer on notice. *Id.* at 828. Furthermore, the employer argued that the employee was "terminated for reasons 'wholly unrelated to the FMLA.'" *Id.* at 827. The district court granted summary judgment to the employer.

In reversing the district court, we first considered whether the employee had put her employer on notice when she spoke with HR during her panic attack or when she provided her employer with a doctor's note and received FMLA paperwork. *Id.* at 827–28. We determined that whether the employer was on notice prior to its termination decision was a material question of fact for the jury. *Id.* Additionally, we held that the panic attack was the cause of the alleged patient abandonment and the reason for her need for FMLA leave. *Id.* at 828–29. We explained: "Given the evidence suggesting a causal connection between [the employee's] condition and her 'patient abandonment,' the district court erred in concluding as a matter of law that [the] 'refusal to work … [was] not related to a medical diagnosis of anxiety.'" *Id.* at 829.

Similarly, we conclude that genuine issues of fact exist here. We cannot determine as a matter of law: (1) whether Westar was on notice of Huber's need for FMLA leave prior to its decision to terminate her; (2) whether Huber notified Westar as soon as practicable; and (3) whether there is a causal connection between Huber's diabetic episode and her failure to abide by Westar's call-in policy. Indeed, viewing the facts in the light most favorable to Huber, a reasonable jury could determine that Westar was on notice of Huber's FMLA needs as early as Kelchen's call with Huber's son. This conclusion is buttressed by the fact that Huber had previously brought her disability to the attention of both Kelchen and Thayer when she requested accommodations related to her diabetes. Likewise, a jury could determine that Huber's call to Kelchen on the morning of December 21 was the soonest she could practicably notify Westar. If Westar was on notice, Rowe's refusal to provide Huber with FMLA paperwork on multiple occasions, along with Westar's termination of Huber, could constitute FMLA interference. Accordingly, we find that genuine issues of fact remain as to Huber's FMLA interference claim.

B.

Huber also asserts an FMLA retaliation claim. "The difference between [interference and retaliation] claims is that the interference claim merely requires proof that the employer denied the employee his entitlements under the FMLA, while the retaliation claim requires proof of retaliatory intent." *Stallings*, 447 F.3d at 1051. "Basing an adverse employment action on an employee's use of leave, or in other words, retaliation for exercise of Leave Act rights, is therefore actionable." *Allen Health Sys., Inc.*, 302 F.3d at 832. Where a plaintiff asserts an FMLA retaliation claim, absent direct evidence, we use the same *McDonnell Douglas* burden-shifting framework as ADA discrimination claims. *Hudson v. Tyson Fresh Meats, Inc.*, 787 F.3d 861, 866 (8th Cir. 2015). A plaintiff must show: (1) they "engaged in protected conduct"; (2) they "suffered a materially adverse employment action"; and (3) "the materially adverse action was causally linked to the protected conduct." *Wierman v. Casey's Gen. Stores*, 638 F.3d 984, 999 (8th Cir. 2011). A "materially adverse action" is one that "deter[s] a reasonable employee from making a charge of employment discrimination." *Id.* (citation omitted). Termination from employment is a materially adverse action. *Id.* If a plaintiff establishes their prima facie case, the burden of production shifts to the employer to "articulate a legitimate, nondiscriminatory reason for its action," after which the burden shifts back to the plaintiff to show the employer's reason is pretextual. *Id.*

Regarding the first element of a plaintiff's prima facie case, an employee must provide their employer with notice as soon as practicable that they may need FMLA leave. *Id.* at 1000. Thus, here, as with Huber's interference claim, a genuine issue of fact exists regarding whether she provided notice to Westar of her need for FMLA leave and, if so, whether she provided Westar with notice as soon as practicable.

Regarding Huber's burden of showing both a causal connection between her FMLA rights and Westar's termination decision, as well as pretext, we are faced with issues of fact similar to Huber's ADA discrimination claim. For example, the very close temporal proximity between Huber's exercise of her FMLA rights and Westar's adverse employment action may support a finding of causation or pretext. *See Allen Health Sys.*,

Inc., 302 F.3d at 833 (finding two weeks between protected FMLA activity and adverse employment action were "extremely close in time" and therefore raised an issue of fact on retaliation). Moreover, because Westar's reason for terminating Huber may be causally connected to her need for FMLA leave, a genuine issue of fact remains. *See Wierman*, 638 F.3d at 1000 (finding that, on an FMLA retaliation claim, an employer's reason for terminating pregnant employee—because she "was tardy or absent from work for pregnancy-related reasons"—was intertwined with the employee's disability); *see also Clinkscale*, 701 F.3d at 828; *Caldwell v. Holland of Texas, Inc.*, 208 F.3d 671, 677 (8th Cir. 2000). Accordingly, we also find that genuine issues of fact remain for Huber's FMLA retaliation claim.

V.

For the foregoing reasons, we reverse and remand the district court's grant of summary judgment to Westar on Huber's ADA, NFEPA, and FMLA claims.

Issues for Consideration

- Was Westar put on notice that Huber had a disability?
- What are the implications of a manager making comments like "that's a you problem, not a me problem" in relation to requests tied to an employee's medical condition?
- Was Waystar's denial of Huber's FMLA claim appropriate under the circumstances?
- Did Waystar interfere with Huber's prospective FMLA claim?

Workforce Changes and Recent Developments Impacting Reasonable Accommodations

Since the passage of the ADA, federal FMLA and most recently, numerous state paid family leave laws across the country, the way work is performed across all industries has changed significantly. The prospect of working from home for many professional jobs was barely prevalent thirty years ago. However, working outside of the traditional office today has been normalized through advances in technology and of course, out of precaution for many jobs during the COVID-19 pandemic. These changes have had a direct impact on how workplace accommodations are considered and more specifically, they've raised new questions about whether an employee can perform the essential functions of the job with more access to technology than ever before. Workplace accommodation requirements under the ADA are designed to remove barriers for employees through a modification or adjustment and many forms of technology have helped on this front. Connection through mobile and video have bridged conventional communication gaps making the concept of "working from anywhere" much more feasible for some jobs.

Advances in technology. The meteoric rise of cell phones since the early 2000's has fundamentally changed the way we communicate with each other. For business, it's bridged a connection that would typically end with leaving the office, or workplace, at the end of a shift. The phone has enabled some employees to continue working at all times of the day, including while traveling. For many roles, the core functions of the job could now be performed both inside and outside of the office. Our ability to communicate with colleagues, team members and leadership has become incredibly easy through these devices and some employers have embraced this transformation by enabling remote work or even hybrid work where employees have the choice of working in an office setting or somewhere else.

In addition to phones, advances with computers and tablets have also enabled many employees to work from anywhere. While this has been wildly beneficial to increasing productivity and expediting projects, it has limited an employer's ability to argue an undue hardship by way of impact to business operations when considering an accommodation asking for flexibility tied to an in-office presence. It is important to remember that with all accommodation requests, there must be a disability and medical justification for needing the accommodation. Therefore, within the purview of the ADA, an employee's personal preference to work from home, or anywhere outside of their workplace, would not qualify them for an accommodation. Deciphering between a personal preference and a medical accommodation has emerged as one of the biggest challenges for employers. Technology has undoubtedly made many jobs easier to perform and it's paved the way for more creative accommodations that keep employees working rather than on leave.

Traditionally speaking, the question of whether in-person attendance is an essential function of the job relied on a few key factors:

(1) whether the job could be performed from home (or outside of the office);

(2) whether face-to-face interactions were required with colleagues or customers to perform the essential functions of the job; and

(3) whether the employee needed to work with tools, or equipment, on-site to perform the job.

While the above list is not an exhaustive list of factors to determine whether an in-office presence is required for an employee to perform the essential functions of the job, it does highlight an example of how technological advances have impacted jobs that have traditionally been performed in an office setting.

Let's use an attorney whose practice focuses on estate planning. This attorney would traditionally meet prospective clients in-person at the firm's offices and if they were signed up as clients, they would work on their case and maintain the documentation in a case file stored in the office. After several years of maintaining paper files, the firm decided to go digital and maintain all case files within a secure, claims management system. This system could be accessed securely from anywhere there is a wi-fi signal and attorneys at the firm could access—and manage—their files online. At around the same time, the court system where this firm was located implemented an electronic filing system where attorneys could submit documentation directly to the court. Clerks and judges now had the ability to review motions and submissions to expedite routine court proceedings. Prior to either of these technological upgrades, this attorney's in-person presence was an essential function of their job so they could manage their claim files and go in person to submit documentation on behalf of their clients.

With both the firm and the court system now enabling case management electronically, it raises the question of whether this specific job as an attorney could be performed outside of the traditional office. Note that in this example, the emphasis here is how technology fundamentally impacted whether in-person presence would still be considered an essential function of the job. The attorney may still be required to meet clients in person, manage a team or appear in court proceedings, so the notion that this role could be performed 100% remote is not absolute. This is merely an example to showcase how a traditional in-office position had changed with the advent of technology.

Evolution of jobs. Over the last three decades, the way in which jobs have been performed has fundamentally changed due in large part to technology. For many roles that relied on in-person or face-to-face connectivity like sales, the core components—or the essential functions—have adjusted accordingly. For example, a direct salesperson may have gone door to door in neighborhoods selling products to prospective customers. This tactic was relatively common before the internet changed the way companies could advertise and sell their products. Having a salesperson go door-to-door to try and sell products became unnecessary when that same customer could be reached through the internet or through email. For this salesperson, their hypothetical job responsibilities selling products to consumers at their home may have shifted to focusing on e-commerce and digital methods in an office setting. As a result, the requirement that they be able to walk or stand for long periods of time became no longer necessary. In the context of workplace accommodations, it is precisely these job functions that are scrutinized when determining whether an accommodation would be reasonable. While it may not have been reasonable for a door-to-door salesperson to work from home before the advent of the internet and email, this very technology raises the question of whether this work could be performed anywhere.

Our ability to communicate well beyond traditional methods like the phone and in-person meetings has had a direct impact upon the reasonableness standard when considering accommodations. For those jobs still requiring in-person attendance like a grocery store clerk, these employers still have an opportunity to think creatively about different ways to accommodate their employees. Modified duty or light duty has become a prospective, temporary way to support employees while they recover before resorting to leave, or job reassignment, which are often seen as accommodations of last resort.

The next frontier of technology is squarely focused on artificial intelligence (AI). There have been a number of productivity gains through new AI technology, but there are still questions about whether this technology will be useful to support medical accommodations. The fundamentals suggest that in certain situations, the right tool could absolutely help an employee with a medical accommodation request but it's far too early to generalize the effectiveness of specific software or products.

COVID-19 impact. The global pandemic upended virtually every assumption we had about how and where work could be performed for many jobs—particularly those in an office setting. For positions that were historically performed inside an office, if it was not expressly stated in a job description, it was universally assumed an in-office presence was an essential function of the job. With that assumption in play, workplace accommodations were, for the most part, focused on modifications and adjustments on-site with the exception of leave and job reassignment. Work-from-home requests prior to the pandemic still had to be considered but they were not nearly as common as they are now. In the early stages of the pandemic (March 2020), many employers quickly transitioned their workforce to work-from-home out of an abundance of caution and in line with several shelter-in-place orders. What we learned over the next few years is that for many roles, the concept of working from home or outside of the traditional office space did not have the presumed detrimental impact that concerned employers in the first place. With the focus of ensuring employee safety and maintaining business operations, enabling employees to operate outside of the office accomplished both goals. The question of whether these employees were more, or less, productive is still very much up for debate. For those employers that have objective metrics to measure the productivity of their employees, this issue of productivity was much easier to decipher during this time. For those employers that assumed productivity through an employee's presence in the office, the issue of productivity was much more difficult to ascertain.

It is critical to point out that the pandemic impacted employers very differently. Depending on their industry, the services provided or the products they sold, many employees were forced to work differently.

Face-to-face meetings were commonly replaced with video meetings and as the pandemic wore on, questions arose as to the effectiveness of video versus in-person. There is still no clear answer to this question, but the issue most certainly had an impact on the essential functions of the job analysis.

Chapter VII

Federal Social Security Disability Benefits

Following the passage of the Social Security Act in 1935, this landmark body of law did not contain provisions for disability insurance. However, twenty years later, in 1956, President Dwight D. Eisenhower signed amendments to the Social Security Act establishing the Social Security Disability Insurance program.[1] Also known as SSDI, the program operates similar to an insurance policy with a portion of an employee's social security taxes set aside to fund the disability program. Unlike private insurance, employees working in the United States cannot opt out of paying social security taxes. And more importantly in terms of eligibility, employees are not automatically entitled to SSDI benefits if they allege disability. As we will explore, there is a formal application process heavily reliant on medical documentation to support and substantiate a claim.

Another disability program within the purview of the Social Security Administration (SSA) is known as Supplemental Security Income (SSI), which was implemented in 1974 under President Richard Nixon.[2] Like the SSDI program, SSI requires a disability but eligibility hinges on "limited income and resources." SSI benefits may also be available for children, which has a specific criteria for meeting the definition of disability based on severe, or marked, limitations of the child. What distinguishes SSI benefits from SSDI are the strict income and asset thresholds where even if a person—or child—could be found disabled, if they exceed the statutory thresholds in place, they would not be eligible for SSI benefits. Alternatively, for eligibility into the SSDI program, a disabled individual could have unlimited assets and still be eligible for disability benefits (actively working and earning income could invalidate these benefits, but generally speaking, assets would not).

Both SSDI and SSI are governed and administered by the Social Security Administration. While eligibility for the program is different, both contain comprehensive application processes handled by a network of claim and hearing offices across the country. In determining whether a person is "disabled" under the Social Security Act, both programs also leverage what's known as the "5 Step Sequential Evaluation," which

1. John R. Kearney, "Social Security and the 'D' in OASDI: The History of a Federal Program Insuring Earners Against Disability," *Social Security Bulletin* 66, no. 3, released August 2006, https://www.ssa.gov/policy/docs/ssb/v66n3/v66n3p1.html.

2. *Id.*

is the SSA's foundational evaluation process for all disability claims. We'll analyze each step of this process later in this section.

The regulations covering both programs can be found in the Code of Federal Regulations. For SSDI, the relevant section is **Part 404—Federal Old-Age, Survivors and Disability Insurance**. For SSI, the relevant section is **Part 416—Supplemental Security Income for the Aged, Blind, and Disabled.** In addition to these regulations, which outline the provisions of the Social Security Act, there are additional texts that help adjudicators and claims processors make decisions on claims. Those include: Social Security Rulings, Social Security Administration's Program Operations Manual System (POMS), the Social Security Handbook and lastly, federal case law.

Qualifying for Social Security Disability Insurance (SSDI) and Supplemental Security Income (SSI)

Social Security Disability Insured (SSDI) Status. Individuals qualify for federal social security disability benefits under the SSDI program through the payment of taxes. A person gains "insured status" by gaining quarters of coverage through the payment of social security taxes throughout the year. You can gain a maximum of 4 quarters each year and each quarter requires a specific dollar amount of earnings. For example, in 2025, the dollar amount needed for 1 credit was $1,810 of earnings. Therefore, a total of $7,240 in covered, taxable earnings was needed to get the maximum 4 credits in 2025. These dollar amount thresholds are always subject to changing each year and as an example, the dollar amount needed for 1 credit in 2023 was $1,510 ($6,040 for the maximum 4 credits in 2023).

As a general rule, Social Security uses a "20/40 requirement" which means a person must have 20 quarters of coverage in a 40-quarter period.[3] This means that generally speaking, a person would have eligibility if they've earned the maximum 4 quarters of coverage in 5 years over a 10-year period (40 quarters of coverage available over 10 years). A person's insured status is often the first step in the disability determination process because before a claim can even be considered on the merits, a person must be insured for the benefits. It must be noted that having insured status does not automatically entitle a person to these disability benefits. This just validates their eligibility for the SSDI program. If a person does not quality for SSDI, however, SSI could be an option if they meet the limited income and resource threshold.

Eligibility under the SSDI program can also be quickly determined by viewing a Social Security Earnings record. Today, these can be accessed online through Social Security's website (ssa.gov) and the report shows a person's monthly retirement and disability benefit calculated by their annual earnings.

3. Social Security Administration, "Code of Federal Regulations § 404.130. How we determine disability insured status." accessed 2025, https://www.ssa.gov/OP_Home/cfr20/404/404-0130.htm.

This calculation of quarters is critical to determining what Social Security refers to as a person's "date last insured (DLI)." Citing § 20 CFR 404.131, Social Security's Program Operations Manual System (POMS) defines the DLI as the "last day of the quarter a claimant meets insured status for disability or blindness."[4] The most practical way to conceptualize this is the claimant's alleged onset of disability must come before their DLI. If their DLI comes before they are claiming when they became disabled, they would not have the requisite insured status and would qualify for SSDI. A claimant's DLI will always be the last day of the calendar quarter (March 31, June 30, September 30 or December 31).

In conjunction with a claimant's DLI is the importance of an established disability onset date. For purposes of filing a claim for disability benefits, a claimant must allege a specific date of disability. Acknowledging the difficulty with pinpointing the specific date that a disability or disabling medical condition began, a claimant can look to when the condition prevented, or significantly hindered, their ability to work and earn quarters of coverage. A common practice here is to use the date that the claimant stopped working or when they began to earn significantly less due to their alleged disabling condition. To illustrate the important relationship between a claimant's DLI and their alleged onset date of disability, here are few examples.

> *Example 1:* Claimant is alleging their disability began on April 1, 2023. They have a DLI of June 30, 2026. This claimant would have insured status through June 30, 2026.
>
> Note that in this example, the claimant's insured status is in the future. This means that they've earned enough quarters to maintain their eligibility through June 30, 2026. If they were to return to work, they could earn more quarters of credit and their DLI would go further out in time.
>
> *Example 2:* Claimant is alleging their disability began on September 10, 2024. They have a DLI of March 31, 2023. This claimant would have insured status through March 31, 2023, but if the alleged disability began after the DLI, they would not be eligible for SSDI benefits with this established onset date.
>
> In this example, when a claimant's DLI is in the past, they can still be eligible for disability benefits if the alleged onset of disability is before the DLI. Here, the claimant is alleging a disability that began over a year after the DLI so they would not qualify for the benefits.

Qualifying for Supplemental Security Income (SSI). SSI is a federal program that pays benefits to disabled adults and children who have "limited income and resources." This program is for individuals applying for disability benefits who have never worked

---

4. Social Security Administration, "Program Operations Manual System (POMS), DI 25501.320 Date Last Insured (DLI) and the Established Onset Date (EOD), Effective 8/12/2015–Present, https://secure.ssa.gov/apps10/poms.nsf/lnx/0425501320.

or who have a limited work history.[5] Once an application for SSI benefits is filed, SSA will conduct a thorough analysis of the individual's household income and resources. This involves a comprehensive review household income and items specifically listed as resources by SSA. The resource limits for 2025 was $2,000 for an individual and $3,000 for a couple. The overall value of income and resources is part of an initial determination of whether a person is even eligible for SSI benefits.[6] Per SSA, resources are things a person owns and include:[7]

- Cash;
- Bank accounts;
- Stocks, mutual funds, and US savings bonds;
- Land;
- Life insurance;
- Personal property;
- Vehicles;
- Anything else you own which could be changed to cash and used for food or shelter; and
- Deemed resources.

Deemed resources are those attributable to an individual who applies for SSI through a spouse, parent, parent's spouse, sponsor of a noncitizen, or sponsor's spouse. According to SSI rules, this deeming of resources uses the same monetary limits ($2000/individual and $3,000/couple) to determine eligibility:

- If a child under age 18 lives with one parent, $2,000 of the parent's total countable resources does not count;
- If the child lives with 2 parents, $3,000 does not count.[8]

SSA also lays out resources that do not count when determining eligibility for the program. These include:[9]

- The home you live in and the land it is on;
- One vehicle, regardless of value, if you or a member of your household use it for transportation;
- Household goods and personal effects (e.g., your wedding and engagement rings);
- Life insurance policies with a combined face value of $1,500 or less;

---

5. Social Security Administration, "Supplemental Security Income (SSI)," accessed 2025, https://www.ssa.gov/ssi.

6. Social Security Administration, "Understanding Supplemental Security Income SSI Resources—2025 Edition," https://www.ssa.gov/ssi/text-resources-ussi.htm.

7. *Id.*

8. *Id.*

9. *Id.*

- Burial spaces for you or your immediate family;
- Burial funds for you and your spouse, each valued at $1,500 or less;
- Property you or your spouse use in a trade or business, or on your job if you work for someone else;
- If you are disabled or blind, money or property you have set aside under a Plan to Achieve Self-Support (PASS); and
- Up to $100,000 of funds in an Achieving a Better Life Experience (ABLE) account established through a State ABLE program.

SSA also includes an additional list of resources that would not count for purposes of SSI eligibility. Some of those include: flexible spending accounts (for health care costs), disaster relief, grants or scholarships and federal tax refunds. This is not an exhaustive list and this list can be found at: https://www.ssa.gov/ssi/text-resources-ussi.htm.

Once an SSI application is filed, SSA will request all available financial information from the claimant to determine eligibility. SSA will review documentation as well as claimant statements about any assets, income and resources. If the claimant meets the household income and resource thresholds, SSA will then determine if the claimant is disabled under their rules.

Definition of disability under the Code of Federal Regulations. Both SSDI and SSI contain the same definition of disability for adults. Under Sections 404.1505 (SSDI) and 416.905 (SSI), the basic definition of disability is defined as:

> the inability to do any substantial gainful activity by reason of any medically determinable physical or mental impairment which can be expected to result in death or which has lasted or can expected to last for a continuous period of not less than 12 months. To meet this definition, you must have a severe impairment that makes you unable to do your past relevant work or any other substantial gainful work that exists in the national economy ...[10]

SSA's definition of disability lays the foundation for how the agency makes a disability determination using what is commonly referred to as the 5-step sequential evaluation. This is the framework for assessing any work activity and associated income, the medical impairment and whether the impairment prevents the claimant from performing any work they performed in the last 5 years[11] or any other work in the local or national economy.

5-Step sequential evaluation of disability. For both SSDI and SSI, this evaluation process serves as the legal formula for determining whether an adult claimant is disabled. While it hinges mostly on the claimant's medical condition, there is also an analysis on the ability to perform any kind of work based on the claimant's limitations, restrictions and overall ability to perform tasks in what Social Security calls a com-

10. Code of Federal Regulations §404.1505 and §416.905.

11. Past relevant work (PRW) previously looked at a claimant's work history over the last 15 years. On June 22, 2024, SSA changed the lookback period to 5 years.

petitive work environment. Social Security follows these steps in a "set order" and depending on the outcome of each step, they will either render a claimant not disabled or move on in the evaluation process. This process is summarily laid out in the Code of Federal Regulations, Sections § 404.1520 for SSDI and § 416.920 for SSI respectively.

Step 1: Is the claimant performing substantial gainful activity (SGA)?

The first step of this evaluation looks at whether the claimant is working. SSA has simplified this analysis by attaching dollar amounts to the question of whether the claimant is working. In 2025, the SGA limit for non-blind individuals was $1,620 per month and $2,700 per month for blind individuals. This means that if a claimant earned over this amount for any month during the time they are claiming to be disabled, the inference is that they were in a working capacity and performing SGA. While there are a variety of exceptions to the technical performance of SGA, a claimant must explain and justify their earnings if they have a dollar amount that exceeds the set monthly SGA amounts. SGA includes all wages (from an employer or self-employment), royalties, bonuses and any income that may not have been reported to the Internal Revenue Service (off-the-books wages).

If a claimant has wages that on their earnings record that don't exceed SGA limits, they may be entitled to disability benefits for that month and it may even help their claim as indication that although they tried, they were not able to perform work in a competitive environment. SGA limits are typically set by SSA in the 4th quarter of the year for the following year. For example, SSA has set the monthly SGA limit at $1,690 per month for non-blind individuals and $2,830 per month for blind individuals. Here is a chart to illustrate the annual fluctuation of these limits:

Year	SGA (Non-Blind)	SGA (Blind)
2024	$1,550	$2,590
2025	$1,620	$2,700
2026	$1,690	$2,830

Social Security adds additional clarity around SGA by defining "substantial work activity" and "gainful work activity" in CFR § 404.1572. The regulations define "substantial work activity" as "work activity that involves doing significant physical or mental activity" even if performed on a part-time basis. "Gainful work activity" is work that is "performed for pay or profit," whether or not financial profit is actually achieved. Activities like household tasks, taking care of yourself, attending school or social activities are generally not considered as substantial or gainful.[12]

Another critical component of the SGA analysis is that any portion of a claimant's apparent income that is not directly tied to the claimant's productivity is not con-

12. Social Security Administration, "Code of Federal Regulations § 404.1572, What we mean by substantial gainful activity," accessed 2025, https://www.ssa.gov/OP_Home/cfr20/404/404-1572.htm.

sidered to be income for purposes of SGA. More specifically, if a person is receiving taxable income, but not through actual physical or mental work activity, this may not be considered income. The most common examples of this involve pensions, annuities, rental income or interest from investments. In these examples, claimants may have dollar amounts on their earnings records, but the income may not have been gained through work activity. Therefore, they may still have eligibility for disability benefits if they can provide evidence that explains how the passive income was obtained.

Note that the analysis here is quite different for an SSI claim. While SSA is interested in any kind of work activity even for an SSI claim, any kind of passive income could make a claimant ineligible for SSI benefits because of the strict income thresholds. Overall, the agency is interested in whether there is any kind of work activity and what, if any, earnings were associated with it.

If SSA determines that the claimant either earned, or is earning, over SGA limits, the evaluation process ends with a finding of not disabled per SSA rules. If SSA determines that the claimant has not performed SGA dating back to their alleged disability onset date, the evaluation process will move to step 2.

Step 2: Does the claimant have a severe medical impairment?

At this step, SSA shifts their evaluation to the merits of the disability claim. Here, they are specifically looking at the severity of claimant's medical condition (or multiple conditions if applicable). When factoring in the agency's duration requirement[13] set forth in their definition of disability, the key question whether the claimant's impairment(s) are "severe" turns on whether it interferes with the claimant's ability to perform a full-time, 8-hour per day, 40-hours per week, job. If the condition is not expected to last for more than 12 months (and has not lasted or is expected to result in death) or it has a marginal impact on a claimant's ability to perform work, the evaluation will end at step 2. Alternatively, if the claimant's physical or mental impairment(s) have any impact on their ability to perform their job and their condition meets the duration requirements, the evaluation process will proceed to step 3.

Step 3: Does the physical or mental impairment(s) meet or equal a medical listing in CFR 404, Appendix 1, subpart P?

As part of the disability evaluation overall, SSA created what is commonly referred to as the medical listings. This listing of these impairments and medical conditions apply to both adults (Part A) and children (Part B) and are all published online. Each listing contains specific criteria to indicate an impairment severe enough to prevent a claimant from doing any gainful activity—or in the case of a child, severe enough to cause marked to severe functional limitations.[14] If a claimant's medical condition "meets" or "equals" the criteria listed within the relevant listing, they typically can

13. The condition must last for 12 months, expect to last 12 months or expect to result in death.

14. Social Security Administration, "Disability Evaluation Under Social Security, Part III—Listing of Impairments," accessed 2025, https://www.ssa.gov/disability/professionals/bluebook/listing-impairments.htm.

be found disabled at this step without the need to move in the evaluation process. This can only happen through medical documentation that substantiates meeting the specific listing.

To explain how these listings operate within the framework from the evaluation process, Social Security provides the following overview:

> The criteria in the Listing of Impairments apply only to one step of the multi-step sequential evaluation process. At that step, the presence of an impairment that meets the criteria in the Listing of Impairments (or that is of equal severity) is usually sufficient to establish that an individual who is not working is disabled. However, the absence of a listing-level impairment does not mean the individual is not disabled. Rather, it merely requires the adjudicator to move on to the next step of the process and apply other rules in order to resolve the issue of disability.[15]

Listing of Impairments—Adult Listings (Part A)[16]

1.00 Musculoskeletal Disorders	2.00 Special Senses and Speech	3.00 Respiratory Disorders
4.00 Cardiovascular System	5.00 Digestive Disorders	6.00 Genitourinary Disorders
7.00 Hematological Disorders	8.00 Skin Disorders	9.00 Endocrine Disorders
10.00 Congenital Disorders that Affect Multiple Body Systems	11.00 Neurological Disorders	12.00 Mental Disorders
13.00 Cancer (Malignant Neoplastic Diseases)	14.00 Immune System Disorders	

Simply put, a finding of disability at step 3 by meeting or equaling a medical listing is rather difficult. Each listing is comprised of very specific medical criteria where claimants often need to substantiate multiple components of the listing to be found medically disabled at step 3.

To put the difficulty of meeting a Social Security medical listing into perspective, here is an example of a current medical listing related to a back condition—typically one of the highest claim types along with other musculoskeletal conditions:

15. *Id.*

16. Social Security Administration, "Disability Evaluation Under Social Security; Medical/Professional Relations; Listing of Impairments—Adult Listings (Part A)," https://www.ssa.gov/disability/professionals/bluebook/AdultListings.htm.

1.15 Disorders of the skeletal spine resulting in compromise of a nerve root(s), documented by A, B, C and D:

A. Neuro-anatomic (radicular) distribution of one or more of the following symptoms consistent with compromise of the affected nerve root(s):

1. Pain; or
2. Paresthesia; or
3. Muscle fatigue.

AND

B. Radicular distribution of neurological signs present during physical examination or on a diagnostic test and evidenced by 1, 2, and either 3 or 4:

1. Muscle weakness and
2. Sign(s) of nerve root irritation, tension, or compression, consistent with compromise of the affected nerve root; and
3. Sensory changes evidenced by:
   a. Decreased sensation; or
   b. Sensory nerve deficit (abnormal sensory nerve latency) or electrodiagnostic testing; or
4. Decreased deep tendon reflexes.

AND

C. Findings on imaging consistent with compromise of a nerve root(s) in the cervical or lumbosacral spine.

AND

D. Impairment-related physical limitation of musculoskeletal functioning that has lasted, or is expected to last, for a continuous period of at least 12 months, and medical documentation of at least *one* of the following:

1. A documented medical need for a walker, bilateral canes or bilateral crutches or a wheeled and seated mobility device involving the use of both hands; or
2. An inability to use *one* upper extremity to independently initiate, sustain, and complete work-related activities involving fine and gross movements *and* a documented medical need for a one-handed, hand-held assistive device that requires the use of the other upper extremity or a wheeled and seated mobility device involving the use of one hand; or
3. An inability to use *both* upper extremities to the extent that neither can be used to independently initiate, sustain, and complete work-related activities involving fine and gross movements.

As you can see from medical listing 1.15, a lower back condition would have to be accompanied by several associated symptoms that are well documented in alignment with this specific listing. Simply having consistent pain or functional limitations from the condition would not justify a finding of disabled at this step of the evaluation process. This listing is not necessary representative of all of the listings, but it does illustrate how rigorous the medical documentation requirements are to be found disabled at this step.

If the claimant's medical condition does meet or equal a listing, it typically means that their condition(s) is severe enough to be found disabled without an analysis of their ability to work. The implication of meeting or equaling the specific medical listing is that the impairment is so severe, it would render the claimant incapable of performing any kind of work. In contrast, if the claimant's medical condition(s) is not substantiated with documentation that would be sufficient to meet or equal a listing, the evaluation process shifts to looking at whether the claimant is capable of performing jobs they may have previously performed or any other kind of work.

Step 4: Can the claimant perform their past relevant work?

At step 4, the analysis shifts to a focus on the claimant's functional capacity and their ability to perform the work they've done in the last 5 years. Past relevant work previously used a lookback period of 15 years but in 2024, SSA issued a policy change to reducing the lookback period to 5 years. This means that at step 4, SSA will only look at the jobs performed in the prior 5 years and whether the claimant could perform those jobs even with their impairments. For a claimant with several jobs over the last 15 years, the agency previously had to assess all of these jobs in conjunction with their functional limitations. So in effect, the 2024 policy change simplified the evaluation process at step 4. If the claimant is declared able to perform their past relevant work, SSA will find the claimant is not disabled and the evaluation will not proceed to step 5.

A critical part of determining whether a claimant can perform their past relevant work is ascertaining the claimant's "residual functional capacity," or more commonly referred to as the claimant's RFC. CFR § 404.1545 (SSDI) and § 416.945 (SSI) address this respectively by defining it as the most a claimant can do in a work setting despite any physical or mental limitations. A claimant's RFC is one of the most important aspects of their disability claim because it indicates what they can, or cannot do, in a competitive work environment across the full spectrum of jobs. In looking at the claimant's physical and mental capabilities, SSA will review medical documentation to assess the ability to perform routine work activities throughout the day. On the physical side, this would include sitting, standing, walking, pushing, pulling, etc. On the mental side, an assessment would include ability to focus and concentrate during the day or ability to understand and follow simple to complex instructions.[17] The claimant's RFC plays a major role in a disability claim because it incorporates all alleged restrictions and limitations into a hypothetical work setting for the purposes of determining whether the claimant could perform past work or any other kind of work.

Social Security Ruling 24-2p contains a policy interpretation ruling specific to how SSA evaluates past relevant work. Within this ruling, SSA provides some important characteristics of past relevant work:[18]

---

17. Social Security Administration, "CFR § 404.1545 and § 416.945, Your Residual Functional Capacity," accessed 2025, https://www.ssa.gov/OP_Home/cfr20/404/404-1545.htm; https://www.ssa.gov/OP_Home/cfr20/416/416-0945.htm.

18. Social Security Administration, "Social Security Ruling 24-2p: Titles II and XVI: How we evaluate Past Relevant Work: Policy Interpretation Ruling, *Federal Register* 89, no. 110, page 48479, effective date June 22, 2024, https://www.ssa.gov/OP_Home/rulings/di/02/SSR2024-02-di-02.html.

- Work started and stopped in fewer than 30 days—SSA will not consider to be past relevant work if it lasted less than 30 days.
- RFC and past relevant work—SSA will consider a claimant's RFC to determine whether they could meet the functional demands of performing their past relevant work in the last 5 years.
- A claimant's work history—SSA acknowledges the claimant is the primary source of information for purposes of their work history but things like an SSA earnings record or previous employer records can help with determining whether the work can be classified as past relevant work.

Per SSR 24-2p, if SSA finds the claimant has the capacity to perform past relevant work, their findings must include: an established RFC, their past relevant work, consideration of their physical or mental limitations/restrictions in relation to their past relevant work and ultimately, a finding that the claimant possesses an RFC to perform their past relevant work as they performed it or as the job is generally performed in the national economy.[19]

Through this analysis at step 4, if SSA finds the claimant is not capable of performing their past relevant work, the evaluation moves onto step 5 where the preeminent question is whether the claimant is capable of performing any other kind of work in the local or national economy.

Step 5: Can the claimant perform any other work in the local or national economy?

At this stage of the evaluation process, the claimant's insured status has been validated along with findings that their impairments have met the durational requirements and have been found to be severe enough to prevent them from performing their past relevant work (last 5 years). Making it to this step also means the claimant's condition did not meet or equal a medical listing. It is important to note that for steps 1–4, the burden of proof rests with the claimant but at step 5, this burden actually shifts to SSA to show that the claimant may be able to perform some kind of work in the local or national economy. Like step 4's evaluation of past relevant work, SSA will consider the claimant's RFC but will also consider the claimant's age, education and overall work experience "to determine if [the claimant] can make an adjustment to other work."[20] This step incorporates age and education for the purpose of determining whether the claimant can adjust to another kind of job or whether they possess transferable skills from their past relevant work that would enable them to perform a different kind of job.

Age is relevant at step 5 because once a claimant reaches 50 years old, SSA acknowledges that adjusting to another kind of job becomes more difficult. Education is also important to determine whether the claimant possesses knowledge (through their education level) that would help them adjust to other work. SSA leverages a set of

---

19. *Id.*

20. Social Security Administration, "Code of Federal Regulations § 404.1520, Evaluation of disability in general," accessed 2025, https://www.ssa.gov/OP_Home/cfr20/404/404-1520.htm.

guidelines that take into account age, education and previous work experience and it operates like a formula to determine whether a claimant can be found disabled or not. These guidelines are known as the Medical Vocational Guidelines and are part of the Code of Federal Regulations, Appendix 2 to Subpart P of Part 404.

Under the Medical Vocational Guidelines, age categories include a younger individual (18–49), closely approaching advanced age (50–54) and advanced age (55 and over). Education is classified as "limited or less" (referring to less than a high school education), high school graduate or more, along with some specificity of each level based on assumed entry into skilled or semi-skilled work. Lastly, previous work experience under the guidelines includes unskilled or none, skilled or semi-skilled without transferable skills and skilled or semi-skilled with transferable skills. When a claimant's age, education level and previous work experience are plugged into the Medical Vocational Guidelines, a decision of disabled or not disabled is directed.

Note that the Medical Vocational Guidelines do not have to be used at step 5 for every single claim. This is one way to determine whether a claimant can be found disabled based solely on their age, education and previous work experience. A claimant's medical condition and related symptoms, restrictions and limitations, which dictate their RFC, will also be taken under consideration to determine what, if any, work can be performed. Consider these following examples of how the Medical Vocational Guidelines are used:

> *Example 1:* Claimant is 52 years old with less than a high school education (8th grade) and worked as a general laborer for the past 25 years.
>
> Under this example, if we assume that this claimant's previous work experience is classified as skilled or semi-skilled but these skills are not transferable, a finding of disabled can be found pursuant to Rule 201.10.

Rule	Age	Education	Previous Work Experience	Decision
201.10	Closely approaching advanced age	Limited or less	Skilled or semi-skilled—skills not transferable	Disabled

> *Example 2*: Claimant is 41 years old with a high school education and worked as a grocery store clerk for the last 5 years.
>
> Under this example, if we assume that this claimant's work experience is classified as unskilled, a finding of not disabled would be found pursuant to 201.27.

Rule	Age	Education	Previous Work Experience	Decision
201.27	Younger individual age 18–44	High school graduate or more	Unskilled	Not disabled

> Note that in this previous example, while the Medical Vocational Guidelines would render a decision of not disabled, these guidelines are specifically looking at age, education and previous work experience. The claimant in this example may have an RFC that would significantly hinder their ability to perform other jobs or even render them incapable of performing any kind of work due to the severity of their medical condition(s). The focus of these guidelines are vocational patterns that assume a claimant's capabilities based on their age, education and previous work experience. For SSA and claimant's representatives, they provide a viable option to substantiate and justify a particular finding or legal theory.[21]
>
> If at any step of the sequential evaluation process, a claimant is found capable of performing some other kind of work based on their RFC or they are capable of adjusting to another kind of work based on their age, education and previous work experience, they will be found not disabled at this step. If they are rendered incapable of performing their past work or any other kind of work, they may be found disabled at this step.

Child SSI and the 6 domains for consideration. A key distinction with SSI benefits when compared to SSDI is eligibility for children. While both require disability, the SSDI program's eligibility is based solely on taxable earnings. SSDI's insured status is dictated by quarterly credits based solely the claimant's taxed social security contributions. Therefore, children under the age of 18 and without any kind of work history would only be eligible for SSI benefits. Like adults, children are also subject to the "limited income and resources" threshold but through the household, rather than themselves. Parents and/or caretakers of the child claimant alleging disability would be taken into account for purposes of calculating eligibility for the SSI benefit.

Another distinguishing component of child SSI is the definition of disability per CFR § 416.906, Basic definition of disability for children:

> If you are under 18, we will consider you disabled if you have a medically determinable physical or mental impairment or combination of impairments that causes marked and severe functional limitations, and that can be expected to cause death or that has lasted or can be expected to last for a continuous period of not less than 12 months. Notwithstanding the preceding sentence, if you file a new application for benefits and you are engaging in substantial gainful activity, we will not consider you disabled. We discuss our rules for determining disability in children who file new applications in §§ 416.924 through 416.924b and §§ 416.925 through 416.926a.[22]

21. Social Security Administration, "Code of Federal Regulations, Appendix to Subpart P of Part 404—Medical Vocational Guidelines, Sections 200.00–204.00," accessed 2025, https://www.ssa.gov/OP_Home/cfr20/404/404-app-p02.htm.

22. Social Security Administration, "CFR § 416.906. Basic definition of disability for children," accessed 2025, https://www.ssa.gov/OP_Home/cfr20/416/416-0906.htm.

This definition of disability uses "marked and severe functional limitations" as the cornerstone of its criteria for a finding of disability for children. In contrast, adult SSI defines disability as the inability to perform any kind of work. Acknowledging this significant difference in how to evaluate a child's SSI claim, SSA uses the following 6 domains or "broad areas of functioning intended to capture all of what a child can or cannot do."[23] These areas include:

1. Acquiring and using information,
2. Attending and completing tasks,
3. Interacting and relating with others,
4. Moving about and manipulating objects,
5. Caring for yourself, and
6. Health and physical well-being.

The SSI regulations address functional equivalence for children at § 416.926a and go into detail around how a child would "functionally equal the listings," which means their condition meets or equals functional severity to be found disabled under the rules.[24] For context, this would be similar to an adult claimant whose medical condition is so severe that it meets or equals one of the medical listings at step 3 of the 5-step sequential evaluation. Within these domains, SSA is specifically looking at what the child's capabilities are (both at home and in school if applicable), how they function in specific situations, their physical and mental capabilities and their ability to care for themselves (not an exhaustive list but these are key areas).

For a child to be found disabled under the analysis of the 6 domains, the impairment, or range of impairments, must result in "marked" limitations in two domains of functioning or an "extreme" limitation in one domain.[25] This is a critical aspect of any child SSI claim because it is both the medical and legal standard for the child claimant to be found disabled under the regulations. SSA defines "marked" and "extreme" limitations within § 416.926a and they provide context for this level of severity. To summarize the key parts of this regulation, here is how they define each one:

> *Marked limitation*: [SSA] will find that [a child] has a "marked" limitation in a domain when [their] impairment(s) interferes seriously with [their] ability to independently initiate, sustain, or complete activities. SSA goes on to say that a "marked" limitation is more than "moderate" but less than "extreme."

---

23. Social Security Administration, "Social Security Ruling 09-7p: Title XVI: Determining Childhood Disability—The Functional Equivalence Doman of "Caring for Yourself: Policy Interpretation Ruling," *Federal Register* 74, no. 36, page 7521, published date February 17, 2009, https://www.ssa.gov/OP_Home/rulings/ssi/02/SSR2009-07-ssi-02.html.

24. Social Security Administration, "CFR § 416.926a, Functional equivalence for children, accessed 2025, https://www.ssa.gov/OP_Home/cfr20/416/416-0926a.htm#b1.

25. Social Security Administration, "Social Security Ruling 09-7p: Title XVI: Determining Childhood Disability—The Functional Equivalence Doman of "Caring for Yourself: Policy Interpretation Ruling," *Federal Register* 74, no. 36 page 7521, published date February 17, 2009, https://www.ssa.gov/OP_Home/rulings/ssi/02/SSR2009-07-ssi-02.html.

> *Extreme limitation*: [SSA] will find that [a child] has an "extreme" limitation in a domain when [their] impairments interferes very seriously with [their] ability to independently initiate, sustain, or complete activities. SSA expressly states that an "extreme" limitation is the rating given to the most severe, or worst, limitations. The regulations also state that an "extreme" limitation doesn't necessarily mean total loss of function, but it would be greater than both moderate and marked.[26]

These domains are covered in great detail within § 416.926a and SSR 09-7p but from an evidentiary standpoint, the regulations are somewhat ambiguous as to how to actually substantiate a "marked" or "extreme" limitation stemming from any of the child's impairments. They do, however, provide examples of relevant pieces of evidence that will help in determining whether the child's limitations rise to the level of marked or extreme. Things such as standardized test scores, classroom reports, professional observations or even lay witness testimony are called out in the regulations to help with the evaluation. As a practical matter, a claimant can provide just about anything to help substantiate the severity of their limitation and the evidentiary ambiguity within the regulations could actually help a claim through the creative illustration of limitation severity by showcasing a child's capabilities through many modalities. Medical records are always prioritized but there are no strict evidentiary rules around what can be submitted to support a claim. The weight of such evidence will be evaluated in accordance with the type of submission. For example, medical records of the child's condition and related symptoms may be given more weight than a neighbor's observation of the child and how they interact with other children in the neighborhood. The weight that each piece of evidence is given is at the discretion of the claim's examiner or at the hearing level, by the administrative law judge.

Some common forms of evidence with a child claim include: medical records, detailed narrative reports, physical therapy records, occupational health records and documentation from school therapists or social workers. Witness testimony, either written or verbal, can also be helpful to illustrate the severity of the child's limitations. Observations by family members or caretakers observing the child on a daily basis can be very impactful to show how the child's limitations impact their daily life.

Child SSI claims are unique and very dependent on a variety of factors with the 6 domains of functioning. If household income eligibility requirements are met, compiling medical records and any kind of documentation that substantiates the child's functional limitations across the domains is essential for proving disability.

26. Social Security Administration, "CFR § 416.926a, Functional equivalence for children," accessed 2025, https://www.ssa.gov/OP_Home/cfr20/416/416-0926a.htm#b1.

Drug Addiction, Alcoholism and Social Security Disability

A common question associated with federal disability benefits is whether a claimant's drug, alcohol or substance abuse addiction would still qualify them for benefits. This is addressed in the regulations at sections § 404.1535 and § 416.935 with the key determining factor being whether the drug or alcohol addiction is a contributing factor material to the determination of disability.

Both CFR § 404.1535 and § 416.935 expressly state the process of evaluating claims where drug or alcoholism is present:

(1) The key factor we will examine in determining whether drug addiction or alcoholism is a contributing factor material to the determination of disability is whether we would still find you disabled if you stopped using drugs or alcohol.

(2) In making this determination, we will evaluate which of your current physical and mental limitations, upon which we based our current disability determination, would remain if you stopped using drugs or alcohol and then determine whether any or all of your remaining limitations would be disabling.

(i) If we determine that your remaining limitations would not be disabling, we will find that your drug addiction or alcoholism is a contributing factor material to the determination of disability.

(ii) If we determine that your remaining limitations would be disabling, you are disabled independent of your drug addiction or alcoholism and we will find that your drug addiction or alcoholism is not a contributing factor material to the determination of disability.[27]

The general rule with disability claims involving drug or alcohol abuse is whether it is a material factor contributing to the disability. To be specific here, if the drug or alcohol addiction is the underlying disability or a material contributing factor, the claimant will not be found disabled. Alternatively, if the claimant's associated medical condition(s) would meet the severity requirements under SSA's evaluation process without factoring in the drug or alcohol abuse, the claimant may be found disabled under the rules. They key piece here with drug or alcohol abuse is whether it's a contributing factor material to the claimant's disability.

In many cases, this is not so clear. A common example of this involves a claimant who has a degenerative back condition that was worsened over the years and has now prevented the claimant from working. While treating for their back condition, the claimant becomes addicted to narcotic medication, which is also evident in the medical records. The question for SSA is whether the back condition on its own would

27. Social Security Administration, "CFR § 404.1535 [SSDI] and § 416.935 [SSI], How we will determine whether your drug addiction or alcoholism is a contributing factor material to the determination of disability," accessed 2025, https://www.ssa.gov/OP_Home/cfr20/404/404-1535.htm, https://www.ssa.gov/OP_Home/cfr20/416/416-0935.htm.

render the claimant disabled under the rules. If the narcotic abuse is a contributing factor, but the back condition by itself would render the claimant disabled, they may be entitled to disability benefits. But if the narcotic abuse is found to be a contributing factor where only the disability criteria is met with both the back condition and the narcotic abuse, then the claimant may not qualify for benefits. This analysis is not always simple. It involves a close review of the medical records and treating provider opinions as to what specifically is preventing the claimant from working.

In addition to the determination of disability and whether the drug or alcohol abuse is material to the disability, if the claimant is rendered disabled despite drug or alcohol abuse, SSA requires the claimant actively participate in treatment for their drug addiction or alcoholism. CFR § 404.1536 and § 416.936 state:

> If we determine that you are disabled and drug addiction or alcoholism is a contributing factor material to the determination of disability, you must avail yourself of appropriate treatment for your drug addiction or alcoholism at an institution or facility approved by us when this treatment is available and make progress in your treatment. Generally, you are not expected to pay for this treatment.[28]

A claimant can either prove they are undergoing appropriate treatment through documentation of their treatment or through a express willingness to seek treatment when they are receiving benefits. The latter is typically seen at the hearing level through claimant testimony since they are under oath when they appear for a disability hearing.

The Disability Claim Review Process

A claim for SSDI or SSI benefits commences with a formal application process that can be completed online or at a local SSA field office. SSA's website has an abundance of information online at ssa.gov to prepare claimants for submitting an application. A claimant can also seek assistance from an attorney, a licensed representative, family member, friend or caretaker to submit their application. Once a claim is properly filed with SSA, all information and evidence is reviewed to determine eligibility, entitlement and whether the claimant's alleged disability meets or exceeds the disability criteria. The SSDI and SSI claims procedure is different than traditional legal proceedings and follows a unique administrative process. In summary, here are the various levels of a disability claim adjudication process (this is covered in detail at CFR § 404.000–404.996 and § 416.1400–416.1494).

Initial application. A claim for disability benefits begins with an application containing personal information, work history, earnings records, alleged onset of disability and why the claimant is unable to work. For a child SSI case, the merits will focus on

28. Social Security Administration, "Code of Federal Regulations § 404.1536 [SSDI] and § 416.936 [SSI], Treatment required for individuals whose drug addiction or alcoholism is a contributing factor material to the determination of disability, accessed 2025, https://www.ssa.gov/OP_Home/cfr20/404/404-1536.htm, https://www.ssa.gov/OP_Home/cfr20/416/416-0936.htm.

the claimant's functional limitations in their daily life. Once a decision has been rendered on a claim, SSA will mail out a notice of determination with an explanation of the decision. If a claim is denied, a claimant has 60 days to file an appeal and requests reconsideration of the claim. The timing for SSA to make a decision on an initial application will vary by claim and often times jurisdiction depending on the claim backlog.

Reconsideration. If a claimant's disability claim is denied, a claimant can appeal this decision and the reconsideration stage "is the first step in the administrative review process."[29] This is essentially a re-review of the disability claim following a denial to ensure the decision and the review process was followed appropriately. Once SSA receives the formal request disputing their denial, they will proceed with a review of the claim. At this stage, claimants can provide additional evidence to support their claim. Like the initial application stage, when a decision is rendered on the claim, SSA will mail out a determination notice (approval or denial). If the claim is denied at this stage, claimants have 60 days to file an appeal but this time the request is for their claim to be heard in front of an SSA administrative law judge (ALJ). This is commonly referred to as the hearing level. Like the initial application stage, the timing for SSA to make a decision will vary by jurisdiction.

Hearing level. If a claim is denied upon initial application and then affirmed at the reconsideration stage, a claimant can appeal these denials and choose to have their claim heard before an federal ALJ in an administrative judicial proceeding. Hearings for SSDI and SSI benefit allow a claimant to present their disability claim in an informal judicial proceeding. The claimant, or their representative, will submit evidence in advance and provide anything that helps to substantiate their claim. At the hearing itself, testimony of the claimant is typically elicited through a series of questions related to the following: work history, education and/or trade skills, whether any skills are transferrable, then a large focus on the claimant's medical condition, symptoms, frequency and duration of those symptoms and how the impairment, or culmination of impairments, functionally limit the claimant in their daily life and in a hypothetical work setting. If the claimant is a child, testimony may be provided by a parent, guardian or caretaker.

Hearings in front of an administrative law judge are addressed in the regulations for SSDI claims at: CFR § 404.929 through § 404.961 and for SSI claims at: CFR § 416.1429 through § 416.1461.

The purpose of claimant testimony at the hearing is to gather additional evidence and allow the claimant to explain how their medical condition prevents them from working (or in the case of a child, how their functional limitations have a severe impact on their daily life). Claimant testimony is also important so that ALJs can perform a credibility assessment based on the evidence contained in the file. If the testimony matches up with what is contained in the file, the claimant may be found credible

---

29. Social Security Administration, "Code of Federal Regulations § 404.907 [SSDI] and § 416.1407 [SSI], Reconsideration—general, accessed 2025, https://www.ssa.gov/OP_Home/cfr20/404/404-0907.htm, https://www.ssa.gov/OP_Home/cfr20/416/416-1407.htm.

although that does not always mean they will be found disabled. If the claimant's testimony conflicts with evidence in the file, the ALJ is tasked with clarifying or resolving any conflicts or inconsistencies. The credibility assessment is just part of the disability determination but the hearing provides an opportunity for the claimant to essentially state their disability case and provide clarity on issues around earnings, work history, medical treatment and overall medical condition.

In advance of a hearing, ALJs have the discretion of including either a medical and/or vocational expert to provide additional testimony about the medical evidence in the file and ability to perform work based on hypothetical functional limitations. These experts are hired by SSA and used by ALJs to gather additional information helpful to making a disability determination. While there is no requirement to do so, the claimant's attorney or representative may cross-examine these experts in the hearing.

A medical expert will perform a review of the medical evidence in the file and testify specifically to whether the claimant's condition or culmination of impairments meet, or equal, a medical listing. Often times, medical experts will add additional information related to symptoms and treatment, but their testimony is relegated to the medical evidence. A claimant's attorney or representative should always have an opportunity to cross-examine a medical expert.

Vocational experts are used by ALJs to provide information about jobs in the local or national economy that could be performed by a hypothetical claimant with specific functional limitations. When eliciting testimony from a vocational expert, an ALJ will ask the vocational expert to assume a claimant with the same age, education and relevant work experience along with a specific physical and/or mental functional capacity[30] to be applied in a hypothetical work setting. A claimant's attorney or representative should always have an opportunity to cross-examine here as well. Although, it should be noted if a vocational expert testifies there are no jobs that can be performed based on the hypothetical provided by the ALJ, there is no need to elicit further testimony from the expert.

The hearing level is often referred to as a critical juncture of the disability determination process because it involves a thorough review of the evidence along with claimant and/or witness testimony that can offer up an explanation why a claimant is disabled. In a hearing, a claimant may be able to bolster their evidence through credible testimony that is sometimes missed in a review of medical evidence. Historically, these

30. To flesh out a claimant's residual functional capacity (RFC), ALJs will commonly use physical capabilities such as the amount of time a hypothetical claimant can sit and/or stand throughout the day, the maximum amount of pounds a hypothetical claimant can lift, push or pull. For a mental RFC, an ALJ may ask the vocational expert to assume a hypothetical claimant that can follow simple instructions or requires sporadic breaks throughout the day to help with focus and concentration. The vocational expert will take these hypothetical scenarios and provide testimony referring to what, if any, jobs this hypothetical claimant could perform taking into account the claimant's age, education, work experience, transferable skills and functional limitations. The actual direct examination by an ALJ will vary with the goal of securing additional evidence about the claimant's ability to perform their last job or any other jobs in the local or national economy.

hearings were performed in person but over the last few decades, SSA has incorporated video hearings to help reduce claim backlog and speed up the time it takes to the actual hearing.

Once the hearing is completed and the ALJ has all of the evidence they need to make a decision, a written notice of determination will be mailed to the claimant and their attorney or representative. If the claim is approved, the claimant will receive instructions about upcoming benefit payments. If the claim is denied, a claimant can request that the Appeals Council review their decision.[31]

Appeals council review. If a claimant is denied benefits following their hearing, they can have one more opportunity to appeal their claim before filing a claim in federal court. This is known as the Appeals Council review and the claim is essentially reviewed in total. The Appeals Council has the authority to affirm the hearing level decision, reverse the hearing level decision and grant benefits or remand the case back to an ALJ in part or in total.[32] Upon review, there are five reasons why the Appeals Council may overturn a decision at the hearing level (CFR § 404.970 and § 416.1470):

(1) There appears to be an abuse of discretion by the ALJ or administrative appeals judge who heard the case;
(2) There is an error of law;
(3) The action, findings or conclusions in the hearing decision or dismissal order are not supported by substantial evidence;
(4) There is a broad policy or procedural issue that may affect the general public interest; or
(5) The Appeals Council receives additional evidence that is new, material, and relates to the period on or before the date of hearing decision, and there is a reasonable probability that the additional evidence would change the outcome of the decision.[33]

The Appeals Council is not performing a review to determine if they agree or disagree with the ALJ's decision following the hearing. Rather, they are reviewing the case in entirety to determine if legal errors or abuse of discretion was evident. New and material evidence that was not presented at the hearing *may* be accepted by the Appeals Council but not always. CFR § 404.970 and § 416.1470, subsection (b) lay out specific reasons for why the Appeals Council may accept new evidence at this stage. The timeframe for receiving a decision from the Appeals Council has varied over the years. Factors impacting this are mostly claim backlog, but this is anecdotal. Per CFR

---

31. Social Security Administration, "Code of Federal Regulations § 404.967 [SSDI] and § 416.1467 [SSI], Appeals Council review—general," accessed 2025, https://www.ssa.gov/OP_Home/cfr20/404/404-0967.htm, https://www.ssa.gov/OP_Home/cfr20/416/416-1467.htm.

32. *Id.*

33. Social Security Administration, "Code of Federal Regulations § 404.970 [SSDI] and § 416.1470 [SSI]: Cases the Appeals Council will review," accessed 2025, https://www.ssa.gov/OP_Home/cfr20/404/404-0970.htm, https://www.ssa.gov/OP_Home/cfr20/416/416-1470.htm.

§ 404.979 and § 416.1479, "the Appeals Council may affirm, modify or reverse, the administrative law judge hearing decision or it may adopt, modify or reject a recommended decision."[34] Once a decision is rendered by the Appeals Council, it will be mailed to the claimant. If the claim is affirmed by the Appeals Council (resulting in another denial of benefits), a claimant has 60 days to file an action in federal district court if they wish to further pursue their appeal.[35]

Legal Roles, Responsibilities and Effective Representation

Claimants for SSDI and SSI claims may be represented by an attorney, or a non-attorney representative may assist. Regardless of licensure or professional affiliation, both attorneys and non-attorney representatives who are well versed with SSA rules and regulations will be advantageous to a claimant navigating the complexities of a disability claim. Claimants can also choose to represent themselves pro se with a disability claim and since the proceedings are non-adversarial by nature, a legal representative is not required.

Attorneys, by way of background, may possess additional skills with creative ways to elicit testimony, cross-examining witnesses and advising claimants with other related areas of law like workers compensation, personal injury or estate law (among others).

CFR § 404.1740 and § 416.1540 address standards of responsibility for representatives and cover general rules of conduct, duties, affirmative disclosures and prohibited actions, such as knowingly misrepresenting the court. Generally speaking, attorneys and representatives must act as "an agent and fiduciary" on behalf of the claimant. The regulations also emphasize that representatives should not knowingly misrepresent the administration while advocating for their claimant. Overall, a claimant's representative must be "forthright in their dealings with [SSA]" and this code of conduct also requires the claimant to be similarly honest and straightforward with their claim and testimony (if applicable). Although somewhat ambiguous as to what "misrepresentation" could look like, this would include withholding medical evidence or making false statements about work experience or earnings.[36]

34. Social Security Administration, "Code of Federal Regulations § 404.979 [SSDI] and § 416.1479 [SSI], Decision of Appeals Council," accessed 2025, https://www.ssa.gov/OP_Home/cfr20/404/404-0979.htm, https://www.ssa.gov/OP_Home/cfr20/416/416-1479.htm.

35. Social Security Administration, "Code of Federal Regulations § 404.981 [SSDI] and § 416.1481 [SSI], Effect of Appeals Council's decision or denial of review," accessed 2025, https://www.ssa.gov/OP_Home/cfr20/404/404-0981.htm, https://www.ssa.gov/OP_Home/cfr20/416/416-1481.htm.

36. Social Security Administration, "Code of Federal Regulations § 404.1740 [SSDI] and § 416.1540 [SSI], Rules of conduct and standards of responsibility for representatives," accessed 2025, https://www.ssa.gov/OP_Home/cfr20/404/404-1740.htm, https://www.ssa.gov/OP_Home/cfr20/416/416-1540.htm.

While CFR § 404.1740 and § 416.1540 provide a foundation for the conduct of representatives handling a disability claim, there are a number of key responsibilities and ethical considerations to be aware of throughout the course of a claim. The following is a list illustrating effective ways to advocate while navigating legal and ethical responsibilities to claimants and the administration.

Responsibilities to a claimant. Claimants that elect to hire[37] an attorney or representative are choosing to enlist a professional that can help them with their claim for disability benefits. A representative's primary responsibility is to provide transparent representation and assistance with securing benefits on behalf of their client. It should be noted that hiring an attorney or representative does not guarantee disability benefits for a claimant but anecdotally, claimants may increase their chances of securing benefits. Attorneys and representatives have primary responsibilities of developing a claim, acquiring medical and non-medical evidence, preparing an application, filing appeals in a timely fashion, developing legal theories of disability and communicating clearly and consistently. Attorneys and representatives should provide the claimant with visibility of any issues that may impact the claim and provide the claimant with enough information to make any key decisions with the claim (i.e., the decision to appeal sits with a claimant).

A common question claimants often have is how strong their case is or what their likelihood is of securing benefits. For attorneys, this hinges on an important ethical consideration of guaranteeing any kind of outcome in a legal proceeding. Like most legal claims (both civil and criminal) it is unethical for an attorney to guarantee any kind of outcome or result. Therefore, when confronted with this type of question from a claimant, attorneys can walk a claimant through their case, any pertinent issues and present potential outcomes based on the evidence contained in the file. While this may not directly answer the claimant's question, attorneys may leverage their own experience to inform the claimant of previous outcomes with cases containing similar facts and/or issues. It is important for attorneys to set expectations with claimants by noting that previous results do not guarantee any kind of outcome in their claim.

Effective forms of advocacy. There are several ways to provide effective representation for a claimant seeking disability benefits. The type of advocacy by an attorney or representative will typically depend on what stage the claimant is at in the application process. For context, here is a table that breaks down different ways to proactively advocate for claimants at each specific stage in the process. Note that these are not exhaustive lists and merely examples of zealous representation at each stage.

37. Most fee arrangements with attorneys or representatives are through a contingency agreement. This means that payment to a lawyer or representative is contingent upon winning or securing benefits for a claimant. SSA uses a formal, written fee agreement that must be approved by SSA. A contingency fee under this arrangement is the lesser of 25% of past due benefits or a maximum amount designated by SSA (as of May 30, 2024, this maximum amount is $9,200).

Claim Stage	Effective Forms of Advocacy
Initial Application	*Assisting with application*—attorneys and representatives may assist with completing forms and ensuring accuracy of information. *Submitting medical and non-medical evidence*—the acquisition of medical records is typically paramount to a disability claim but non-medical evidence like police reports (i.e., car accident), injury reports (i.e., workers compensation) or written witness testimony can be useful to substantiate a claim. *Legal guidance*—at the beginning of the claims process, attorneys and representatives can play a key role in highlighting specific aspects of a claim such as work experience and how it might impact a claim. They can also provide an overview of the claims process, expected timeframes and implications of decisions.
Reconsideration	When a claim is denied upon an initial application, the reconsideration stage provides claimants with an opportunity to submit new or material evidence that may not have been reviewed initially. New evidence could potentially help in reversing an initial claim denial.
Hearing Level	*Ensure development of claim file*—SSA uses an electronic filing system where attorneys and representatives can review, submit and confirm evidence in the file. Claimants may have to wait several months for an actual hearing in front of an ALJ, attorneys and representatives should continue to submit evidence as it becomes available. *Identify key issues*—if there are questions or conflicts with a claimant's work history, education level or medical history, attorneys and representatives should be prepared to explain these issues to an ALJ in an effort to resolve any inconsistencies. Hearings are informal, non-adversarial proceedings, with the goal of understanding why a claimant cannot work so clearing up any questions, conflicts or inconsistencies through written or verbal submissions to an ALJ can be helpful to a claimant's case. *Develop legal theory of disability*—this can include meeting a medical listing, inability to perform any kind of work or a finding of disability through the Medical Vocational Guidelines (factoring in age, education and work experience). Multiple theories can be proffered, and they will depend solely on the facts of each case. *Submit a pre-hearing brief*—legal memorandums can help to summarize a claimant's case. Attorneys and representatives can highlight medical evidence, work experience, earnings history, legal theories and reasons why certain evidence should be given more weight. There is no required format for these briefs and they should be tailored to a claimant's facts and circumstances. *Claimant preparation*—disability hearings are held to provide the claimant with an opportunity to explain why they are disabled. Claimants should be prepared to answer a series of questions from the ALJ or their representative with the focus on work experience, medical condition, functional capacity and ability to perform activities of daily living (not an exhaustive list). Attorneys and representatives can help claimants

	to understand that their credibility will be evaluated in a hearing. Ethically, attorneys must be careful not to tell claimants what to say or even influence their testimony, but they can prepare them with sample questions to practice in advance. *Conduct hearing*—attorneys and representatives are often critical pieces inside the hearing. SSA records each hearing so the preservation of the record and a complete claim file could be important for an appeal. Attorneys and representatives may need to clarify things on the record and can do so with strategic examination of their client. They may also need to cross-examine an expert if the expert testimony is unfavorable to the claimant's case. Lastly, if there is evidence that did not make it into the claimant's electronic file for some reason, a formal request to the ALJ at the hearing can be made to hold the record open for a specific period of time to ensure the submission of evidence. *Post-hearing activity*—depending on what actually happens in the hearing, attorneys and representatives may wish to submit additional evidence or even a post-hearing brief. Although it is not required, post-hearing briefs can help to explain any conflicts or inconsistencies that weren't resolved in the hearing. They can also follow up with the status of a decision which could take several weeks (or months) depending on the backlog of cases sitting with a specific ALJ.
Appeals Council	When a claimant appeals a denial of benefits at the hearing level, they can request an appeal to the Appeals Council. The claim will be reviewed in full, but an attorney or representative should focus on why the denial of benefits at the hearing level was incorrect or not supported by the facts, evidence and hearing testimony. In addition to a full review of the claimant's file, attorneys and representatives should listen to the hearing recording and determine whether the finding included an abuse of discretion by the ALJ, errors of law in the decision, or the conclusions were simply not supported by the evidence. *Appeals Council Brief*—similar to a pre-hearing or post-hearing brief, a memorandum of law to the Appeals Council can be helpful for a more expeditious review. Attorneys and representatives at this stage should emphasize why the claimant should be found disabled but also whether there were any errors with the ALJ's decision that would warrant a reversal or remand back to an ALJ.
Federal District Court	If a claimant's disability claim is denied by the Appeals Council and their decision affirmed the findings of the ALJ, the final appeal is to federal district court. At this stage, the federal court's review is not a review of the disability claim in total, but rather a specific review of whether SSA or the ALJ made any procedural or evidentiary errors in previous findings. Licensed attorneys are well positioned to file this civil suit in federal district court and submit a comprehensive brief focusing on why the ALJ wrongfully denied the claimant's disability claim. There is no hearing at this stage and additional testimony is not proffered to the judge overseeing the case. Instead, a decision will be rendered on the evidence in the claim and arguments made in the legal brief(s) to the court.

Scope of representation. It is not uncommon for a claimant applying for disability benefits to have various other legal claims related to the disability claim. For example, if an individual was involved in an accident at work, they could have a claim for workers compensation. Furthermore, if this work injury occurred because of a car accident, they may also have a personal injury claim. And while these claims may be related to a single incident, each case requires specific legal expertise to advocate on behalf of the individual. For social security disability claims, it is important to set expectations with the claimant on what the scope of representation is for the pursuit of disability benefits. A successful claim for disability benefits may result in monthly financial benefits and potentially medical benefits through Medicare or Medicaid (these programs depend on eligibility, income, current coverage but are associated SSDI and SSI benefits). Attorneys and representatives should be transparent in that a finding of disability under Social Security's rules does not mean they will also be entitled to compensation for their other claims. Alternatively, legal findings with other claims may factor into a disability determination, but they will not dictate a specific finding. For example, a workers compensation finding of total or partial disability does not automatically mean that a claimant will be found disabled under SSA's rules.

A best practice for attorneys representing claimants with multiple legal claims is to ensure they have appropriate representation for each claim. Appropriate representation involves an advocate that is well versed in the legal and procedural elements of the specific claim. A lawyer with social security disability claim expertise should only handle a claimant's workers compensation or personal injury claim if they have expertise in those areas too. They should not represent the claimant in these other claims just because they are handling the disability claim. This could be a disservice to the claimant and for attorneys specifically, this could equate to malpractice. Although it may not be ideal for a claimant to have multiple attorneys or representatives stemming from their injury, or inability to work, if they choose to be represented by counsel for each cause of action, optimal representation by someone with relevant expertise is the most advantageous for the claimant.

Social Security Disability Hypothetical Scenarios

Scenario #1— Handling a client that withholds information

While preparing your client to testify at their upcoming disability hearing, your review of the medical evidence reveals a treating provider opinion that says your client is unable to sit for prolonged periods of time without the need to stand up or lay down. The treating provider estimates this would occur every 15 minutes. Before the hearing, you ask your client if they've traveled on an airplane since their alleged onset date of disability. Your client says "no" and adds they have not traveled out of the state since their disability onset date.

At the actual hearing and while under oath when testifying, your client states that they took a trip overseas after their disability onset date. This information was never revealed to you before the hearing.

Considerations

1. Does traveling on an airplane negate a claim for disability benefits?
2. Why would this information be relevant to a disability claim?
3. How would this information impact a claimant's residual functional capacity?
4. Does this impact a claimant's credibility?
5. Upon learning this information inside the hearing, what options does an attorney or representative have to reconcile this new information?

Scenario #2—
Unsupportive medical evidence

While gathering evidence for your client's case, you request a functional capacity evaluation from your client's treating orthopedic surgeon. This evaluation asks the doctor to opine on your client's ability to perform physical activities such as: sitting, standing, walking, pushing, pulling and lifting. As part of the residual functional capacity analysis, these opinions help to ascertain whether a claimant could perform in a hypothetical work environment. The doctor completes the form but the opinions are unsupportive to your client's claim for disability benefits.

Considerations

1. How should an attorney or representative handle this piece of evidence? Should it be submitted?
2. What options exist to seek clarification from the doctor?
3. Should an attorney or representative communicate with the claimant to explain the implications of this report?
4. How can a doctor's opinion on "disability" be reconciled with their opinions as to the claimant's functional capacity?
5. How should attorneys or representatives handle conflicting medical opinions?

Scenario #3—
Earnings after an alleged onset of disability

As you prepare your client to testify at their hearing, you learn that they did some work for a friend "off-the-books" and earned $800 cash. Your client requests that this information should be considered privileged.

Considerations

1. How should "off-the-books" work activity be handled with a claim for disability benefits?
2. Should this information be privileged between you and the client? As an attorney, should you be prohibited from sharing this information?

3. What are the ramifications of disclosing or not disclosing this information?
4. Would the disability claim be forfeited now that this information has surfaced?
5. How would this impact a claim overall?

Chapter VIII

Corporate Absence Management Models

Since the FMLA was passed in 1993, the management of disability and leave of absence claims have matured into sophisticated models built to track and monitor primarily utilization and duration so that employers can provide any legally required leave. Historically, many employers leveraged internal teams to support employee leave of absence requests and may have leveraged an insurance carrier or third-party administrator for short-term and long-term disability claims. Employers had the discretion to choose how they managed these requests within the confines of any applicable laws, and they still do today. That said, the regulatory environment has dramatically changed and an influx of legislation at both the federal and state levels have made it difficult for all employers to keep up. Complicating matters more for employers has been the steady increase of leave and disability claims over the last two decades. The pressure to maintain compliance combined with rising employee claims has created a swirl of risk for all employers.

A key decision for employers of all sizes is how they choose to structure the management of their leave and disability programs. With most employer-sponsored benefit programs, employers have the choice to offer—and administer—the program on their own or partner with an external vendor to provide the service delivery to their employees. For disability and leave claims, service delivery includes but is not limited to: claim intake, medical record acquisition, employee follow-up, claim determination and consistent communication with the employee. This also requires appropriate application of internal policy and procedures in compliance with any federal or state mandates. This ultimately equates to a substantial amount of administrative work that often sits within a human resource function if handled internally or with an external vendor partner. The decision to insource (keep the work in-house) or outsource (leverage an external vendor) hinges on things such as cost, headcount, company culture, absence program design, claim volume and more recently, data privacy and security.

Additionally, employees have significantly more options for leave and disability than ever before. As workforce demographics have shifted, new private and state paid leave programs beyond disability have become commonplace. But while these programs have ushered in new and provocative benefit offerings, foundational leave options under the FMLA and ADA still need to be complied with. This has caused confusion for both employees and employers around things like entitlement, job protection and eligibility.

Compliance mandates have forced employers to develop programs and processes that not only meet legal requirements but also enable their employees to request and use applicable disability and leave programs when they need it. Employers have forged partnerships with insurance carriers, third-party administrators (TPAs), consultants and other external vendors to stay ahead of a rapidly changing regulatory environment to meet the needs of their employees and to mitigate organizational risk.

Technological advances have also played a major role in the transformation of the absence management industry. Employers have gained the ability to automate time tracking and eligibility, making it mutually beneficial to an employee filing a claim. Although an employee still typically needs to apply for—and be approved—for a leave or disability claim, the use of electronic records, two-way claim platforms and mobile submission of documentation is quickly becoming the norm.

Over the last two decades, three primary absence management models have emerged. These models are not absolute, and some employers have chosen to incorporate multiple models depending on the programs they offer (hybrid models). Employers have the ultimate discretion to manage their absence programs and there is no one-size-fits-all approach to the strategy they pursue. Within each of these models there are pros, cons and key factors to consider when making decisions on design and strategy. This will be addressed within each model, and they are not exhaustive lists as there are a variety of things to consider when choosing how to manage absence (i.e., cost, workforce, company culture).

Following a summary of each specific model will be a chart summarizing the components of each absence model based on key characteristics.

In-Sourced Model

An in-sourced model involves the internal management of all leave and disability claims. Under this approach, employers assume the management and risk associated with these claims. Employers will typically create a team to manage, track, monitor and follow up on claim activity. Traditional in-sourced models often involved the use of internal systems to manage claims but with the emergence of more technology platforms, many employers have chosen to implement external systems but have their internal team manage and oversee the claim processes (overlap with a co-sourced model).

The essence of an in-sourced model enables full control by the employer to develop fine-tune strategy, process, communications and other components of the claims process. This model also enables the development of policy which often serves as the foundation for leave and disability programs.

With in-sourced models, employers carry all the risks associated with disability and leave claims including, but certainly not limited to, discrimination lawsuits and EEOC charges related to a leave or disability claim. Following the passage of the ADA and FMLA, this risk has grown over the years and involves monetary liability for disability discrimination or adverse employment actions, as well as reputational harm towards the employer. The latter can often be more detrimental to an organization with lofty talent acquisition and retention aspirations.

Model Characteristic	IN-SOURCED model specifics
Claim administration	Internal management of all leave of absence claims
Risk	Assumed by employer
External Partners	Limited; employers may still leverage external consultants for compliance guidance and process development
Associated Costs	Staffing, internal systems to track and monitor claims, data repositories, litigation costs
Advantages	Total control of policy (within the confines of the law), process development, strategy, claims management procedures
Disadvantages	Employers carry all of the risk in this model; claims management can be burdensome, time consuming and involve internal reconciliation of claim escalations

Co-Sourced Model

A co-sourced absence management model can take shape in a few different ways but typically involves one or more vendor partners to help with claims administration and compliance requirements. Here are a few examples of how a co-sourced model works with different types of vendors:

> **Software Platform**—employers with an internal absence management team can partner with an external vendor to leverage a technology platform or web-based solution to manage, track and monitor leave and disability requests. These solutions typically come with reporting capabilities to gain insights into utilization, average durations of leaves and even return-to-work rates. Many vendors have also added compliance solutions to help mitigate risk for the employer and to ensure the most up-to-date information around federal and state requirements. Under this arrangement, the external vendor is responsible for maintaining and updating the technology platform and the employer is responsible for administering the actual claims through an internal leave team or human resource function.
>
> Some of the more sophisticated platforms have developed the capability to integrate with other systems like payroll or time-tracking. This has become increasingly valuable to employers required to compensate employees for specific leaves under new state paid family leave mandates.
>
> The partnership and level of collaboration with the external vendor will differ depending on the employer's needs and the vendor's capabilities. Many ven-

dors have added personnel with leave and disability expertise to help with program design, process development and compliance guidance.

Insurance Carrier or TPA Collaboration—another example of a co-sourced model involves a partnership with a supplier organization that specializes in claims management. Unlike a fully outsourced model, employers can select specific leave types to be managed by an external vendor while retaining other leave types. This is often used by employers offering short and long-term disability benefits, which can be fully insured products. Under this example, an employer may decide to handle FMLA and workplace accommodations internally but use an insurance carrier to insure and administer short and long-term disability benefits for their employees. If the employer offers short-term disability benefits that are self-insured, through a payroll practice rather than an insurance premium, they could leverage a TPA to administer the short-term disability and choose to have an insurance carrier insure and administer the long-term disability benefits. Employers have several vendor options to choose from and common considerations include cost, technology and compliance capabilities.

Co-sourced models have become quite popular over the years because employers can pick and choose which pieces they'd like to outsource. Whether it's a leave of absence software platform to be used by internal staff or the outsourcing of a specific leave type like long-term disability, employers can still retain control of their programs but still be creative with their absence management strategy.

Model Characteristic	CO-SOURCED Model Specifics
Claim Administration	Internal management + vendor(s) for leave of absence claims
Risk	Assumed by employer but potentially shared with vendor partner depending on the facts and circumstances around a dispute
External Partners	Technology platform, insurance carrier, TPA or other vendors related to the management of disability and leave claims (analytics, compliance assistance)
Associated Costs	Staffing, vendor costs, data repositories, litigation costs
Advantages	Total control of policy (within the confines of the law), process development, strategy but in collaboration with any external vendors
Disadvantages	Employers still carry the majority of the risk in this model with any external vendors typically operating as an agent for the employer; any liability attributed to an external vendor is usually contained in a contract between the parties including any reasons for liability (i.e., negligence). Costs aren't always higher in this model since an employer may be able to offset any vendor costs with a smaller team internally; there is a lot of variance around structure, costs and program design

Outsourced Model

If an employer opts to use an external vendor for the full, end-to-end management of disability and leave claims, this is known as an outsourced model. The primary reason for choosing this model is to reduce the administrative burdens associated with leave of absence claims. Outsourcing can deliver a variety of services to an employer but most focus on customized management of individual claims and regulatory compliance rigor.

There are several reasons why an employer may choose to outsource their management of leave and disability claims. First, employers with large claim volumes can benefit from an external vendor's consistent processes and policy application. Second, employers with operations in multiple states may be subject to additional state and local mandates tied to leave and sick time. This heightens their need to stay compliant in all jurisdictions where they operate. While FMLA regulations are uniform and can be applied consistently across the US, paid family leave mandates vary at the state level. This complex patchwork of state laws has caused many employers to seek customized service delivery models from insurance carriers, TPAs and the vendor community at large.

Although outsourcing can be advantageous for employers looking to free up their internal teams from the administrative work associated with claims management, it does come with costs. Vendor service delivery models, staffing a team of claims examiners and subject matter experts, technology platforms and analytic insights represent a few of the cost drivers for these models. Offerings will greatly depend on the vendor, their technology and their specific services and products.

For disability claims, employers have historically had the option of fully insuring their short and long-term disability offerings with an insurance carrier. These products have grown tremendously over the years and enable employers to offer disability insurance to their employees by paying premiums to an insurance carrier in exchange for the administration of the benefit. Unlike FMLA, which requires eligible employers to provide unpaid leave, private disability plans are offered at the discretion of the employer. But these insurance arrangements are an example of outsourcing. It should be noted with fully insured disability benefits, the carrier retains decisional independence with claims. This is an important distinction because if a claimant is denied benefits, their dispute is with the insurance carrier, not the employer. This is a significant distinction when disability claims are outsourced in a fully insured arrangement. To differentiate a self-insured disability benefit that is handled in an in-sourced model, the employer has full control over decision making and administration.

Over the last two decades, the outsourcing of FMLA and disability claims have been commonplace. Insurance carriers and TPAs have systematized their processes and procedures to comply with applicable legal mandates and at the employer level, they've been able to scale customized service models to apply and interpret employer-specific short and long-term disability policies. Newer lines of outsourced administration have included: workplace accommodations under the ADA, parental leave, caregiving leave, bereavement and more. Some of these programs overlap with FMLA or disability so employers may elect to consolidate their claim administration or keep them separate and apart.

The outsourced administration of workplace accommodations under the ADA has emerged as a popular choice for employers already outsourcing disability benefits and leave under the FMLA. A primary reason for this is the frequent overlap of accommodation requests with disability and FMLA claims. Here are a few examples that illustrate this:

Example 1: Short-term disability and an accommodation request

John is a floor clerk at a large home improvement retailer. Common responsibilities include lifting over 50 pounds and being on his feet for 6–8 hours per day. John applies for and is approved for short-term disability benefits while he undergoes back surgery. John will be out on disability benefits for 8 weeks while he recovers. Upon his return-to-work date, John is released to return to work but with the following restrictions:

- He cannot lift over 20 pounds
- He will need to sit down throughout the day

John's employer must now engage with him around a potential accommodation that will still enable him to perform the essential functions of the job. Let's assume that John's employer was able to come up with a solution that allowed him to return to work with accommodations enabling John to perform his essential functions.

This example highlights the interplay of a short-term disability claim that transitioned into an accommodation request because his provider released him to return to work with restrictions. In a fully outsourced model where the disability claims and the accommodation requests are handled by the same vendor, there is an opportunity to automate this transition from a disability claim to an accommodation request based on John's return-to-work note. The restrictions would hypothetically trigger the outsourced vendor to proceed with the accommodation request.

Example 2: FMLA exhaust and the request for more leave

Katie was out on family medical leave (FMLA) for her own serious medical condition. She was approaching being out for 12 weeks at which point she would exhaust her unpaid leave under the FMLA. Katie contacted her employer and asked for an additional 2 months of medical leave to allow her to recover from her serious health condition.

In this example, Katie has exhausted her leave under the FMLA. Assuming her employer is an ADA eligible employer, Katie's request for more leave becomes a medical accommodation request for leave and needs to be considered accordingly. At a minimum, it requires Katie's employer to engage with her to better understand her request, the need for leave and whether there are alternative solutions that could be accommodated. This differs from an FMLA request where a claim depends on eligibility and whether the condition is a serious health condition (if it's for their own illness/injury).

Like the first example, if Katie's employer chose to outsource FMLA and workplace accommodations, the vendor can automate the transition from an FMLA claim to an accommodation request based on her ask for 2 months of additional leave. The difference with the accommodation request is an approval hinges on a reasonableness standard that takes things like impact to business operations, cost and whether her ask for more leave constitutes an undue hardship (not an exhaustive list) into account.

The above examples illustrate why some employers have chosen to outsource their accommodation requests in combination with their disability and leave claims. But it is critical to point out that an accommodation request is completely different than a claim for disability, leave under the FMLA, parental leave or caregiving leave (the last two represent relatively newer leave programs). Unlike a disability or leave program, claims management is fully dependent on specific regulations or an internal policy. These claims result in an approval or denial based on whether they meet the requisite criteria for disability or leave. An accommodation request is an employee asking for support to be able to perform the essential functions of the job. The request can often be unique and consideration by the employer depends on several factors within the confines of a reasonableness standard. Simply put, an accommodation for a call center representative may very well differ from an accommodation for a construction worker. And unlike a disability or leave claim that requires medical information or proof of birth (parental leave), an accommodation request requires an interactive dialogue between the employer and employer (and possibly medical documentation). These conversations serve as the foundation for trying to come up with a reasonable accommodation that enables the employee to perform their job. For this reason, a strong knowledgebase of the jobs—specifically the essential functions—and what an employer might be willing to accommodate is vital for an external vendor to be successful when administering accommodation claims. Without this information, the external vendor will require the employer to make decisions on accommodation approvals, creating potential inefficiencies with the model (if the intent is to fully outsource).

Workplace accommodation requests have grown steadily over the last decade. Some theories for this include employees feeling more comfortable self-identifying as a person with a disability or they have felt more comfortable asking for help. As workforce demographics have shifted and ushered in new generations of employees, accommodation requests have grown and become somewhat normalized with employers. Accommodation statistics are not as prevalent as disability or FMLA data, but in a recent accommodation study published by AbsenceSoft, a technology provider for leave of absence and accommodations, 60% of the respondents saw an increase in their accommodation requests.[1] Although each employer would have a better sense of how much their requests have increased, the general industry consensus is that volumes continue to rise.

The COVID-19 pandemic also contributed to the increase with accommodation requests mostly as a result of many employees working from home for an extended period of time. The aforementioned study by AbsenceSoft revealed that remote work or telework was the most popular type of accommodation request over intermittent leave, reduced schedules, specialized equipment, additional breaks and changes in the workplace.[2] As external vendors get more sophisticated with the managing of accommodation requests, there should be more credible data to validate the impact of rising accommodation requests.

Model Characteristic	OUTSOURCED model specifics
Claim Administration	Full claims administration by an external vendor(s)
Risk	Still assumed by employer but potentially shared with vendor partner depending on the facts and circumstances around a dispute (similar to a co-sourced model) Employers cannot absolve themselves of liability by outsourcing claims administration to an external vendor; vendors operate as agents for the employer and liability clauses are negotiated in contracts
External Partners	Typically, an insurance carrier or TPA
Associated Costs	Staffing, vendor costs, data repositories, litigation costs
Advantages	Employers can leverage the expertise and skillsets of external vendor that specializes in claims management; employer will collaborate with the external vendor and benefit from their best practice recommendations, repeatable processes, compliance expertise and reporting capabilities The external vendor will lead the work and own the actual management of claims
Disadvantages	Cost is the biggest factor with this model; employee populations, claim volumes and service model add-ons will dictate pricing (other factors here as well) Even in an outsourced model, employers still carry the majority of the risk with any external vendors since they are operating as agents for the employer

1. The 2025 State of Leave and Accommodations, published by AbsenceSoft. The survey was comprised of 2,400 respondents and included employees, HR and leaders at companies with 500 or more people.

2. *Id.*

Chapter IX

Business Implications of Managing Leave and Disability

Absence management in the workplace continues to evolve for employers and the supplier community. The regulatory landscape has changed dramatically over the last thirty years and employee entitlements have changed with it. In the 90s, prior to the passage of the ADA and FMLA, employers had the discretion to offer disability or company-sponsored leave, but it was not overly prevalent. The FMLA brought in the concept of mandated leave and the need to accommodate employees included a potential medical leave of absence. By the early 2000s, paid family and medical leave laws were gaining momentum in state legislatures across the country. Further, local and municipal sick leave laws flooded the regulatory landscape creating a complex and elaborate patchwork of interstate compliance requirements. For employers with multistate operations, this became a real business impacting challenge.

Within this section, I'll analyze some of the implications tied to absence management within industry's growth over the years and how employers have sought to combat rising claims, compliance, impact to business operations and the constant threat of litigation.

Industry growth. Disability insurance carriers have been in existence for well over a hundred years. TPAs emerged in the 1970s to help insurance carriers with large claim volumes and employers with self-funded health plans. Following the passage of the FMLA, both carriers and TPAs saw an opportunity to streamline leave and disability administration for employers. Since FMLA often ran concurrently with a disability claim, carriers and TPAs were well positioned to perform intake, then track, monitor and manage these claims simultaneously. There was immediate growth for these suppliers in the wake of mandated unpaid leave through FMLA.

The administration of FMLA claims by insurance carriers and TPAs was just the beginning of the industry's expansion. Its tremendous growth would be fueled by the influx of state paid family leave laws, employer-sponsored parental leave and caregiving leave programs, workplace accommodations, sick leave laws and a plethora of other employer-sponsored leave options effectively creating new opportunities for vendor-driven service delivery models. Even longstanding disability programs underwent a transformation with many employers opting to self-insure a program giving them more control over the benefit offering. In turn, this gave employers the choice to partner with a TPA rather than an insurance company giving them some control over the operation of their claims.

Since 2000, the absence management industry has experienced somewhat of a renaissance because of technological advances, new claim software, creative service models and new tools to guide employees and employers around all things related to leave.

Employers seeking assistance with the design of their absence management program and overall compliance have also leveraged the broker and consultant community. These subject matter experts have a broad range of expertise useful to an employer looking to structure their program, set up policy and come up with new ways to manage absence. They can play a key role vetting leave administration options for employers and leading the competitive process known as a Request for Proposal (RFP).

The broker and consultant community has also been instrumental with a popular practice in the benefits space known as benchmarking. This is the practice of compiling de-identified leave and disability data from employers to illustrate emerging trends, leave utilization, plan designs and a variety of other, customized data points that help employers to answer the question of what other employers are doing in the space. For employers, benchmarking studies are an effective way to compare disability and absence programs within a similar industry. It enables them to see how they stack up against similar employers.

A perfect storm of rising claims, increased compliance risks and a patchwork of state and local regulation created the need for employers to leverage consultants and advisory firms to ensure they are providing market competitive programs to their employees.

Productivity, absenteeism and presenteeism. Between mandated leave programs and employer-sponsored leave offerings, employers now have healthy portfolios of leave options for employees. Whether an employee is taking leave to care for their own medical condition, caring for a loved one, starting or expanding their family (parental leave) or is requesting leave as an accommodation under the ADA, employers have begun to recognize the importance of understanding how employee leave of absence impacts their business operations and even bottom line.

An employee's ability to perform their job and produce goods and services is quantified as their productivity. In layman's terms, if employees are outperforming in their job, exceeding sales expectations and completing projects expeditiously, they are considered highly productive. In contrast, if they missing sales targets or project deadlines, they may be considered unproductive. In the context of leave of absence, when the employee is not working, there is no productivity for the employee. This isn't necessarily a negative connection to leave of absence—especially when an employee is taking advantage of an employer-sponsored leave program—but when looking at an employer's full slate of leave of absence utilization, it can tell a story about why employees are taking leave. It is important to note that there is not one, single way to measure productivity. Any measurements or metrics associated with an employee's productivity will depend heavily on the specific job. For example, a retail sales associate's productivity will vastly differ from that of a professional consultant.

Absenteeism in the workplace refers to frequent absences. The overall absenteeism rate for employers is a useful statistic that provides an objective picture of leave of absence utilization. For employers, understanding the makeup and drivers of their absenteeism rates are critical to assessing the impact. Looking at the overall absenteeism rate may not tell the whole story so it's advantageous for an employer to better understand what's causing any increase or decrease in absenteeism. For example, disability claims, leave under the FMLA, leave as an accommodation and any employer-sponsored leave programs will all contribute to an absenteeism rate. Therefore, knowing the utilization, duration and absenteeism rates for each of these leave entitlements is crucial to understanding what is driving overall leave within a workplace.

Another concept impacting overall productivity is presenteeism, "which refers to the lost productivity that occurs when employees are not fully functioning in the workplace because of an illness, injury, or other condition."[1] Presenteeism represents the idea that although the employee is at work, they may not be performing at optimal levels due to a physical or mental limitation. Presenteeism is arguably more impactful than absenteeism because this is far more difficult to manage than securing a temporary replacement or contractor when someone is out on leave. The assumption with leave is that the employee can leverage the time off to recover, care for a loved one or just simply use the time off before returning to work. But with presenteeism, employers have to decipher whether lack of performance is the result of a medical condition or something else. This is far more difficult to reconcile.

Measuring presenteeism is also very challenging to measure. Unlike an absenteeism rate that is objectively based on leave utilization whereas presenteeism depends on employee productivity and maintaining performance levels while at work. In many cases, employers may not know whether a dip in performance is due to a medical condition, caregiving responsibilities or something else. Without a full understanding of why the employee might be struggling, any data sets suggesting a presenteeism rate would not be credible.

Reducing both absenteeism and presenteeism is typically a business priority as they both cost employers time and money. Employers have leveraged their health and well-being programs to provide holistic support for employees in all situations. In somewhat of an irony, employer-sponsored leave programs like parental leave or caregiving leave encourage employees to utilize paid leave to handle caregiving responsibilities. But it is precisely this kind of leave that could very well reduce presenteeism when the parent returns to work. In developing a methodology to measure absenteeism rates, some employers have chosen to exclude any leave programs that are encouraged because they are counterintuitive to creating strategies that look to reduce absenteeism.

In short, a sound disability and absence strategy is central to reducing absenteeism and presenteeism. Employers will typically look at their leave data to help them make

1. Will Kenton, reviewed by Gordon Scott and fact checked by David Rubin, "Presenteeism: What It Is and How it Works," *Investopedia,* January 6, 2025, https://www.investopedia.com/terms/p/presenteeism.asp.

strategic decisions around targeting specific leave types impacting their organization. Dashboards and statistical summaries are very helpful for long-term planning and often key to driving employee behaviors.

Analytics. Comprehensive data sets that illustrate leave of absence have matured over the last two decades. Insurance carriers, TPAs, consultants and technology vendors have come up with new ways to measure, track and monitor leave utilization. Today, employers can customize their disability and leave analytics to show not only impact, but potentially predict utilization based on historical patterns. Big data has delivered new, statistical insights that enable predictive modeling for employers.

Here are some examples of leave of absence data points (not an exhaustive list):

Data Point	Rationale for Metric
Disability Utilization	Claim volumes based on type of illness, injury or condition Shows number of days lost to disability
Disability Claim Type	Insights into what is causing disability among employee population (physical vs mental health claims)
Disability Durations	Insights into how long employees are out on claim (10, 20, 30 days or more for each specific claim type)
FMLA Utilization	Claim volumes based on caring for own condition, caring for loved one, military leave
FMLA Intermittent Use	Claim volumes and rate of intermittent use (number of days per week or month)
Recidivism Rate	Repeat claims by type (this shows patterns and whether specific claim types are more likely to repeat themselves)
Claim Approval Rate	Percentage of claims approved
Claim Denial Rate	Percentage of claims denied; some employers also track why claims were denied (medical vs eligibility)
Accommodation Request Type	Insights into what kind of accommodation employees are asking for (i.e., telecommute, additional breaks, etc.)
Type of Accommodation Approved	Insights into what an employer has approved

Another useful data set that has been particularly useful for employers that outsource leave and disability claims involves operational metrics tied to claims management. Insurance carriers and TPAs that are administering claims for employers have the ability to measure their overall administration efficiency. These statistics typically focus on call center operations but also include employee self-service options through portals.

Operational metrics look at the speed and effectiveness of managing individual claims that may also play a part in reducing durations or helping employees return to work.

Here are some examples of operational metrics related to the actual administration of claims (not an exhaustive list):

Data Point	Rationale for Metric
Call Center Volumes	Number of incoming and outgoing calls to and from supplier call center
Self-Service Data	Number of claims opened through portal versus phone call
Speed to Answer Calls	Time it takes for examiner to connect with employee
Call Abandon Rate	Number of calls dropped (either by employee or examiner)
Examiner Claim Volume	Average number of cases handled by examiner
Case Development Rates	Speed to conduct initial intake and acquire medical records
Closure Rates	Speed to close a claim
Escalation Rate	Number of escalations directed at claims administrator; this requires a mutually agreed upon definition of what an escalation is

Operational metrics will hinge on what the supplier can measure, track and monitor. These metrics will often vary as well depending on what kind of service delivery model they are using for the employer. These are typically customized models tailored to the type of workforce. For example, if an employer has a workforce that doesn't have access to a computer or technology throughout the workday, self-service options through a portal may not be a popular option for employees to start a claim. Nevertheless, these metrics do provide statistical insights into efficiency opportunities with the claims administrator.

Cost considerations. Before the FMLA was passed, leave of absence cost drivers were mostly relegated disability claims, and ancillary costs associated with lost productivity from employees taking miscellaneous, unpaid time away from work. Today, the leave of absence landscape has grown to include a variety of both paid and unpaid leave options for employees. As a result, costs associated with these leave and disability claims have grown tremendously. A larger focus by employers has also clarified direct and indirect costs associated with leave of absence. Lastly, better analytics have illuminated these costs so employers can identify strategic options for effectively managing costs while simultaneously mitigating organization risk. The simplest way to identify costs associated with absence management is to separate direct from indirect costs. The examples below highlight some of the more common cost drivers but do not represent an exhaustive list.

Direct Costs

Disability payments through a short or long-term disability plan are a tangible dollar amount paid to employees. These can be tracked by claim and in the aggregate. Elevated dollar amounts paid to employees on claim doesn't necessarily mean that claim volume is rising since employees with higher salaries could be contributing to the rise in cost. Changes in disability plan design like moving from partial pay to full pay could also be a driver of cost. Therefore, it's important to look at claim volumes in conjunction with benefits paid out each year. If the employer's disability plan is a fully insured model where an insurance carrier is responsible for insuring and administering the benefit, the insurance premiums would be considered the direct cost for the employer. If claim volumes increase, premium rates would likely increase when the contract is up for renewal.

Vendor costs are a major contributor to overall spend in a co-sourced or outsourced model because the employer is paying an external partner to help with the administration of leave and disability. Contractual terms and conditions will dictate the overall cost of the relationship and some employers have included contractual incentives for vendors that meet specific criteria with their administration. If key performance indicators (KPIs) are met, a contractual provision is enforced to pay that vendor additional fees. Alternatively, if the vendor does not meet the agreed upon KPIs, the stated fees are retained by the employer.

The use of brokers and consultants is related to vendor costs especially when they are often the bridge between employer and chosen vendor. Brokers and consultants are often leveraged to perform any formal Request for Proposal (RFP) or Request for Information (RFI), which provides the employer with a fair, competitive process to acquire the services of a vendor. For claims administration, RFPs and RFIs are comprehensive processes that give vendors an opportunity to answer a variety of questions related to their services and this selection process gives employers visibility to vendor capabilities and strengths. This process typically includes finalist meetings where vendors will make their final pitch to offer their products and services. If selected, the employer and vendor will engage in contract negotiations. This process can be lengthy and is typically led by brokers and consultants.

Staffing costs for an employer's internal leave management team are also a contributor to overall spend. In-sourced models will typically involve larger teams and in addition to salary and performance-based bonuses, other labor costs like health benefits and insurance increase the overall cost. In a co-sourced or outsourced model, employers may elect to maintain a smaller team responsible for vendor management, program design and policy development.

Indirect Costs (non-tangible costs)

Lost productivity is arguably the biggest indirect cost of leave and disability claims in the workplace. When employees are absent from work and unable to perform their job, there is an immediate impact to productivity that may or may not be reconciled by other employees at the company. Presenteeism is also an indirect, often hidden, cost driver that is far more difficult to measure. Presenteeism is typically associated with lower work quality, underperformance and service level impacts. Depending on the employer and the industry they operate in, this could lead to things like missed sales targets, delayed deliverables and customer attrition (just to name a few examples).

Employers can choose to apply an average fixed cost for each day lost from an employee's leave of absence claim, but again, it may not represent the most accurate picture of how leave and disability claims are impacting the organization. This methodology is also unique to that employer since the actual cost will vary by employer, type of job and compensation levels. A more sensible approach may be to carve out the leave types that are encouraged by the employer—like parental or caregiving leave—so that these absence rates are factored into the overall absenteeism rate for the employer. It's still a best practice to track these leaves that are encouraged by the employer, but utilization for these leaves represent popularity of the program or workforce demographic trends rather than a leave of absence trend.

Turnover and talent attrition is another implication, or symptom, of leave and disability in the workplace. Inflexible leave policies or lack of leave options may cause an employee to leave the company. This can cause a domino effect of the employer needing a replacement and related actions like searching for the replacement and training a new employee. Depending on the criticality of the role, the employer may also have immediate needs that require a contractor or temporary hire while searching for a replacement. There are consequential dollars at stake here as well and for larger employers, it can involve different parts of the organization like labor, human resources and talent acquisition teams.

Compliance. In general, disability and leave of absence programs are heavily regulated by federal, state and local law. In addition to these regulatory mandates, these programs are also governed by program and employer policy. Maintaining compliance is paramount with an absence management program and since 2000, it has become a daunting challenge for employers. State paid family and medical leave continues to evolve with states launching unique and individualized laws making it very complicated for multistate employers. Dozens of local and municipal paid sick laws have further confounded the ability to maintain an absence program's full compliance.

The regulatory frameworks serve as a foundation for employers and claims administrators, but claims compliance is also a large requirement. Whether it's an employer's internal team or external administrator, the individual examiners handling the claims need to be aware of key regulatory provisions that govern a claim. For example, under the FMLA, employees generally have at least 15 calendar days to return a health care provider certification, or the claim can be denied.[2] If the employer, in partnership with

2. US Department of Labor, "Fact Sheet #28G: Medical Certification under the Family and Medical Leave Act: Wage and Hour Division," dated March 2025, https://www.dol.gov/agencies/whd/fact-sheets/28g-fmla-serious-healthcondition#:~:text=When%20the%20deadline%20is%20not,after%20her%20employer%20requests%20it.

a claims vendor, did not stand up a process indicating time windows for returning medical certifications, they are subject to FMLA rules by default. If the examiner in this case denied a claim before the 15 calendar days, this would be in violation of FMLA regulations. Similarly, if the claim vendor stood up a process giving employees only 10 days to return a medical certification, that too would be in violation of FMLA regulations.

Many disability programs are governed by the Employee Retirement Income Security Act (ERISA), a federal law setting forth regulations that govern the administration of claims. In addition to disability claims, ERISA covers employer-sponsored health, pension, welfare benefit plans and well-being offerings. ERISA compliance is highly complex, and employers may choose to have a combination of in-house experts (usually attorneys), external counsel and/or consultants to help with maintaining compliance and updating associated policy documentation when regulatory changes happen.

Employer disability and leave policies are fundamental to ensuring transparency with leave programs. Disability summary plan descriptions and employee guides can be helpful to lay out eligibility requirements, criteria for approval and clarity around the process for employees. These policies and guidance documents are of course also subject to all federal and state regulatory requirements. As these laws are passed or revised over time, all policies and employee guidance need to be updated accordingly.

Artificial Intelligence (AI) has infiltrated just about every aspect of the workplace and how work is performed. In the leave, absence and disability arena, the supplier community has introduced AI tools that appear to help with claims administration, employee education and speeding up the time it takes to make a decision. From automation to enhanced decision-making, AI has become a transformative tool to help claims administrators improve efficiency while reducing manual errors.

While it appears to have several advantages, employers should be cautious about how AI is used with respect to their leave and disability claims or accommodation requests. Inaccurate eligibility calculations or sporadic claims management mistakes that result in denials could create liability for employers. Human oversight remains a critical part of the claims process and employers need to be aware of how AI is deployed on their processes. An employer's claim that they were not aware of how AI was used would likely be a weak defense in a court of law.

To date (April 2026), there is very little data to suggest that AI has directly contributed to a decrease in disability and/or leave durations. While AI is certainly a valuable tool for summarizing medical records or developing employee communications, we have yet to see if it can actually help return an employee back to work faster. Another related question is whether deploying AI technology has helped employers expedite the accommodations process. There is certainly the potential for it to help navigate a traditionally arduous process, but if deployed in a methodical, appropriate manner, employers may be in a position to speed up the time it takes to effectuate an accommodation request. That said, employers still need to be mindful of the ADA's requirements around the interactive process and ultimately, decision-making. Deploying AI will certainly require human oversight at key parts of the process.

Chapter X

COVID-19 Impact on Leave and Disability in the Workplace

The COVID-19 pandemic had a significant impact on employee leave of absence and employer absence management programs. In March of 2020, the World Health Organization declared COVID-19 a pandemic and around this time, employers were grappling with how to guide their workforces in the wake of numerous shelter-in-place mandates. Many employers with offices transitioned their office populations to work remotely, but for other, non-office roles, employers did their best to implement occupational safety initiatives designed to keep employees safe.

With COVID-19 being a highly contagious virus, leave of absence considerations were thrust into the spotlight and employers were faced with an abundance of questions related to their leave and disability programs. Below are some questions that employers faced.

Does a positive COVID-19 test qualify me for short-term disability benefits?

Is a COVID-19 diagnosis considered a "serious health condition" for purposes of FMLA?

If I am experiencing COVID-19 symptoms but don't have the ability to test for it, would I qualify for short-term disability or FMLA?

Is long COVID a disabling condition for purposes of long-term disability?

If I am caring for someone with an autoimmune disorder that is now classified as "high-risk" if they are infected with COVID-19, can I take leave under the FMLA even if they do not currently have a "serious health condition" as defined under the regulations?

Can I ask my employer to remain working in an office setting if my home is not equipped to enable me to perform the essential functions of the job?

Can I take leave under the FMLA if my child's school has ceased operations?

These are just a handful of the endless scenarios that employers had to consider at the start of the pandemic. To delve further into how the COVID-19 pandemic impacted leave and disability claims, consider the following leave and disability types with novel questions around claims.

Short-term disability (STD). Most STD plans incorporate an initial waiting period (usually 7 days) before benefits can be paid. This effectively means that an employee's illness or injury must last for at least 7 days to qualify for disability benefits. For the most part, any illness or short-term incapacity is covered by an employer's sick time or sick leave. Some employers might bake sick time into an all-compassing paid-time-off bucket but either way, a short-term illness was typically covered through another time-off program. When the pandemic hit, if an employee did not have sick time, questions poured in as to whether STD would be an option if their condition lasted longer than the 7-day waiting period.

A person's experience, symptoms and severity varied with COVID-19, so a positive test wouldn't necessarily automate an approval under a traditional policy. Under most STD plans, qualifying for a disability goes beyond a diagnosis and hinges on why the person is incapacitated or otherwise not able to perform their job.

Another aspect of a traditional STD claim is the requirement to substantiate a claim with medical documentation (for most claims). In March of 2020, it became increasingly difficult to treat in-person with medical providers. Hospitals were inundated and many physicians transitioned their practice to telehealth out of an abundance of caution. This prevented employees filing for STD benefits from getting medical records to substantiate their claim. So, while a traditional STD claim process would require medical documentation to be approved, employers and their administrators had to make difficult decisions as to whether they would approve COVID-19 claims, lasting longer than 7 days, without requisite documentation.

These early considerations around STD claims led many employers to explore administrative leave for employees with a positive COVID-19 test or were experiencing COVID-19 symptoms. Employers also had to factor in time windows for quarantining measures following guidance from the Centers for Disease Control and Prevention (CDC).

Lastly, it should be noted that if an employee was forced to work from home during the early stages of the pandemic, a positive COVID-19 diagnosis and associated symptoms may have prevented them from working but it also may not have (they may have been able to continue working at home). This varied by person and really depended on the severity of symptoms. That said, employers could not make assumptions on the ability to work.

Long-term disability (LTD). Most LTD policies don't kick in until an individual has been disabled for a specific period of time (e.g., 6 months) or in the case of employer-sponsored disability programs, at least through the exhaustion of STD benefits. Note that STD and LTD programs tend to be employer specific so the benefit windows will vary. A typical STD policy that allows for 26 weeks of benefits (6 months) will coincide with an LTD policy that requires at least 6 months of disability or STD exhaustion before a claim can begin. This context is important for the introduction of Long COVID. According to the CDC, "Long COVID is a serious illness that can result in chronic conditions requiring comprehensive care and may cause disability."[1] The CDC goes onto say that "Long COVID can include a wide range of ongoing symptoms and conditions that can last weeks, months, or even years after COVID-19 illness."[2] While this is just guidance from the CDC, it does validate that Long COVID is a medical condition and from a claims perspective, should be treated like any other physical or mental condition.

Long COVID was a relatively new concept for claims examiners and obtaining medical documentation between 2020 and 2022 was a real challenge for some people. Adding to these challenges was a large degree of uncertainty around a treatment plan and estimated return-to-work timeframes. Long COVID was a novel concept to many medical professionals so opining on things like disability and return-to-work was extremely difficult.

Recognition of long COVID as a disability was not really in question. In addition to the CDC, the US Department of Health and Human Services (HHS) recognized long COVID as a disability under the ADA if it substantially limits a major life activity and labeled it a "physiological condition affecting one or more body systems."[3] The bigger issue for LTD claims involved substantiating the condition with medical documentation beyond the individual's description of how they experienced the symptoms and the frequency and duration of these symptoms. For LTD insurance carriers and claims administrators, there were a lot of inconsistencies in the early days of the pandemic because there were no formal processes in place to adjudicate these claims.

A best practice did emerge but was not new or necessarily unique. Many claims administrators recognized Long COVID as a disabling condition but adjudicated the claim as they would any other—looking at how the medical condition impacted the individual's ability to perform their specific job or any other kind of job. Following the same process of other claims, medical documentation remained a critical component of the disability determination. The primary question for insurance carriers and claims administrators during the early stages of the pandemic was whether they would be flexible with medical documentation challenges and whether the claimant's allegations of disability due to Long COVID would be given enough weight for approval.

FMLA and state paid family leave. Arguably the most applicable leave types for employees impacted by COVID-19 were FMLA and state paid family and medical leave claims. COVID-19 infections ranged from short-term illnesses with cold or flu-like symptoms to long-term infections and battles with Long COVID. FMLA's "serious health condition" standard applied to an employee's own medical condition and when

1. Center of Disease Control and Prevention, "Long Covid Basics," dated July 24, 2025, https://www.cdc.gov/long-covid/about/index.html.

2. *Id.*

3. US Department of Health and Human Services, "Guidance on 'Long COVID' as a Disability Under the ADA, Section 504, and Section 1557," content last reviewed July 30, 2025, https://www.hhs.gov/civil-rights/for-providers/civil-rights-covid19/guidance-long-covid-disability/index.html.

caring for a loved one. Most state paid family and medical leave programs have similar standards and like the FMLA, the leave can be taken intermittently. In the early stages of the pandemic, FMLA and state paid leave programs could cover both short and long-term absences. But issues arose related to the handling of employees that may have been exposed to someone with COVID-19 and the evolving guidance from the CDC to quarantine if a person was exposed. Employers began to face a flurry of questions as to whether FMLA or similar state paid leave programs would apply in these scenarios where an employee may not be sick, but was recommended to quarantine if they were exposed to someone with COVID-19.

With respect to one's own illness or caring for a family member, many employees raised concerns about underlying medical conditions or auto-immune disorders that made them "high-risk" if they contracted COVID-19. These employees may have had conditions that were controlled through medication management, or their symptoms were sporadic in nature, but with the spread of COVID-19, they were at greater risk (sometimes fatal) if they contracted it. This raised the question of whether an individual, or their family member, through their medical condition, would be classified as having a "serious health condition" under the FMLA or any applicable state paid family leave law because they are at greater risk if they contract COVID-19. A classification of "high-risk" due to an underlying medical condition would not technically qualify someone as having a "serious health condition" so employers began to face a tsunami of employee requests to work from home (if feasible) or be granted leave as an accommodation under the circumstances (high-risk or at-risk individuals would also not technically qualify someone for an accommodation under the ADA). Employers did have discretion to formulate more flexible FMLA policies for situations like this so there was a lot of parity in the early stages of the pandemic.

Another very common issue related to FMLA and state paid family leave was childcare. FMLA provides unpaid leave to employees for their own medical condition or to care for a family member (parent, child, spouse) with a serious health condition or bonding. Technically, FMLA does not cover employees for leave related to childcare or school/daycare closures. Some state paid family leave programs[4] did include provisions to cover leave for school or childcare closures, but not every state.

In March 2020, mostly due to shelter-in-place mandates, many schools, daycare and childcare facilities closed their doors out of an abundance of caution to prevent the spread of COVID-19. For many employees, working from home while their children were home became commonplace. But for those employees that could not work from home, childcare became an increasingly difficult challenge with large scale ramifications to employers. On the claims front, FMLA did not technically apply and for those employees outside of state that offered leave for this scenario, they looked to their employers for guidance. For states in the midst of crafting state paid family and

4. For reference, a few states that included paid leave for childcare closures are California, New York and Maine (just to name a few).

medical leave laws during this time, childcare became an instant consideration due to the COVID-19 pandemic.

Workplace accommodations under the ADA. At the outset of the pandemic in 2020, many employers transitioned large portions of the workforce to be able to work from home. In 2021, some employers began to bring their office populations back into a physical workspaces and by 2023, more employers were implementing "return-to-office" (RTO) mandates. After approximately two years of working from home for some employees, this transition was not welcomed by everyone. It was a rather polarizing topic and raised a lot of questions as to whether an employee was more productive working from home or in a physical workplace.

As RTO mandates become more common, employers saw an influx of work from home requests. It became immediately incumbent for employers to separate a work from home request by way of personal preference and a medical accommodation request to work from home. This continues to be an extremely difficult distinction when the employee has medical documentation backing up their request to work from home.

According to a "2026 State of Leave and Accommodations" survey published by AbsenceSoft, an absence management technology company, remote work or telework was the most common accommodation request above leave, additional breaks, specialized equipment and changes in the workplace (there were others on the list, but these ranked the highest).[5] Work from home requests in general are in direct conflict with an RTO mandate but with respect to medical accommodation requests, employers had to proceed with caution before issuing a blanket rejection because of an RTO policy. To remain compliant with the ADA, employers need to engage in an interactive dialogue with employees to better understand accommodation needs and why they are requesting to work from home. ADA regulations are clear that while an employee can suggest a preferred accommodation, employers are obligated to consider and provide an effective one that is reasonable under the circumstances and one that does not create an undue hardship. This remains a contentious issue that the courts are still sorting out.

In addition to the variety of issues impacting individual claims, COVID-19 had a large impact on the absence management industry itself. Suppliers and claims administrators seized opportunities to offer new services like 24/7 COVID-19 helplines that triaged employee questions and concerns around a possible infection or exposure. Some suppliers added clinical personnel to claims management teams in an effort to bolster their claims management.

One of the more innovative services that was around long before COVID-19, but which rose to prominence during the pandemic, was the use of telehealth. This enabled patients to interact with a medical professional through digital means rather than in person. Services included medical guidance and the ability to prescribe certain medications. Employers began to offer this service as a way for employees and their family

5. The 2026 State of Leave and Accommodations survey, published by AbsenceSoft.

members to connect with medical providers for mild or minor illnesses like a cold, flu-like symptoms or a rash. During the pandemic, many doctors and medical professionals transitioned their practice to telehealth only to help prevent the spread of COVID-19. While telehealth could resolve all medical issues, it certainly bridged an access gap during a time when getting into see a physician or medical professional was extremely challenging.

Although telehealth proved to be beneficial to patients for a number of reasons, there were novel issues raised about medical providers opining on disability and work capabilities in conjunction with applications for disability benefits and leave of absence requests. Traditionally speaking, most telehealth services shied away from providing individuals with disability evaluations or medical certifications because of the short interactions with the patient (i.e., some telehealth sessions were no longer than 20 minutes). But without the ability to treat in person with medical providers for disability evaluations, employees had no way of obtaining medical records to substantiate their claims.

Employers had some discretion here to accept opinions from medical professionals providing opinions related to disability evaluations or leave of absence claims. If their disability programs were self-insured, employers and their claims administrator could have flexed their administration policies to accept such evaluations. Alternatively, if the disability programs were fully insured, this decision rested with the insurance carrier.

For leave of absence claims under the FMLA and accommodation requests, documentation through telehealth visits was much more palatable. The approval threshold for an FMLA claim and disability standard for an accommodation request is much lower than a short-term or long-term disability claim, so many employers were amenable to the idea of accepting documentation through telehealth. Again, like most impacts from COVID-19, employers had discretion to go above and beyond regulatory requirements if it meant providing more leniency and flexibility for employees.

Chapter XI

Conclusion

The expansion and growth of leave, disability and accommodation programs in the United States have evolved into a complex matrix of options for employees. For employers, it's created a myriad of compliance issues requiring a high level of expertise both internally and externally to deliver sound, effective programs. The regulatory climate is hotter than it's ever been in the wake of COVID-19 and rapidly changing workforce demographics are impacting the volume and nature of employee requests. Compliance requirements and legal considerations have become increasingly vital to maintaining the spirit, intent and sustainability of programs either mandated by law or sponsored by employers.

As options have expanded, the overlap of leave and disability programs have stifled human resource teams and, in many instances, created more confusion for employees. Compounding this trend is the consistent increase in leave requests over the last decade. The steady rise in leave claims and accommodation requests can be attributed to more leave options, increased mental health needs and a rise in caregiving responsibilities, but this is by no means an exhaustive list. Modern analytics have played a major role in helping employers identify opportunities based on their leave, disability and accommodation data. More importantly, its enabled employers to consider health, wellness and benefit initiatives to help target the reasons employees are seeking leave of absence.

Workforce and even workplace changes have had direct and indirect impacts on leave of absence utilization and accommodation requests. On a positive note, these changes have led to the introduction of new, innovative benefit programs that provide employees with the ability to pursue leave or disability without having to immediately exit the workforce.

As this cycle of change presumably continues, employers will need to react with vigilance to ensure compliance and the ability to deliver a seamless, transparent employee experience. History suggests that in the coming years, employer leave and disability programs will continue to evolve creating new opportunities for creative benefit options in line with changing employee needs.

Table of Authorities

Cases

Statutes

Regulations

Secondary Sources

Index